Alexei Elfimov

Russian Intellectual Culture in Transition

TRANS
anthropologische texte/anthropological texts

herausgegeben von/edited by

Ina-Maria Greverus and George Marcus

Band/volume 2

LIT

Alexei Elfimov

Russian Intellectual Culture in Transition

The Future in the Past

LIT

Bibliographic information published by Die Deutsche Bibliothek
Die Deutsche Bibliothek lists this publication in the Deutsche
Nationalbibliografie; detailed bibliographic data are available in the
Internet at http://dnb.ddb.de.

ISBN 3-8258-6820-6

© LIT VERLAG Münster – Hamburg – London   2003
Grevener Str./Fresnostr. 2   48159 Münster
Tel. 0251-23 50 91   Fax 0251-23 19 72
e-Mail: lit@lit-verlag.de   http://www.lit-verlag.de

Distributed in North America by:

Transaction Publishers
New Brunswick (U.S.A.) and London (U.K.)

Transaction Publishers
Rutgers University
35 Berrue Circle
Piscataway, NJ 08854

Tel.: (732) 445 - 2280
Fax: (732) 445 - 3138
for orders (U. S. only):
toll free (888) 999 - 6778

Contents

	Acknowledgements	6
	Introduction	7
1	The Problem of Modernity, Intellectuals and the Humanities	19
2	Discourses of History, Architecture, and the New Paradigm in Intellectual World-Views	41

    Discourse of History / 46
    Discourse of Architecture / 65
    Effects of the New Paradigm / 93

3	Power, Culture, and Changes in Values and Ideals	103
4	Restoring the Humanities	137
	Conclusion	189
	Bibliography	201
	Index	206

Acknowledgements

This work is modest in its scope, but, as it is said, any scholarly work these days, no matter how modest, is a collective endeavor in some sense, and I would like to acknowledge a number of individuals and institutions that have helped me carry out this project in one or another manner. The Department of Anthropology at Rice University, where I had a privilege to study and subsequently teach, was a wonderful place and fascinating academic environment. Thank you all, folks over there, I think of you as my second home. George Marcus deserves credit for so many things that, at this point, I cannot remember all of them anymore – you know, George, I am deeply grateful for everything. Thanks go to Patricia Seed who commented on separate chapters of the work, while it was in progress, and provided valuable critical reflections. I am indebted to Bruce Grant for taking time to scrutinize the manuscript and offer extensive criticism, as well as for all the help and useful advice over the course of many years that have frequently crossed our research paths on two continents. Finally, I am grateful to a group of colleagues in Russia who took a live interest in the project and facilitated my research in various ways. Alexei Nikishenkov, Olga Vainshtein, Sergei Sokolovski, and Sergei Cheshko provided me with hours of exciting intellectual conversations and made a valuable contribution to the present work. A word of acknowledgement goes to Andrew Elez whose supportiveness, friendship, and wit had been very special – thanks, Andrew, I still think of you as a great friend. Svetlana Usacheva and Radik Makhmutov were immensely helpful in every regard during the year 1995 in Moscow, and Svetlana Mikhasenok has been so ever since. Once again, thank you all.

Introduction

In September of 1997, Russian journal *Itogi* published in its section on culture and the humanities an article under a telling title, "The Majestic Russian Past Will Surpass the Most Daring Expectations in the Future".[1] The article dealt with the issue of architectural and cultural restoration in the city of Moscow and with the reconstruction of the main exposition in the Russian State Historical Museum. What is remarkable about the title of the article, however, is that it subtly reflected not just the subject matter of that particular narrative, but the dimensions of the entire paradigm of intellectual discourse on culture and the humanities, as it formed in Russia of the 1990s. This paradigm, which gradually evolved from the general intellectual moods in the late Soviet Union, being successfully propelled by the efforts of academics in the humanities and later, in the post-perestroika Russia, strengthened and legalized by political authorities, came to represent the major trial of cultural ideology in Russian society of the end of the twentieth century.

Perhaps the most essential feature of this paradigm consisted in the fact that, after more than half a century of persistent socialist ideological utopias of the future, it reversed the cornerstones of social mentality, having directed broad intellectual and cultural interests primarily toward the past. The future now became addressed in all kinds of cultural discourses almost exclusively through the prism of the past, as if in the specific tense "Futur dans le Passé" (Future in the Past) that exists in the French grammar. There was virtually no sphere in Russian cultural life of the post-

---

[1] Nikita Sokolov, "Pravoslavie, samoderzhavie, elektorat: Velichestvennoe proshloe Rossii v budushchem prevzoidet samye smelye ozhidania," *Itogi*, no.37 (23 September 1997), p.66.

perestroika era that remained unaffected by the new paradigm. The area that was, perhaps not surprisingly, most heavily influenced was that of humanities and social sciences. The practices of scholars, their understanding of the object of scholarly inquiry, and the subject of the humanities and social sciences itself noticeably changed, according to the new principles of intellectual and cultural ideology. Most of the disciplines in the humanities and social sciences assumed a historical genre of inquiry as their disciplinary model and the specificity of that model often consisted in the idea of return to, or revival of, the old and presumably lost or abandoned knowledge. The ideals of research and scholarship in the humanities and social sciences became associated with various nineteenth-century Russian figures that had been generally neglected in the tradition of Soviet university education. In the discipline of history, for example, the methodological ideals of treating the object of inquiry were all of a sudden seen in the works of renowned nineteenth-century Russian historians V. O. Kliuchevskii and S. M. Soloviev who had been formally regarded during the Soviet time as "bourgeois or tsarist historians who had no clear understanding of Marxism." The complete multi-volume hard-covered editions of works by both historians were published by major Russian publishing houses during the late 1980s and 1990s.

Anthropologists started to associate the high points in their discipline with their own intellectual heroes from the pre-revolutionary Russia, such as L. Shternberg, K. Kavelin, N. Nadezhdin, and others. Similarly, a number of nineteenth-century ethnographic books were reprinted during the 1980s–90s.[2] Even sociologists, who, as one might think, should have been primarily interested in the contemporary developments in social theory, revoked old disciplinary authorities of their own. Works by many pre-

---

[2] For example, a book by V. V. Radlov, *From Siberia* (Moscow, 1989, in Russian), and several books by D. K. Zelenin: *East-Slavic Ethnography* (Moscow, 1991, in Russian) and *Collected Works* (Moscow, 1994, in Russian). Many more editions were planned and announced in catalogs, but never came out because of the financial hardships that academic publishers had to face in the 1990s.

revolutionary Russian sociologists, such as M. Kovalevskii, V. Khvostov, B. Kistiakovskii, V. Chernov, K. Takhtarev, and others, were included in new sociology textbooks and introduced in university curricula, regardless of the fact that most of them had had no particular theoretical importance already at the end of the nineteenth century.

The academic infatuation with the past was part of a larger cultural trend which from the early perestroika years became an object of active political interest and regular ideological investment. This political interest, which was identified by many scholars and analysts of Gorbachev's and Yeltsin's Russia as an expressed attempt to appeal to, and as a matter of fact revive, Orthodox nationalistic feelings, was highly conducive to the re-emergence in the intellectual milieu of what had been traditionally known in Russia as a Slavophile social attitude. The spreading and strengthening of this attitude over the course of the late 1980s and 1990s determined the basic character of intellectual debates and discourses in the humanities and social sciences, which thus assumed by and large an ideologically conservative shape.

Although ideological contradictions and scholarly disagreements between the followers of the Slavophile trend and those of the opposing conviction, frequently called Westernizers, are still seen by a large number of intellectuals as a distinctive mark of the present situation in Russia, I try to argue in this book that it is not a struggle between the two cultural poles but rather the dominance and growing influence of the Slavophile one that has actually come to constitute the essence of the moment at the turn of the centuries. The struggle, to the extent that it took and still takes place, remains mostly uncreative and generally occurs at the level of mutual complaints. Characteristically, the Slavophile side often acts aggressively, whereas the Westernizers are typically reluctant to respond, and tend to think that the battle itself is pointless and not worth the trouble.

The discord in intellectual discourse is frequently deepened by the predicament of intellectual identities, which perhaps has troubled the Russian society for over a century in its different manifestations. "Intellectuals," skeptically remarked Alexei Nikishenkov in one of the interviews, cited at full length in the following chapters, "are evolving in very strange ways; a revolutionary yesterday is a conservative today and will probably become a religious fanatic tomorrow – that's what the intelligentsia is all about." Indeed, having never quite found their place in the labyrinth of the Soviet society (although having successfully adapted to it in many instances), the intelligentsia suddenly found themselves in a chaotic social reality of the last decade of the twentieth century, in which neither their former roles, nor their imaginary ideals turned out to matter much. The desire of intellectuals to establish themselves as a significant cultural stratum, to find a prestigious cultural niche in the new social environment became another distinctive mark of the post-communist Russian reality.

The predicament of identity became especially salient in the case of academics, particularly scholars in the humanities who started to feel that they were losing their proper place in the new Russian intellectual culture. One should understand that, unlike discourse in the West, in which the terms *academic* and *intellectual* normally appear firmly associated, in Russian cultural discourse the association is not so firm and points, perhaps, to one of the major predicaments of Russian academics, which is going to be the subject of discussion in the following chapters. Academics in Russia (and the tradition stems from the days of the Soviet Union) are not generally thought to be genuine intellectual producers, as opposed to, for example, writers, poets, theater directors, and others who belong to the so-called creative professions. In fact, academics are not always at all thought to be intellectuals as such. Their involvement in the production of what, for the lack of a better phrase, could be called an intellectual discourse of modernity – which always only takes the form of reappreciation of the past in Russia – remains often unnoticed or neglected. This predicament – which is deeply rooted in decades, or perhaps centuries, of Russian history – is by no means a new development. Rather it represents an old development that has come to dwarf the attempts at establishing a normal, critically oriented discourse in the humanities in the 1990s. Although the past decade in Russia has surely witnessed an unprecedented amount of social change, it has also kept much of the cultural conservatism of the former years in what the Soviet ideolanguage used to describe as *dukhovnaia sfera* ("social mentality," for our purposes; but literally, "spiritual sphere," an interesting term that could easily extend its meaning to cover the whole of "culture," for example).[3] As a result, mainstream intellectual discourse still reminds one of the first years of perestroika, being more aggressive than critical, predominantly centered on, if not obsessed with, the past, and persistently dismissive of the subject of modernity. At the same time, there might be observed an increasing desire on the part of academics to surmount their traditional intellectual alienation and assume a more important role in the process of broad cultural production, which has been long dominated by writers, artists, and other creative elites that were, as such, thought to be intelligentsia.

The encounter of academics and other intellectuals with an array of such cultural and political issues in the 1990s by and large constitutes the subject of this book. The aim of this work is to present a contextualized

---

[3] *Dukhovnaia sfera* was indeed an enormously charged notion that could absorb virtually all cultural phenomena, magically lifting and separating them from the earthly ground of *material'naia sfera* (material sphere), which implied a "mundane" realm of money, work, production, food, actual living conditions, and other things "real." An interplay between the two "spheres" was employed by the ideology sometimes to a highest degree of inconsistency. Thus, in the use of Marxist philosophy, the "material" sphere had natural priority over the "spiritual" one (as a matter of priority of *being* over *thinking*), so it was usually said that in no society a good "spiritual" sphere could be built without a proper "material" one. But to justify a more immediate and less philosophical reality, the ideology easily granted the "spiritual" priority over the "material," asserting that Soviet people were mainly interested in a "spiritual" achievement in life, while the "material" side was for them just something to come along, and that that order of things made their life richer than, for example, life in the West. People in the West, as it was taught perhaps in every school, were actually after the "material" ("low" things like money, careers), which was why their "spiritual" life (literally meaning "culture") was incomparably poorer and less interesting than that in the Soviet society.

account of some of the major trends that shaped intellectual and academic discourses in Russian, and formerly Soviet, society in the last quarter of the twentieth century and to a large extent continue to shape them today. It seeks to provide answers to such questions as: Why has in the post-perestroika Russia, a decade after the demise of the communist ideological regime, no substantial revitalization in the humanities and broader intellectual discourses taken place and the latter are remaining locked within a paradigm of expressed conservative character? What are the major traits of this paradigm, its cultural grounds and ideological implications, and how it came to dominate over intellectual practices and worldview? What are the particular social conditions that impede the development of critically oriented discourse in the humanities and social sciences after perestroika? How have intellectual identities changed within the past decade, what are the ideological and political preferences of the intelligentsia, particularly academics, their new values and cultural ideals?

The analysis presented in the following chapters is based on several years of research and personal observation, conducted in Russia during the last decade. Although the main site of my research was the academic institutional setting of the city of Moscow, particularly (but not exclusively) Moscow State University, Russian State University for the Humanities, and various institutions of the Russian Academy of Sciences, some complementary work was done both outside the academic setting, among different strata of the intellectuals, and outside the limits of the Russian capital. Several interviews involved academics from the cities of Cheliabinsk and Omsk. The academic institutional setting of Moscow itself was rather a virtual site, hardly a traditional field site in the anthropological sense, for due to the character of contemporary academic activity, well portrayed by David Lodge in his novel *Small World* and sociologically analyzed by Pierre Bourdieu in *Homo Academicus* and elsewhere, it was in too many instances the social space of discourse and relationships, rather then the physical space of location, that could render an explanation of why things were happening the way they were. Indeed, even within a single locality of an academic department, much of what appeared to be a matter of purely internal importance could be in fact determined by the same space of external social network. Methodologically, therefore (if I have to identify my positions from the anthropological point of view), I would describe my research as loosely adhering to conventions of the emerging genre in anthropological practice, sometimes called multi-sited ethnography, which is strategically focused upon examining "the circulation of cultural meanings, objects, and identities in diffuse time-space ... and tracing a cultural formation across and within multiple sites of activity."[4]

Although much of my work focused on the analysis of texts, and in the following chapters I quote extensively from the printed sources, I see my approach to the reading and interpreting of such sources as essentially anthropological, rather than what is understood in sociological methodology as "discourse analysis." I do not engage in the comparison of texts with other texts as a way to discover some patterns of public opinion – instead, as an anthropologist by training, I reason that the actual patterns of public opinion typically lie behind the text and can be more effectively analyzed through the comparison or juxtaposition of texts with the unprinted routine of everyday life. I attempt, therefore, to ground the texts that I use in the more general context of my ethnographic observations, and consider them only as a manifestation of larger structures of cultural reality that define social discourse as a phenomenon.

The present account is interpretive and descriptive in character, rather than theoretical, due to the nature of my research task. An extended discussion of literature in social theory is omitted intentionally, and theoretical matters are addressed throughout the course of the book in so far as they appear methodologically and conceptually useful. Thus, I specifically address Foucault's discussion of the rules of discursive formation, as it pro-

---

[4] George E. Marcus, "Ethnography in/of the World System: The Emergence of Multi-Sited Ethnography," *Annual Review of Anthropology* 24 (1995): 96.

vides a set of analytical categories that help me explicate the difference between what I try to delineate as the normative discourse of history and the broader cultural historical discourse. On the other hand, for example, I do not specifically address Bourdieu's ideas, as much as they might seem relevant to the subject of intellectuals and academics, primarily because they do not always apply well to the context of what is generally defined by socialist cultural order. This point was well taken by Katherine Verdery in her frequently quoted book on Romanian intellectuals, and I do not find it necessary to repeat her argument here.[5] Similarly, in my discussion of architecture and its relation to the ideology of cultural discourse, I do not invoke recent (mostly, US-oriented) theoretical debates or works, such as Jameson's *Architecture and the Critique of Ideology* and others written in a similar vein, even though they might seem obviously related to the subject.[6] The fact is, the common take on the issue that largely characterizes these debates and that is mainly centered around the question of new spatial geographies is heavily influenced by the particular kind of socioeconomic development in the Western culture (again, particularly the US culture), generally referred to as "postmodern condition." Russian culture, which has not witnessed yet this kind of development, cannot be effectively analyzed on such grounds. As I argue in the following chapters, the entire dimension of architectural discourse in Russia is different from that in the West and represents primarily the collision of a certain primordial tradition with modernity, whereas in the West, especially in the US, the discourse of architecture reflects rather the collision of modernity with postmodernity. For this reason, I find it more appropriate to analyze the architectural discourse in Russia within a conceptual scheme somewhat different from that provided by the recent Western debates on culture and

---

[5] See: Katherine Verdery, *National Ideology Under Socialism: Identity and Cultural Politics in Ceausescu's Romania* (Berkeley: University of California Press, 1991), p.5.

[6] Fredric Jameson, "Architecture and the Critique of Ideology," in *The Ideologies of Theory*, vol.2 (Minneapolis: University of Minnesota Press, 1988).

space. I do resort, however, to frequent comparisons between the academic realities in Russia and the US, because they provide much more tangible grounds for juxtaposition, or perhaps because I am torn between these realities, having spent equal periods of my professional life in both.

Throughout the course of the book, particularly in the concluding chapters, I make extensive use of interviews and conversations with various Russian scholars, many of whom are prominent in their fields, as well as with graduate students in the humanities and other people. Following the idea of privileging the voice of the observed at a certain expense of the authorial voice – idea informally encouraged in the anthropological community of Rice University which to a large extent shaped my vision of the project – I allowed some full-length quotations in the text, although in some instances I felt a need to break or cut the interviews and render them in my own words. In some instances, on the other hand, the interviews delivered perhaps an even more consistent view of discussed issues than the one I could have expressed myself.

Although some twenty five interviews were recorded during the course of my research, not all of them directly appear in the text of the following chapters. Some of the responses were repetitive and I chose the most informative and consistent or otherwise important answers for quotations. The rest of the interviews are rendered in one or another way in my own remarks or indirectly used in my analysis. Apart from the recorded interviews, I drew on many informal conversations with my respondents, which happened in a spontaneous manner. A few people who took a live interest in my project and provided me with long hours of audio tape transcriptions should be perhaps introduced from the beginning, since excerpts from their interviews are used on many occasions in the following text. Olga Vainshtein is a professor currently teaching in the graduate program in the humanities at Russian State University for the Humanities, and a research associate at the Center for Advanced Studies in the Humanities, a very interesting institution that has gathered a group of respected scholars, most of whom came from the interdisciplinary tradition of Moscow-Tartu School of Studies in Culture and Semiotics, formerly associated with Yuri Lotman. Alexei Nikishenkov is a professor teaching at the History Faculty of Moscow State University, and a senior scholar who has been one of the most respected and popular figures among the students at that school. Sergei Sokolovski is a professor of anthropology at the Russian Academy of Sciences and one of the few scholars in the discipline who has been trying to shift research to the interdisciplinary frontiers, writing on the subjects of modernity, reflexivity, and reproduction of knowledge. Sergei Cheshko is also a professor of anthropology at the Russian Academy of Sciences, and the editor of the major anthropological journal in Russia, *Etnograficheskoe Obozrenie* [Ethnographic Survey]. Aleksandr Saltykov is a recent graduate of the History Faculty of Moscow State University, who currently works for a small Russian-American firm. He was a talented and promising student who was offered, upon his graduation, a position of assistant professor, but chose to decline the offer and quit the academy. I found that his career path and his statements in the interviews quite adequately reflected both the attitude of the younger generation toward the academic sphere and the state of the academy in its many aspects.

The organization of the present work is more or less straightforward. The first chapter undertakes a short excursus into the history of the Russian and Soviet intelligentsia. Although much of the following discussion will be focused on academics, they still should be seen as part of a broader intellectual community, however particular or specific their intellectual status might be. The predicaments of academics, likewise, are part of more general predicaments to which the intelligentsia in the Soviet Union and Russia has been exposed over the course of the century. Furthermore, in Russian culture, which is enigmatically rooted in the past in its every aspect, a little history sometimes explains much about what is going on today. The strategic aim of the chapter, however, is to delineate the contours of the problem of modernity – one of the central problems of Russian culture, as I argue, which is essential to understanding the specificity not just of intellectual life in Russia, but also of many current political and cultural processes in the country.

In the second chapter, I attempt to develop my main argument about the specific character of intellectual environment in Russia of the last quarter of the twentieth century. Within this period of time a crucial shift occurred in the intellectual climate of Russian society, which consisted principally in the emergence and rapid spreading of what I identify as a "new historical/cultural paradigm" in intellectual thinking. Focusing on two important social discourses in Russia and the Soviet Union, that of history and that of architecture, I explain how this particular paradigm came to be and what consequences it brought about.

The third chapter elaborates on the issue of cultural impact of the new paradigm. A set of interrelated issues, such as new values of the intelligentsia and the notorious predicament of power, is discussed in this chapter. Typical examples of the new intellectual rhetoric are presented here and their place in the broader cultural discourse in contemporary Russian society is analyzed.

The final chapter focuses specifically on the changes in the humanities that have been taking place in the last decade. Interviews with Russian scholars, who discuss current problems of scholarship, the object of the humanities, and the state of the academy in Russia, are presented in this chapter. Special attention is paid to the discussion of *culturology*, a newly forged university discipline, loosely associated with the Western "cultural studies." Several scholars express in the quoted interviews their personal opinion of the trajectory of culturology's institutional development and its promises and failures. Other important issues, such as current ideological and political moods in the academic milieu, Slavophile and Westernizing trends, and an array of related questions are touched upon in this chapter.

Once again, this book is neither an anthropological monograph, nor a sociological treatise. Much of the research for it was done by various anthropological and sociological means, but in the final genre of presentation it is rather a critical statement or critical reflection that attempts to map, so to speak, a certain cultural territory and invites scholars to further explore the situation behind the charted map. Moreover, it attempts not so much to map an unfamiliar territory, as to re-map a territory that, on the contrary, seems too familiar and maybe too taken-for-granted. I believe there is still much to discover in this territory. The project of cultural critique carried on for some time in the tradition of American anthropology – the project of exposing the strangeness of the familiar – in my opinion, retains its usefulness, no matter how modest and limited in scope it is. In the American academia, as well as to some degree in European academic traditions, this project has been variously praised and variously criticized, but in Russian social sciences and humanities, where it was never undertaken and never existed as such, the absence of reflective self-critical inquiry on any socially meaningful scale remains a trademark of the scholarly discourse. This is the fact which is, fortunately, acknowledged today by a growing – still insignificant on the social scale, but nevertheless growing – number of critically minded intellectuals in Russia. The present account, therefore, is a contribution to the growing fund of critical studies of contemporary Russia, and I hope that this fund will continue to grow. One of my reviewers felt that there was a sentiment of cynicism detectable in this account, and I would like to clarify that no cynicism was intended – there was a sentiment of bitter irony and regret I could not avoid, but hardly was there that of cynicism. Any person familiar with Russian reality of the last decade will acknowledge that life in Russia has been immeasurably more cynical than any account that tries to depict it. If an element of cynicism did sneak into my description of it, that is surely due to the nature of the reality described, not due to some grouchy mood of the author. This is in the first and last instance a book about the society that I personally love and that I wish to see improving and getting rid of certain dogmas that arrest the potentialities of its development.

Chapter 1
The Problem of Modernity, Intellectuals, and the Humanities

> Dear to me is sleep and better to be stone
> So long as shame and sorrow is our portion.
> Not to see, not to feel is my great fortune;
> Hence, do not wake me; hush, leave me alone.
>
> *Michelangelo*

The first and the last problem – at which, one way or another, every other cultural issue in Russia stops and which is essential for understanding how things work in Russian society – is the problem of modernity. In this chapter, I will start outlining the contours of the issue to lay the ground upon which to rest the discussion in the subsequent chapters. Because of the fundamental gravity of this problem, one has to begin with it right from the start, rather than making it a matter of conclusion.

Modernity is a topic that is generally unpopular among Russian intellectuals and tends to be persistently dismissed in intellectual discussions. The system of discursive rules and cultural practices, which embrace Russian society, whether we choose to see it as Foucauldian discursive formation or Kuhnian paradigm, is deeply embedded in the past, and it shows itself in a variety of cultural details, apart from the mainstream discourse with its traditional topics and subjects, which dictate that the correct understanding of the past is the most essential requirement for being in the present, or for arriving at a better future. If, for instance, one should just watch the public in a bookstore for a while (save for a couple of central megastores in Moscow or St. Petersburg), one will unmistakably notice that the history section will be permanently crowded, while the section where they sell contemporary criticism will see a rare customer and a salesperson will just stand there yawning, if there at all.

The lack of interest in modernity, curiously enough, is characteristically reflected in language. *Sovremennost'*, a Russian term for modernity, is not as loaded a word as its English correlate (or, say, French *modernité*, for that matter). Although in rare contexts it may be forced to represent a partial, or even the full array of meanings, covered by the term *modernity*; in regular use or as a stand-alone word, *sovremennost'* conveys little meaning to the ear of a Russian intellectual and points out to a most banal, routine, and uninteresting moment in the life of humankind. Both by origin and its actual meaning, the word stands closer to the English adjective *contemporary*. In fact, the words *sovremennost'* and *contemporary* use exactly the same morphological structure, employing an adequate set of morphemes:

$$[con] + [temp]$$
$$[so] + [vrem]$$
(together, with + time)

Thus while in English or some other European languages, there is a certain line of distinction, drawn between the notions *contemporary* and *modern*, it is not so in Russian, where we find only one term, called into service for all occasions; its counterpart that would stand strictly analogous to *modernity*, as it appears in Western discourse, is missing. (This, incidentally, is a cause of perennial problems and inconsistencies in translations of scholarly and literary works.) The use Russian language makes of the root *modern* is restricted (with the exception of the recently borrowed term *postmodern*, which means nothing in the realities of Russia but comes, as a matter of fashion, into increasingly frequent use among writers, artists, and some avant-garde-minded scholars) by and large to two words: *Modérn*

(Russian architectural style of the beginning of the twentieth century); and *modernizatsiia* ("modernization," "improvement"). Neither of the words in Russian has a straight temporal connotation; both rather imply a sort of technological advance (one of the peculiarities of the style *Modérn* is indeed its employment of convoluted architectural forms on the basis of elaborated engineering design).

It is interesting why the word *modern*, in its temporal function, was not borrowed from French and incorporated into Russian in the nineteenth or the beginning of the twentieth century, given the persistent Francophile spirits among the Russian intelligentsia (tremendous numbers of French words were brought into Russian during the period). It is even surprising to a degree, considering the fact that Baudelaire – a great French poet who was among the first to praise the experience of modernity – was one of the most adored figures in the artistic and literary circles of the Russian Silver Age. His poems and writings were widely read and translated and apparently constituted a "must-know" subject within the intellectual discourse of the day. A curious detail, though, which should not escape the attention of a sensitive literary scholar is that the interest in Baudelaire's works, which the Silver Age manifested so openly, was not comprehensive and the choice of the poet's writings as such fell apart into two major categories: one contained poems that can be loosely described as eschatological in character; the other represented an array of works that dealt with art and symbols. Both were dictated by the retreat of Silver Age intelligentsia from reality to the realm of "pure art," in which an excessive value was always attached to symbolism and the idea of the return to the past, to the "stones of antiquity" as a source of eternal values. (Michelangelo's famous sonnet "Sleep," quoted in the beginning of this chapter, served as a condensed expression of Russian intellectual moods at the turn of the century; the reason I used it as an epigraph is because many years later the same moods and the same sonnet would reappear in literary circles of the 1960s and 1970s in Soviet Russia.) As a result, an essential part of Baudelaire's heritage was dismissed by the Russian intelligentsia, which is also clear from the fact that, in the Silver Age hierarchy, Baudelaire was placed in the same row along with German romanticist Novalis, English symbolist Swinburne, and other French poets of symbolic orientation. Experience of modernity was alien to Russian culture and did not translate well into it.

The experience of modernity has never become part of Russian cultural spirit – Russia lives in another temporal dimension. This was rarely well understood by so-called "sovietologists" in the West, especially in the US. The fact is not surprising per se: people in the US do not remember any other experience, except that of modernity, because, strictly speaking, every time in the US history was modernity. As long ago as in the mid-nineteenth century, Walt Whitman could say things like "The Modern Man I sing," or "I know that the best time and the best place are mine." If one should search through the vast body of Russian literature, one will fail to find a similar praise to time. Russian literary thought of all times has been equally sick with the present, haunted by the past, and longing for a better future. This paradigm in thinking has become deeply entwined in the fabric of Russian culture over the centuries. As a consequence, the past and the future have polarized into a major meaningful dualistic opposition, while the meaningfulness of the present has been substantially reduced. In Russian society, therefore, the loaded categories are the past and the future, while the present, *sovremennost'*, possesses a minimal value – it would not be much of an exaggeration to say that the present is socially perceived by and large as just an annoying transitional moment on the way from the past to the future.

The paradox is, of course, that Russia has been stuck in this "transitional" moment for several centuries by now. As a matter of fact, the idea of Russian history being caught in some sort of time loop reappears fairly frequently in the thoughts of the most insightful Russian thinkers. In the nineteenth century Russian state politician and brilliant philosopher Piotr Chaadaev criticized Russian culture for its ultimate ignorance of the present. In the beginning of the twentieth century prominent philosopher Nikolai Berdiaev seconded his thoughts and wrote in one of his memoirs, "Among us the intelligentsia could not live in the present; it lived in the future and sometimes in the past."[1] This was a common perception of time among the liberal intelligentsia who, much like the Silver Age writers and artists, in their thoughts and deeds (which were, again, mostly writings) sought to live for the future, desperately trying to separate and free it from the haunting past, while remaining disdainful of the present moment. Baudelaire's famous warning, "You have no right to despise the present," scattered throughout his writings here and there, was again and again dismissed by the same Russian intelligentsia that was so fond of the poet. It rarely occurred to a mind of the intelligentsia that something was to be changed in the present in order for the future to be rid of the past. So strong and pervasive was this belief that the political system was corrupt to the bones and nothing could be changed in the present, that the only valid course of action, seen by the intelligentsia, was to not collaborate with the bureaucracy, withdraw, and hope that one day clever people would come to power, or maybe, better still, Christ would come down to Earth and things would finally change. Berdiaev perhaps meant this intelligentsia's blindness, saying that he felt they all had hardly lived in the present. In fact, among the intellectuals who survived the revolution in emigration or elsewhere, this feeling eventually grew into the complex of guilt and words of repentance that "we failed to notice the present, and let the Bolsheviks ruin Russia" became a commonplace in memoirs written after 1917.

This pattern of treating the present remained essentially the same throughout the Soviet period of Russian history. What once had been the intelligentsia's dream was made by the Bolsheviks an ideology. Now life entered a new cultural epoch, the present of which was horrifying to people. So the ideology crossed the present out of history. From now on, peo-

---

[1] Nikolai Berdiaev, *The Russian Idea* (Hudson, N.Y.: Lindisfarne Press, 1992), p.43.

ple were supposed to forget about the present and work hard to death in order to achieve the future that would liberate them from the evil past (that is, that of tsarism and imperialism). People worked hard, but the future never came; and sixty years later, they still remained in the same horrifying present they had started with. Suspicions were rising and the new intelligentsia began to guess that "something must have been wrong with the past (this time, the Bolshevik one), that is why we are still here and cannot arrive at a future." In other words, the cycle repeated itself. The perception of time by new Soviet intellectuals fell into the same trap as the one that the Silver Age intelligentsia failed to avoid. The problems of the present were thought to be related to the inability to work out the right attitude toward the past. A new future was again secretly longed for. But nobody was going to change anything in the present because long decades of exiles, expatriations, and gulags brought back to life the old belief that the political system was totally corrupt and would not allow any change in life, or even just tolerate a hint of it, for that matter. The intelligentsia became absorbed in moral and spiritual self-searching; reappraisal of the past became one of the ultimate goals of personal development, and symbolic means of expression assumed again utmost importance. Thus, in the sixties, Soviet poet Andrei Voznesensky, then avant-garde minded, opened his collection of poems, symbolically entitled *I am Goya*, with his new translation of Michelangelo's sonnet "Sleep."[2] The pattern of the Silver Age, with minor deviations, was reproduced in the Soviet society almost precisely.

---

[2] The symbolism of the title *I am Goya*, for example, was obvious to critically minded intellectuals and, at the same time, could hardly be detected by the Communist Party censorship. To party officials Goya was known at best as a "poor Spanish painter who criticized the evils of bourgeois society in his paintings," so Goya's name was, so to speak, a positive signifier, from the party's point of view. The intellectuals, of course, would see a deeper meaning behind the name Goya, meaningfully exposed on the cover of the book, and would unmistakably associate it with the critic who unmasked and bitterly censured the hidden truth of the day. But then again, behind the title, the hidden truth of the day, from the intellectuals' standpoint, was best depicted in Michelangelo's sonnet "Sleep."

* * *

It should be said that one major difference between the old pattern of the intelligentsia's behavior and the new one lay in the course of action that the intellectuals resorted to. If the old intelligentsia refused to cooperate with the government and chose to either oppose the state or just withdraw from participation in any political activities whatsoever, the new intellectuals, trying to keep an informal image of themselves as some sort of "dissidents," often went into cooperation with the communist state, or one way or another did what the party wanted them to. Voznesensky, for example, in addition to his "dissident" poetry,[3] wrote a series of procommunist, patriotically oriented poems in which he praised Lenin and for which he was eventually awarded the Lenin Komsomol Prize, the second most important state award, after the State Lenin Prize, in the Soviet hierarchy of honorary distinction. Although the image of a "dissident" and the fact of being a recipient of a major communist award did not go over well, this was one of the paradoxes of the new condition in which intellectuals found themselves under the Soviet regime.

One important change related to the intelligentsia's life had taken place since the Silver Age. In the new society of workers and peasants, the intelligentsia was debased, declassed, and deprived of all social privileges. If the nineteenth-century intellectuals constituted a class of a kind, a social group that possessed certain rights and certain wealth (after all, most of those people came from aristocratic noble families), under the new regime the intelligentsia was purposefully made the poorest group of individuals and was deliberately opposed to "workers" and "peasants" in the language

---

[3] Here, I put "dissident" in quotation marks because Voznesensky's poems, just like writings by many other Soviet authors, were never really dissident in the full sense of the word. Nevertheless, there was always this pretense of being a dissident of some sort among the intellectuals, for the idea of cooperating with the state was still a very unpopular one and, like a hundred years before, there was the same strong and unpleasant bad-conscience ring to it.

of the Soviet constitution.[4] Unlike the intellectuals, who did not learn much from history, the new rulers of the Soviet state learned well that the intelligentsia's brain, on the one hand, could pose a threat to the state but, on the other, was needed by it. So they came up with a simple solution – they turned the intelligentsia into a servant with no actual rights, having lowered it, by the power of the constitution, to a classless status of a "layer" that was supposed to accentuate the marginal grounds, upon which the existence of the intellectuals in a new society was built. The famous novel by Russian writers of the 1920s and 1930s Ilya Il'f and Evgenii Petrov *Twelve Chairs* [*Dvenadtzat' stuliev*], one of the most popular literary works ever in Russia, drew a sarcastic picture of the proletarian society that made the existence of an intelligent individual an absolute utopia. In this society the intellectuals, in a fine phrase from the novel, were made "proletarians of the mental labor." (I should add that there is perhaps no single intellectual in Russia who would not know this phrase; we will return to it later, in a

---

[4] The Soviet constitution made truly amazing use of language. Instead of referring to all people of the country as "citizens," the constitution made a distinction between a class of "workers," obviously given a priority in the system and often referred to as "the leading force of the society"; a class of "collective-farm peasantry," allotted equal rights but sort of put in the second place; and what was called a "friendly layer of people's intelligentsia [*druzhestvennaia prosloika narodnoi intelligentsii*]," an amazingly smart and concise phrase that said everything about the intelligentsia's status in society. Thus the intelligentsia was emphatically denied a class status and reduced to the humiliating word *layer* once and for all. The only comprehensible goal of the adjective *friendly* was to stress that, originally and by definition, the layer was unfriendly and was not really needed in this cake at all; but, since it accepted the friendly terms of serving the cause of the working class, it was allowed to legally stay under some kind of "alien resident" status, for no legal room had been allegedly envisaged for this group from the beginning. Finally, the possessive *people's* was added to make the clear even clearer, that is, to emphasize that the intelligentsia belonged to people, that it was actually in people's *possession*, simultaneously drawing an astonishing line of opposition between the terms *people* and *intelligentsia* and, therefore, excluding the latter category from the former. The rest of the constitution by all rhetorical means supported what was laconically stated in this short and sweet phrase. The words *workers, peasants, collective farmers* would consistently pop up in every chapter of the text, in some tricky ways alternating with the notions *citizen* and *people*, whereas the word *intelligentsia* would be meaningfully dropped out in every case.

discussion of the academic community, because it can tell much about the social perception of academics and intellectuals in Russia.)

The idea of making the intelligentsia the party's servant was, in fact, rooted in Lenin's revolutionary theory. One of the most frequently repeated thoughts in Lenin's works was that the point was not to exterminate the intellectuals, but to make them work for the cause of the working class. Shortly after Lenin, as it is known, suspicious rulers of the communist state worked out a more efficient strategy: to make the intellectuals work for the party and *then* exterminate them. During the 1920s, before the beginning of the notorious Stalinist mass terror, this policy was already pursued, sometimes to a very strange end. Even such personalities as Aleksandr Blok, a famous Russian poet who was married to a daughter of the acclaimed chemist Dmitrii Mendeleev and who was openly against the tsarist regime, and for that reason welcomed the revolution; or, for example, Maxim Gorky, a writer who came from the proletarian walks of life and who was highly regarded by Lenin for his literary work – even these people, who in fact were extremely important in molding a new nation's cultural consciousness, were confined by the communists to the atmosphere of highest ingratitude, constant poverty and hardships, and were allowed to die under unclear circumstances. Recent inquiries into the matter do not exclude the possibility that both Blok and Gorky were deliberately poisoned by the doctors who were assigned to "treat" their tuberculosis. Although there is still no conclusive evidence to prove this point, it is a proven fact that both writers were categorically denied permission to go to Europe for treatment. An interesting issue is the involvement of Lunacharsky, the head of the State Committee for Education, in this matter.[5] The

---

[5] "The State Committee for Education" is an accepted translation for *Narodnyi Komissariat Prosveshchenia*, also known in Russian as *Narkompros*. The literal meaning of the phrase, which in this case would probably represent a more culturally sensitive translation, is "The People's Commissariat for the Enlightenment" (a bizarre combination of words, in which *commissariat* is a military term for "enlistment or registration office," *enlightenment* is still "enlightenment," and all this is embraced by *the people's*).

traditional Soviet version of the story, as retold in many literature and history textbooks, pictured a half-heroic, half-pathetic episode, according to which Blok, for instance, simply did not want to inform the government authorities or anybody of his illness, being too modest and aware that at the moment the whole country was "ill," not just himself, and that the government had more important matters to attend to. When Blok's relatives and friends somehow found out that his health was getting worse, they interceded with the authorities for the poet, asking to let him go to Europe for medical treatment, but some bad guys in the bureaucracy allegedly never passed their request to the government, which thus was left again unaware of the illness of the first poet of the nation. It was, as the myth goes, only when the news of Blok's serious condition reached Lunacharsky that the matter was immediately attended to. Lunacharsky supposedly rushed to the highest government officials and obtained the permission for Blok to leave in a matter of hours, but it was too late since the poet happened to die the same night.

This mythical story was placed in Soviet school and university textbooks not as an excuse but rather as an object lesson that was supposed to show just how many bourgeois saboteurs there were in the young Soviet society, how difficult it was to fight them, and how high the price to pay was sometimes. At the same time, it demonstrated the heroism of communist leaders, such as Lunacharsky, who at the drop of a hat were ready to help Soviet people with all their needs and troubles.

Of course, things probably did not seem quite as heroic in reality, as they were pictured afterward. Recent archival research has revealed that Lunacharsky knew about Blok's illness all along and that other government officials were kept informed about the state of his health as well. Writers and artists constantly reminded Lunacharsky of the need to send Blok abroad, and, in fact, it was only when the state of the poet's health became apparently hopeless that the measures (or the appearance of measures) were taken.

This is, of course, just a single example of what became a rather typical practice under the socialist regime. No intellectual was considered worth a penny, and anyone, regardless of one's importance in the eyes of the public or even one's services to the party, could be tossed away at any moment. Therefore, the trap was not just that the intelligentsia was given an unambiguous choice – either to serve the party or go to the gulag – it was rather that even serving the party, it could not be sure that it was doing the right thing and that its position was secure. A secure position was not envisaged for the intelligentsia in socialist society simply because, by definition, the intelligentsia was bourgeois in its interests and aspirations. It was allowed to stay and live in this society, so to speak, "on parole" and "until further notice."

That is why the Soviet intelligentsia, which was allowed some freedom of expression at the time of Khrushchev's "thaw" in the sixties, still could not counterpose itself to the state bureaucracy in the way the nineteenth-century intelligentsia had done. Soviet intelligentsia was unconditionally employed by the bureaucracy, and it had to work for it one way or another, otherwise it would have been "released" to the KGB's hands. Even during Khrushchev's short rule, when the official reevaluation of Stalin's personality cult and mass terror started and, for the time being, the risk of being thrown in the gulag was substantially reduced, intellectuals could not allow themselves more than several bold words, wrapped in a veil of historical metaphors or symbolically disguised in some other manner. They did not think about assuming an actual oppositional stance and openly standing up to the humiliating bureaucratic system. Unlike nineteenth-century intellectuals, they had nothing to stand on, and they were afraid. This is, of course, understandable. However, much like the old aristocrats, the idea of struggle with and, more importantly, *for* the present was alien to their consciousness, as some impossible and fatalistically unaccomplishable task. Intellectuals now occupied nothing more than isolated cells in the structure, firmly held by the communist bureaucracy. Besides, as a rigid rule, all those places in which the concentration of intellectuals exceeded a safe level (universities, pedagogical institutes, research institutes, high schools, literary and artistic unions and organizations, newspaper, journal and book publishing houses, and so on) were prudently injected with an enforced dose of communist *nomenklatura*, which maintained close surveillance and set not just the rules for intellectual discourse, but the standards of intellectual behavior as such. Anyone who displayed a deviant tendency became subject to punishment or at any rate official censure, and the criteria for "deviant" could be indeed cunningly loose, because they were never written out in black and white, being deliberately placed at local *nomenklatura's* exclusive disposal and thus made, in essence, a subject to oracular interpretation.

This condition explains why intellectuals would not want to take any risk related to their jobs or their behavior at work, for being punished at work or losing a job was not the end of the road down but just the beginning of it, and one could never be sure where exactly it would lead. There is a remarkable episode in Andrei Tarkovsky's film *The Mirror* [*Zerkalo*], which subtly illustrates the point. A woman who works as a journalist in a newspaper publishing house is awakened early in the morning and informed that, due to a type-setting misprint, a line in her article about some high government official has acquired an obscure double meaning and that the issue is about to come out. The woman gets up and, having grabbed some random clothes, rushes to the printing house. What follows is just a long silent scene of her running, which conveys all the profound psychological contents of the moment. Tarkovsky's camera captures the full measure of this constant fear of a regular Soviet intellectual, showing that the woman is not just scared to lose her job, but is rather experiencing a feeling of the beginning of the end of the world. The universe is about to start falling, in her eyes – and this chilling experience, Tarkovsky seems to say, is what constitutes the never-ending pathological horror one can never escape from. An intelligent person was meant to walk a tightrope in this society – one step aside and you begin a long agonizing descent through the seven circles of hell.[6]

* * *

Pressed by social and economic instability on the one hand, and by constant ideological terror on the other, intellectuals certainly went to work for the communist bureaucracy, and they, in the fullest sense, became a part of it. They must have surely felt that, but they were never able to admit it, for so strong was the persuasion that the union of the intelligentsia with the bureaucracy implied bad conscience on the part of the former. Some people could live with that, some could not, and some chose to dismiss the whole point of the contradiction. This seemingly simple delimitation came to mark three distinctive categories of intellectuals, which were steadily reproduced through the 1980s, having gone into the process of mutation with the bankruptcy of the communist regime.

To the first category (where "the first" means essentially "the largest") belonged all those who, one way or another, dismissed the moral implications of the connection with the bureaucracy and, having thus cleared the bad-conscience predicament once and for all, in good conscience assumed the right way of life, prescribed by the communist state. Undoubtedly, this category contained all those who reached, and were allowed in, various positions that involved power, even the slightest amount of it, or some kind of management or control over people and cultural production. That is to say, departmental chairs, deans, section heads in any kind of organization,

---

[6] Tarkovsky's life perhaps exemplified the point he was trying to make in his movies even clearer. *The Mirror* became one of those films that eventually led to his expulsion from the country. His trying to say a word of truth about the present was certainly a step aside. Likewise, after *The Mirror*, the actress Margarita Terekhova, who performed the starring role in the film, was utterly disapproved of by the communist censorship, found herself in deep disgrace in the Union of Soviet Filmmakers, and was offered only unimportant secondary roles for many years ahead, even though she was known as one of the most talented and popular actresses.

journal and newspaper editors, film and art producers, TV and radio newscasters and program hosts, secretaries of the central and local artistic unions (i.e. unions of writers, musicians, painters, and so on), and others of the sort all came to belong in this group. Side by side with them was an even larger part of the same group, which consisted of the intellectuals who had not reached such prominent positions but were aspiring to them. And, finally, the rest of the group was primarily academics (par excellence those in the upper divisions of the academia). All these people, as a general rule, cared very little whether their image corresponded to what was defined by others by that rather demanding term *intelligentsia* (as a matter of fact, most of them were sure they actually were *the* intelligentsia, although they were rarely perceived as such by the public, and perhaps never so by other intellectuals) – this question did not trouble them at all in any form. In other words, this group represented that group of intellectuals who had achieved some success within the framework of the communist social system and felt comfortable with it. The majority of people forming this group were either members of the Communist Party or on the way to joining it – because party membership was a prerequisite for virtually any of the positions mentioned above.

The second category embraced perhaps a somewhat smaller group of intellectuals, most of whom were well educated, in fact often better than those belonging in the first category, but not as successful at moving up the social scale as the representatives of the latter. The reason why they were experiencing social difficulties was in many cases the same. They did cherish some intellectual ideals and adhered to the principle (rather utopian in the communal society) that their success, well-being, rewards, and movement up the social ladder should result from their work and their actual intellectual achievement, not from their place in the communist hierarchy. The tricky way of achieving success by means of joining the party and playing the "bureaucratic game" was not favored among this category of people, and often they saw party membership as an obstacle that was blocking their professional road. Nevertheless, some of them might reluctantly join the party when, upon completion of a certain amount of work, they came to face membership as a last requirement they had to meet in order to advance their professional status. There were also some romantics who joined the party out of sincere conviction that a citizen, especially an intellectual, should be actively engaged (needless to say, this type of enthusiasm was not particularly welcome among the more pragmatic community of party members). Still, many others chose not to compromise their moral principles and remained where they were for years or for ever, considering involvement in ideological structures as a mark of bad conscience and thus following the old pattern of Russian intelligentsia. These intellectuals could be found occupying many positions in society except those reserved for the first category – for example, they could be talented (or not necessarily talented) writers whose works were rarely accepted for publication, journalists of a lower rank, all kinds of assistant and associate professors or junior research assistants[7] in academia (the rank of full professor almost unconditionally required being a member of the party), museum or library assistants, a variety of people in creative arts, freelancers, and so on. Common to all these individuals was that they believed or felt that the intelligentsia – especially genuine intelligentsia – should not be involved with the bureaucracy and should only engage in creative intellectual activities (as opposed to administrative tasks). Moreover, many reasoned that, in

---

[7] Technically, there were no such categories as "assistant" or "associate" professor in the Soviet Union. For those who are into the details of Soviet academic hierarchy, what I am referring to are the positions of *mladshii prepodavatel'* and *starshii prepodavatel'* which, in terms of the usual career track in the academic environment, roughly correspond to the positions of "assistant" and "associate" professor in the US university system. "Junior research assistant" (*mladshii nauchnyi sotrudnik*) was and remains the lowest Soviet/Russian academic position, infamously known as *MNS*. It was intended, in the proper sense, for young non-tenured scholars (i.e. recent college graduates); but, in reality, people could be, were, and still frequently are kept in this position without promotion for decades. Being a *MNS* for someone in their late forties or fifties was humiliating; and so this kind of manipulation with the academic status was certainly one of the rudest disciplinary instruments in *nomenklatura*'s disposal.

the ideal case, the intelligentsia should oppose and criticize the bureaucracy, exposing its oppressive nature. In other words, people in this category were those who, in their beliefs or worldview, maintained a certain standard of what genuine intelligentsia should be like, and that standard very often had a "dissident" ring to it. Furthermore, they were not always sure they conformed to that standard, which was thought to be rather high, and, for that reason, usually did not like to use the word *intelligentsia* when referring to themselves (they certainly never applied it to intellectuals in power, those composing the first category, for whom they usually had the greatest disdain as ignorant people who pretentiously posed as cultural elites or people who betrayed their moral principles). Instead, they had a common habit of referring to themselves as "proletarians of mental labor," in a phrase borrowed from *Twelve Chairs*.[8]

To the third and the smallest category belonged, as it is perhaps easy to guess, those who not only "believed" that intellectuals should oppose the state and act to expose the oppressive nature of bureaucracy, but who in fact did oppose the state and did act the way they felt they should. These were dissidents without quotation marks, and they could mainly be found abroad or in gulags, although a certain number of them always remained scattered here and there in the social maze of socialist society.

So the first group represented an actual intellectual elite, where by *elite* I mean not "intellectually sophisticated" but rather "socially safe." These

---

[8] The phrase "we are not intelligentsia, we are just proletarians of mental labor" indeed enjoyed wide currency among the intellectuals and actually was a modest phrase to reply with. However, it has to be noticed that what was just a popular quotation was at the same time a strategically precise expression that served several tasks simultaneously. First, it was a humble way for an intellectual to refer to his or her social status, emphasizing its inadequacy to the high standard granted to the word *intelligentsia*. Second, it certainly contained a sad social truth hidden behind the humor. Third, and most interesting, it was a simultaneous excuse for the inability to act the way a *genuine* intelligentsia would have acted, and thus allowed "humble intellectuals" to disclaim the burden of intelligentsia's responsibilities at any given moment: "after all, we are not intelligentsia, we are just proletarians of mental labor."

people occupied the highest positions that intellectuals could possibly achieve within the given social system, and they were loyal to the system rather than to their intellectual background in exchange for some power that they were allowed to exercise over the rest of the intellectuals. This was, therefore, the group of intellectuals that most successfully merged with the bureaucracy – or, one may simply say, they *were* the bureaucracy.

The second group essentially represented those who tried to maintain their intellectual identities, their being part of cultural intelligentsia (which unequivocally required them to stay away from the bureaucracy), and at the same time tried to find their way in the system by honest means (which unequivocally required them to work for the bureaucracy one way or another). This was the group by and large producing the intellectual discourse of the day.

The third group represented intellectuals who gave up attempts to find their way in the system, being in radical disagreement with the existing social order, and either were engaged in some underground activity or, if miraculously employed, tried to assume an attitude of defiance toward the bureaucracy, thus taking advantage of their positions. As mentioned earlier, these people often were either abroad or, if at home, under KGB's surveillance. They played a very important part in consolidating the self-identity of the Soviet intelligentsia, serving both as "saints" of informal intellectual culture and certainly as an ideal of a kind for every intellectual unhappy with the oppressive totalitarian system.

The distinction drawn between the groups of intellectuals is an important thing for a researcher to keep in mind because the layer of intellectuals in the cake of Soviet society was never homogenous. When one speaks of *Soviet intelligentsia*, it always makes sense to specify what particular group is being talked about; otherwise, an account may result in a good deal of confusion. It is obvious, too, that one may subdivide the stratum of intellectuals according to different criteria; our subdivision, however, will suffice for our purposes. Here, as we are going to pay special attention to the academics, we will mainly touch upon the first two groups of intellectuals, the more problematic of which appears certainly the one we have placed in the second category, as a group responsible for the basic production of intellectual discourse in the humanities and as a group with the most complex relationship with the bureaucratic structure. Indeed, the relationships of the first ("elites") and the third ("dissidents") groups with the bureaucracy were very much fixed and relatively unproblematic, whereas for the intellectuals of the second category that relationship always constituted an awkward (or perhaps one should say, *the basic*) predicament, which in many aspects shaped their worldview and social position. This was a rather curious group of people, which in fact ideally conformed to the type of intellectuals frequently mentioned by Adorno and perhaps represented by himself to an equal degree (that is, the type, caught in a double bind between seductive powers of bureaucracy and the vanity of intelligentsia); for, within the realm of intellectual discourse, these people essentially liked to pose as intellectuals from the third ("dissident") category, but in their deeds often performed what the intellectuals from the first ("bureaucratized") group did, even without noticing it. So in a sense this was a group most successfully co-opted by the state, because the first group actually already *was* the state and exercised certain power over the second, whereas the latter, being forced to stay in marginal positions and permanently kept at bay, was at the same time allowed to pursue some "dissident-looking" discourse and, thus, experience some excitement of individual freedom – of course, *in exchange* for some good work done for the state. Hence the notorious paradox of the totalitarian state needing the dissidents. It is not just that the state needed the dissidents to satisfy its paranoia, as a psychoanalytic interpretation would tell us; it is rather that the state found it a cheap and efficient coin with which to pay. The state somehow figured that the intelligentsia's work could be best paid off not with money or with career honors or distinctions, but with the mythical experience of freedom. It was not expensive at all to let intellectuals pronounce a few dissident words and make them feel proud, if that was what they wanted. On the contrary, this price could not suit the state better, for by satisfying dissident desires of intellectuals, the state simultaneously gathered evidence against them, so that at any time, should the need arise, the state would have a reason to nail them; and it was also good because it made intellectuals feel somewhat guilty and insecure, which meant that the state did not have to exert extra pressure on intellectuals in a direct way, for now their own feeling of guilt and insecurity would force them to do what the state expected them to.

This ideological device proved very efficient because, for example, a writer, having said a dissident word in one novel, would now feel obliged, solely by power of his or her guilty conscience, to write three other novels, this time ideologically correct and expressly loyal, in order to atone for the misdeed. The state in many instances found the price acceptable, because both on the social and individual scale expression of loyalty substantially exceeded that of disloyalty. In this light it becomes less surprising that such people as Voznesensky, who was publicly denounced by Khrushchev as a "bourgeois formalist, slandering the Party," should be made recipients of outstanding party awards several years later, under Brezhnev (whose coming to power, absurdly enough, marked the end of the "thaw" of the sixties and the beginning of much stricter censorship over cultural production).

The same could be said about another formerly popular, now unpopular, Soviet/Russian poet, Yevtushenko, who had a fairly radical, almost dissident, public image but at the same time was one of the most publishable and well-traveled writers, which again represented a virtually implausible combination of things that, according to common opinion, could not go together. Common opinion certainly was not misleading people, but it never went far enough to reveal the actual roots of what appeared as implausible. Thus many people were apt to reason that the poet was just so popular that his public prestige made the government show some formal regard for him and take his authority seriously. This was nothing but another absurdity in Soviet intellectual thinking, which, having gone through decades of most disrespectful social oppression, still was able to accept that an intellectual voice could possess such authority that would carry some weight with the ruling power. It was hardly a question of some public authority, which mattered little to the political elite, for, according to a number of recent publications, Yevtushenko simply did some kind of minor spying job for the party, watching and denouncing his fellows intellectuals, in exchange for the informal permission to look "dissident" and intellectually bold. Some authors even assert that Yevtushenko was actually involved with the KGB; but at this point it does not really matter whether his activities had to do directly with the KGB or did not go further than some party officials, because both party officials and the KGB were nothing but different hands of a single state machine, and it was all the same in the end. What is remarkable here is, again, the pattern of relationship between intellectuals (those we have marked under the second category, as the basic cultural producers) and the state. The degree of co-optation that pattern has revealed is indeed impressive. What comes to mind is again Adorno's statement, "*Administration is not simply imposed upon the supposedly productive human being from.without; it multiplies within this person himself*" (emphasis added).

It is now time to turn to the academic community after this detour into the history of intelligentsia, which had to be taken into account, for everything that has been said above about the intelligentsia holds pertinent to the academics. Among the intellectuals, academics always held one of the most secure positions in the social maze of society. Journalists, writers, or artists might have to live by constantly switching places and jobs whereas an academic, upon taking his or her job at a university, could really relax in a sense (all it took was to accept the rule of the game, and in the end it was not that much – just behave and write and teach, according to an unsophisticated standard set by the party officials, and you are set and secured for the rest of your career). That is why professors in the Soviet Union rarely changed their places of work (institutions, departments) – which, for example, has been very typical for scholars in the US, where academic mobility is rather high. Getting an assistant professorship at a university in most cases would mean literally that you were secured to spend your entire career at that institution to the day of retirement. As a result, academics became one of the most bureaucratized groups among the intelligentsia. Naturally, they would rarely do anything against the regime. And so, because of all that, because of their being relatively aloof from many common anxieties of the intelligentsia – because of their silence and nonparticipation, noninvolvement in provocative intellectual discussions, but also because of that idea, deeply ingrained in Russian culture, that intellectuals should be writers, poets, or artists – academics, in public perception, somehow slipped out of the notion *intelligentsia* (at least, genuine intelligentsia) and were rather thought as some sort of technical workers of science. Academics never felt uncomfortable with that public image – indeed, one may wonder if they even noticed it – until the perestroika ended academic security and privileges. Now academics have been put on equal terms with all other intellectuals, and they are definitely losing in the eyes of the public because journalists, TV newscasters, and other popular figures have been able to develop a more salient public image in recent years, leaving academics behind the realm of publicity. The media, accordingly, have lost active interest in academics, especially those in the humanities, who are now often thought of as Marxist retrogrades or as figures incapable of any good intellectual discussion. Newspapers and public magazines, for instance, now rarely turn to academics for interviews. And it is strange, but academics still remain conservative in that they still wait for something from the state and think that the state should come to their salvation, while it becomes increasingly apparent that the state does not seem to appreciate their "help" anymore, since with the demise of communist ideology, silent guardians of the ideological values have apparently become unneeded. What the state now needs is proclaimers of new "capitalist" values, and old academics are not good for it, as they are not used to such things as proclamations in principle, being largely accustomed to a quiet style of intellectual activity. The state wants those who do proclamations – and these people are certainly being enrolled from other walks of the population: from the uncompromising (not academics), desirably wealthy (again, not academics), and those with constant public exposure (surely not academics). That is to say, those who qualify to be favored by the state are often journalists, all kinds of media people, businesspeople – but by no means academics. Academics feel increasingly alienated in this situation, and they want to find a way to join the group of the privileged ones, but at the moment it looks like they are likely to remain in the shadow.

Chapter 2
Discourses of History, Architecture, and the New Paradigm in Intellectual World-Views

> Rome makes one feel stifled with sadness ... through the gloomy and lifeless museum atmosphere that it exhales, through the abundance of its pasts, which are brought forth and laboriously held up (pasts on which a tiny present subsists), through the terrible overvaluing, sustained by scholars and philologists and imitated by the ordinary tourist in Italy, of all these disfigured and decaying Things, which, after all, are essentially nothing more than accidental remains from another time and from a life that is not and should not be ours.
> *Rainer Maria Rilke.*[1]

Although it is well known that the discourse of literature played a very important part in the spectacle of intellectual life, and in many ways broader mass culture, in the Soviet Union, and indeed the conclusion Bruce Grant, a good colleague of mine, makes when he says that "members of the elite [Writers'] union had been the main architects of Soviet culture since their profession had been collectivized under Stalin in 1934" is very much to the point,[2] – there have always been two interesting parallel social discourses, to which I would like to draw attention in this chapter: that of history, and that of architecture. These discourses were as much subject to ideological scrutiny as was the literary realm and their connec-

---

[1] Rainer Maria Rilke, *Letters to a Young Poet* (New York: Vintage Books, 1986), pp.46–47.
[2] Bruce Grant, "Dirges for Soviets Passed," in *Perilous States: Conversations on Culture, Politics, and Nation*, ed. George E. Marcus (Chicago: University of Chicago Press, 1993), p.17.

tion to the state regime was also unquestionable, but the ways in which these discourses were employed by the regime were sometimes less obvious – which perhaps accounted for the fact that they survived longer, and actually are still very much in ideological use, several years after the "literary machine" has been dismantled and the discourse of literature has lost its appeal and influence. In fact, not only did they survive, but, as I shall try to show in the course of this chapter, they became the major constituent parts in the shaping of a new paradigm in intellectual thinking, which gradually encompassed and eventually came to dominate the larger structures of social discourse in Russia in the last quarter of the twentieth century.

The major difference between the literary discourse and its neighbor discourses under consideration appears to have been, indeed, in the mode of operation – that is, in the ways these discourses were socially established and culturally appropriated in the Soviet society. (This brings me to think of Foucault's well-known discussion of the rules of discursive formation, which may, as it seems to me, put the subject into an appropriate interpretive analytical framework, and I shall draw on this discussion as I proceed further.) The discourse of literature came to signify one of the major, or arguably but possibly the main field of cultural production in the Soviet Union. As such, it rested on an elaborate institutional infrastructure and an unusually dynamic, for the socialist system, producer-consumer relationship which, in turn, was successfully maintained both at the level of fully functioning symbolic market (the "word" was consumed, produced, and again sought for, i.e. there was a continuous dialectics of symbolic demand and supply), and at the level of no less functioning material commodity market (the book, despite the centralized socialist economy, oddly remained a kind of free-floating commodity, the real value of which was in most cases determined by that very producer-consumer relationship, not by the planned economics of book publishing and nominal selling prices). In short, the discourse of literature had a tangible organizational structure behind it (the notorious Unions of Writers, famous Gorky Institute of Literature, a network of prestigious publishing houses, popular literary newspapers and magazines, including *Literaturnaia Gazeta* [Literary Newspaper] and a "must-read" set of journals, like *Novyi Mir* [New World], *Nash Sovremennik* [Our Contemporary], and others, known to everyone and subscribed in every family that had any intellectual interest in life; and so on).

Contrary to this, neither the discourse of history nor that of architecture did have a clear organizational structure, which would be identifiably responsible for the production of this or that kind of social conversation. There were departments of history at universities and pedagogical institutes, but academics, as it has been mentioned earlier, were not generally considered intellectuals and very few of them had public exposure in the media. Scholarly journals in the field of history were hardly read outside the history departments, not to mention that only a few of them – in fact, perhaps only one, *Voprosy Istorii* ("Questions of History", which was largely ignored by most intellectuals anyway, being associated with the dogmatic version of Marxist-Leninist scholarship) – were known to the public at all;[3] the rest were obscure newsletters with minimum circulation and so called *Vestniki*,[4] published by various divisions of the Soviet Acad-

---

[3] By and large, this was a rather typical public attitude toward all other academic periodicals in the humanities. A professor of philosophy, whom I interviewed in 1995 in Moscow, reflected on the situation in his own discipline: "Yes, we have got journals, but the thing is, they are not popular among the general public. They are simply not known outside the academic community. Stop any person in the streets, who is not an academic, and ask him whether he reads *Voprosy Filosofii* [Questions of Philosophy] – he'll just do those scared eyes, because he has never heard of such thing. Or maybe, better still, he has, because fifteen years ago they probably made him learn some Marxist propaganda from that journal in high school. So, at best, public is unaware of these publications – at worst, it is instinctively afraid of them." (The full text of the interview may be found in: Alexei Elfimov, "Academics and the Production of an Intellectual Discourse of Modernity in Russia," in *Para-Sites: A Casebook against Cynical Reason*, ed. George E. Marcus [Chicago: University of Chicago Press, 2000], p.225–55.)

[4] *Vestnik*, in academic language, stands for "newsletter," "periodic news."

emy of Sciences and a few major universities (such as Moscow State University or Leningrad State University). Generally, even history students found these publications boring and tried to ignore them in their studies, if that was possible.

Even less could be said about architecture. Architecture was mainly considered a technical discipline (apart from its side connection with the history of arts, which will be discussed further). The *disciplinary* discourse of architecture as such was of marginal interest to the broader intellectual public, although it must be noted that however narrow that disciplinary discourse was, it was always directly linked to the highest levels of power, and this is perhaps just another area where Soviet intellectuals overlooked an important target for social criticism. One of the very few serious attempts to analyze the connection between socialist power and disciplinary practices of architecture in cultural terms was undertaken in the late 1970s by a bright young Soviet scholar Vladimir Papernyi in his book *Kul'tura Dva* [Culture Two],[5] which was, to no surprise, recognized by Soviet authorities as anti-socialist, never published, and eventually led Papernyi to emigrate to the US, where he eventually decided to abandon his academic career and pursue his graphic designer talents.

In a word, discourses of history and architecture, as they formed in the realm of Soviet intellectual culture, had no clear referent, unlike the discourse of literature; instead, they assumed fluid omnipresent forms. The literary discourse was salient; it came in tangible "chunks" of journals, newspapers, books, statements, authors, and events. Discourses of history and architecture were almost intangible, they appeared everywhere inconspicuously as an underlying context, evoking indisputable themes of "cultural heritage" and "humanism" – that is to say, they were thoroughly dis-

---

[5] The book was first published in 1985 in the US by *Ardis* (Ann Arbor) who published much of the Soviet immigrant literature during the Cold War years. After the breakdown of the Soviet Union, there finally appeared a Russian edition: Vladimir Papernyi, *Kul'tura Dva* (Moscow: Novoe literaturnoe obozrenie, 1996).

solved in the very fabric of culture and, indeed, were meant to penetrate the realm of taken-for-granted ideological, if not ontological, foundations. While the literary discourse was positioned, so to say, in front of intellectual minds, the latter discourses were passively consumed and led their existence *within* the minds.

Speaking of the rules of discursive formation, Foucault distinguishes between discourses based on a *program*, and those based on what he calls *strategies*. By program, Foucault means certain projects of power, characterized by the normative logic of social planning, where the ways or, as Foucault names them, *technologies* of power intervention are rationally elaborated and the effects of such intervention are calculated in advance. By strategies, in contrast, Foucault defines power maneuvers in the fluid realm of unexpected occurrences within the discursive domain – occurrences that result, often in a spontaneous manner, from the process of complex interactions and transformations of various discourses, power relations, and social forces, among other things. Some discourses, says Foucault, "give rise to certain organizations of concepts, certain regroupings of objects, certain types of enunciation, which form, according to their degree of coherence, rigour, and stability, themes or theories ... Whatever their formal level may be, I shall call these themes and theories 'strategies'."[6] But strategies are also those elusive forms of power exercise that take advantage of everything that was not envisaged or taken into account by the normative tactics of control, such as programs. Strategies are essentially those types of power maneuvers that do not seek to produce a special discourse, but rather rely on existing discursive currents in their manipulative interests.

This conceptual distinction applies rather well to the situation we are dealing with in the Soviet Union. The discourse of literature was indeed a fine example of a program-based discourse, in Foucault's sense: its goals

---

[6] Michel Foucault, *The Archaeology of Knowledge* (New York: Pantheon, 1972), p.64.

and tasks were worked out on the basis of particular needs of the power regime, the forms and methods of its intervention were elaborated, its effects were planned and anticipated, and its fulfillment was controlled. Even the deviant tendencies, expressed in the form of dissident moods, seem to have been taken into account by that smart program. Discourses of history and architecture, on the other hand, come to exemplify Foucault's strategy-based discursive phenomena that form out of various collisions in the discursive realm, regroupings of social forces and objects, and the desire of power to take advantage of all these voluntary and involuntary shifts in one or another manner.

I. Discourse of History

Let us consider first the mechanics of the discourse of history. History, of course, is one of the sacred domains in any national ideology, especially in the societies of socialist orientation, and it is a commonly taken point now that "communism as a political institution has exercised the most rigorous and exclusive control over the political utilization of historical knowledge".[7] A good account of such utilization of historiography by the socialist regime was provided, for example, in the often cited Katherine Verdery's work on Romanian intellectual culture.[8] The Soviet Union was certainly no exception in this regard, and the same planned and thoroughly thought out system of ideological control over the production of history functioned there. This system embraced a variety of social institutions, from censorship to libraries and archives to mass media and various cultural organizations, apart from the obvious institutions of academic schol-

---

[7] Colin Gordon, "Afterword," in *Power/Knowledge: Selected Interviews and Other Writings, 1972–1977*, by Michel Foucault (New York: Pantheon Books, 1980), p.232.
[8] Katherine Verdery, *National Ideology Under Socialism: Identity and Cultural Politics in Ceausescu's Romania* (Berkeley: University of California Press, 1991).

arship and general mass education. Professors and teachers in history were, as a rule, recruited from people who were active members (at any rate, simply members) of political organizations – that is, Communist Party or *Komsomol*, the Young Communist League. In case of recent graduates or young candidates, who had not yet had sufficient time to establish their reputation along the political lines, their joining the party and subsequent participation in its activities was expected.[9] This procedure clearly functioned as a pledge of loyalty to the ideological regime. If, upon certain "grace" period of time, a teacher or professor failed or displayed unwillingness to join the party, she was usually questioned by the dean, principal, or other authorities and asked to explain her motives. Subsequently, she might be either given a choice of joining the party or leaving the job, or, if the authorities found that the person was more or less ideologically reliable and her preference to stay away from political activity was "arbitrary," not dictated by any kind of ideological motives, she might be left alone for some time, after which she would be informally questioned again, and so on. If such person, however, continued to be employed without the party membership – that is, continued to be *bespartiinyi* (literally, "partiless"),[10] as it was usually said in the Soviet Union – her road to promotion, it must

---

[9] Cf. Verdery's remarks on the historical profession in Romania: "...various institutions of history ... were brought more fully under the control of the Party's Central Committee. Subsequent measures allowed Ph.D.s to be given only to persons acceptable to their municipal Party organization, prescribed the precise content of courses to be taught in history, and even fixed by fiat the dates of major events to be celebrated..." (Katherine Verdery, *National Ideology Under Socialism*, p.221).

[10] Word *bespartiinyi*, from a colloquialism, forged in the early years of socialism as a label (surely, somewhat derogatory) for all those who did not belong to the party, gradually grew into a major social status line. All job applications and other more or less important bureaucratic documents in the Soviet Union contained this must-be-filled entry "Party Membership," in which one could either indicate that one was a "member of the Communist Party since such and such year," or write the word "*bespartiinyi*." But, of course, the presence of the word *bespartiinyi*, from the point of view of the authorities, indicated that there was something wrong about the person. So, the derogatory sense, once granted to "partiless," not only remained but was also administratively legalized as a primary social stratification element.

be understood, would be almost certainly closed. For any promotion (at least, more or less important promotion), party membership would serve as a mandatory condition. This situation, incidentally, explains the presence of a fairly large number of middle-aged and older people working as assistant professors or earlier mentioned "junior research assistants" at universities, or as elementary level school teachers who had never been promoted to senior levels.

Such practices, it must be added, constituted a standard mechanism of ideological control, which was widespread in the Soviet society and was employed almost universally as a most elementary form of power exercise and most elementary means of social stratification and differentiation. This mechanism was present and functioning in the historical discipline, just as it was in other humanities and sciences, leave alone other sectors of society. What was distinctive about the discipline of history in this regard was, perhaps, only the amount – that is, enforced doses – of such practices put into action. In such fields, as mathematics or physics, for example, social censorship was always less strict (although physics was actually a difficult case too, for a variety of reasons). An assistant professor in mathematics could safely achieve a promotion on the basis of her scientific skills and talents alone, without having to worry much about party matters (to be promoted to the position of chair in mathematics, though, one still had to meet the party membership criteria). The ability to understand mathematics was not so clearly linked to the necessity of being "ideologically correct," as the ability to understand history.[11] To understand the true laws of history, one had to develop an ideologically correct world view first; and party membership, depending on the perspective one looked from, was either a prerequisite for developing such world view or an indication that one had already developed it.

---

[11] This also partly explains the fact that popular science magazines, like *Nauka i zhizn'* [Science and Life], which were less infected with socialist propaganda, had a larger circulation among the intelligentsia than many journals in the humanities.

The elaborated hierarchy of *rites de passage*, firmly built on the mixture of the moral, the professional, and the political, was not the only evidence of the paramount importance attached by the Soviet state to the field of historical production. Another instance of the same social obsession with the field could be seen in the fact that the discipline of history, as it was shaped in universities under socialism, became the largest division in the humanities, having absorbed a number of different subfields and disciplines and having formally merged them into its own institutional domain. At Moscow State University, which served as a model for all other universities across the country, the Faculty of History eventually came to embrace some dozen departments, only half of which represented an initial disciplinary domain of history (Department of Ancient History, Department of History of the Middle Ages, Department of Old Russian History, Department of Soviet History, and some others). The other half included: Department of History of Arts, Department of Ethnography, Department of Archaeology, Department of Research Methods, Department of History of the Communist Party (which was, in essence, a department of political science), Department of Political Economy (another dose of Marxist-Leninist political science, spiced up with the basics of Marxist philosophy and economics), and even Department of Foreign Languages.

Thus, what had been in the beginning of the twentieth century a joint interdisciplinary Faculty of History and Philology, built on general ideals of Enlightenment and liberal education, was transformed under socialism into a disciplinary institution of power ("disciplinary," one must say, both in the academic and Foucauldian sense). This development unambiguously indicated, on the one hand, a tendency towards the politicization of the historical field (evident in the attempts to merge it with the field of political science); and, on the other hand, a tendency towards the totalitarianization of the field (evident in the efforts to spread it over the entire domain of all those academic disciplines which might be connected, even in some remote manner, to the production of historical knowledge). The appropriation of archaeology, for example, was strategically important because archaeological data bore a direct relationship to the questions of "origins" and historical "authenticity" of culture – questions which, as it is now known, were attached utmost importance under any totalitarian regime.[12] The appropriation of ethnography, by the same token, facilitated the academic "nationalization" of the question of national identity.[13]

Thus, history has become the major discipline in the humanities and social sciences. It needs to be mentioned that in the Soviet Union the divi-

---

[12] Not that these questions were unimportant in so-called democratic and other societies. In fact, they troubled and continue to trouble all societies in one or another form. Preoccupation with these questions is a typical characteristic of all newly independent states in the Eastern Europe and the CIS, which are looking today for reasons and bases to justify their autonomy and cultural integrity. A representative account of how the issue has emerged in some of the republics of the former USSR may be found in: Victor A. Shnirelman, *Who Gets the Past?* (Washington, D.C.: Woodrow Wilson Center Press, 1996).

[13] For the discussion (in English) of the early socialist debates around the concept of nationality and its ideological importance in the Soviet Union, see: Francine Hirsch, "The Soviet Union as a Work-in-Progress," *Slavic Review* 56, no.2 (1997). It is a fairly common opinion, among contemporary Russian ethnographers, that the institutionalization of ethnography as part of the discipline of history was a consequence of general degradation of social sciences under Stalin. Sergei Cheshko, professor at the Russian Academy of Sciences, responding to my question in an interview, says, "Ethnography in this country traditionally belongs in the historical disciplines, due to certain historical and political circumstances. Under Stalin, ethnography, like other sciences, suffered an ideological breakdown. The word *ethnology*, for example, was expelled from the academic vocabulary, because of associations with "bourgeois comparative science," and the discipline had been given the official title of "ethnography." It was introduced into the history faculties and charged with the task of illustrating Marxist historical materialism through a variety of examples." (Quoted from: Alexei Elfimov, "The State of the Discipline in Russia," *American Anthropologist* 99, no.4 [1997]: 776). In my opinion, however, this degradation of social sciences can be seen precisely as a sign of the strengthening of the historical discipline (or, in stricter terms, of the socio-political alliance of history with Marxism-Leninism) as an omnipotent ideological structure, responsible for the production of, as well as surveillance over, social "truth." The social sciences were excluded from high school curricula and, according to the statistics, were not taught at all at the secondary-school level between 1934 and 1962 (Janet G. Vaillant, "Reform in History and Social Studies Education in Russian Secondary Schools," in *Education and Society in the New Russia*, ed. Anthony Jones [Armonk, N.Y.: M. E. Sharpe, 1994], p.142). Eventually, an introductory social science course (so called *Obshchestvovedenie*) was restored at high schools but, as a common practice in the 1970s and 1980s, it was taught, again, by history teachers, not by social scientists.

sion between the humanities (*gumanitarnye nauki*) and the social sciences (*obshchestvennye nauki*) was fairly arbitrary. In any case, it was ruled by what might be appropriately called situational logic. Philosophy, for example, was normally thought of as pertaining to the humanities. But in the official language of Soviet ideology, where the word "philosophy" typically appeared accompanied by the adjective "Marxist," it was spoken of as a social science, for *Marxist philosophy* laid claim not only to the discovery of true ontological foundations of human knowledge, but also to the revealing of the fundamental laws of social development. History, likewise, technically belonged among the humanities. But, in many instances, it was also considered to be one of the social sciences, since *Marxist historical science*, as it was officially asserted, was a "science of society" that was, along with Marxist philosophy, responsible for the discovery of fundamental laws of social development. This sharing of primary responsibilities, again, points out to what was in fact a firm ideological alliance of history with philosophy, which effectively annexed a fraction of what traditionally belongs in the area of social sciences. (A consequence of that is still felt today, especially in the newly established field of cultural studies, which remains by and large a typical Soviet-style mixture of history and philosophy.)

History, therefore, came to cover an unusually wide academic terrain. One could defend a dissertation in art criticism or ancient languages, archaeology or ethnography, political science or political economy and be granted the same uniform degree of "Candidate of Historical Sciences" (*Kandidat istoricheskikh nauk*) or, at what corresponds to the post-doctoral level in the West, "Doctor of Historical Sciences" (*Doktor istoricheskikh nauk*).[14] (The very placement of history among "sciences" is, again, telling too.) Textbooks in history, written during the Soviet period, often started

---

[14] This tradition has survived and this is still the case in many Russian universities today, even though the past decade has witnessed a good deal of disciplinary differentiation and there are many non-accredited schools that may offer alternative titles.

with the phrase "History is mother of all sciences" ("*Istoriia – mat' nauk*"), which was in essence just another manifestation of the same ideological tendency towards universalizing and, so to speak, fundamentalizing the discipline. This was precisely that kind of danger upon which, half a century earlier, Nietzsche had reflected in his *Untimely Meditations*: "Insofar as it stands in the service of life, history stands in the service of an unhistorical power, and, thus subordinate, it can and should never become a pure science such as, for instance, mathematics is".[15] In the Soviet Union, every necessary step was taken to promote history to the level of "pure science" and to mask the fact of its connection or, to use Nietzsche's more appropriate word, *service* to power.

This brings us back to the subject of intellectual discourse. Indeed, from what has been said so far, one might conclude that the historical enterprise appears to be in all respects similar to the literary one, being based on an elaborate project of power, in other words, Foucauldian *program*, and might wonder why I prefer to speak of the discourse of history in terms of *strategies*. This is where the complication starts. The social discourse of history, as it was envisaged and planned by the socialist power, can undoubtedly be categorized as a Foucauldian program-based discourse, insofar as it represented a rational project of power with clear-cut aims and methods. But this program-based, or let us call it *normative*, discourse never assumed a scale and dimensions it was intended to assume. It never quite made it into the sphere of broader intellectual discourse and remained confined to the institutional framework of history departments and research institutes, unlike the literary discourse which far overstepped the boundaries of literature departments and became, in a way, *the* intellectual discourse of the day. The effect that the normative historical discourse really produced in the broader intellectual sphere came later as a result of its unintended collision with the notorious issue of modernity, which has

---

[15] Friedrich Nietzsche, "On the Uses and Disadvantages of History for Life," in *Untimely Meditations* (Cambridge: Cambridge University Press, 1983), p.67.

been discussed in the previous chapter. This effect essentially consisted in the transformation of the normative historical discourse into a broader cultural discourse of a new type, which was characterized by a kind of profound fusion of themes related to history, ethics, humanism, and cultural heritage – fusion that was eventually successfully assimilated into the very consciousness of the Soviet/Russian intellectual culture. This development, which was not a planned part of the initial "program" but turned out to be reaching even farther ends, presented a convenient target and means for ideological maneuvers, and ultimately became both an object and medium of power exercise. This is why this new type of cultural discourse of history (not the normative historical discourse), as it emerged in the Soviet intellectual culture, may be seen as an example of what Foucault defines by "strategy-based" discourse.

The problem with the normative historical discourse, as it was established in the Soviet society, was that it paradoxically turned against the very notion of history. The past before the socialist revolution was denied; while in the epoch after the revolution, there was no past anymore – everything essentially turned into a timeless present. The revolution reversed the whole course of social progress – or, to be more precise, *social regress* – just like the appearance of Christ on Earth. Everything before the revolution was now "B.C." and time in that remote epoch was said to have gone in the opposite direction. The questions of historical and cultural continuity, therefore, were no longer an issue. Furthermore, as Walter Benjamin observed, under the new conditions such questions became simply inappropriate as a reminder of that "triumphal procession, in which the present rulers step over those who today are lying prostrate ... A historical materialist therefore disassociates himself from it as far as possible. He regards it as his task to brush history against the grain".[16] The main preoccupation of

---

[16] Walter Benjamin, "Über den Begriff der Geschichte." Quoted in: Susan Buck-Morss, *The Dialectics of Seeing: Walter Benjamin and the Arcades Project* (Cambridge, MA: MIT Press, 1989), p.288.

that historical materialist became the creation of a new historical narrative, unhistorically placed in a timeless mythological space of the victorious socialist era. The genre of this historical narrative became typologically similar to that of medieval "chronicle of life and times of such and such king," and here it was successfully realized in the form of a "chronicle of life and times of the Communist Party."[17] What this genre provided was a scrupulously detailed, allegedly historically narrated, account of the activities of a powerholder, the relation of which to other historical epochs and events, at the same time, always remained shrouded in a haze of mythological exegesis.

This is to say that the real task of the new socialist historical discipline after the revolution became that of establishing a discourse of the Soviet present, rather than that of pursuing investigations into ambiguities of the past. The past was fixed once and for all as a regressive entity, as an antitime, whereas the present suddenly became an ideological burden and in many ways an awkward subject that required a great deal of justification, interpretation and explanation. That it was precisely the period of Soviet history, i.e. the period from 1917 onward, which constituted the major predicament in the relationship between socialist power and goals of academic scholarship, is now a frequently commented fact and I will not elaborate on

---

[17] Thus, the major treatise – infamously known treatise – on Soviet history, that appeared under Stalin and remained a basic canon for historians to follow for many years after his death, was entitled *A Short Course on History of the Communist Party of the Soviet Union*. Learning and reciting endless and senseless sentences from the party annals became a routine practice for every history student. Accounts of Soviet history in school and university textbooks that were still in use when Gorbachev was carrying out his perestroika reforms were by and large accounts of various conferences, congresses, and executive decisions of the Communist Party. Applicants taking entrance examinations in history at Soviet universities in the late 1980s were asked to summarize Gorbachev's own speech at the 1985 Communist Party Plenum. So, while perestroika years loosened the limits of historical interpretation, having particularly encouraged reevaluation of the Stalinist past, the genre of history as "Party chronicle" remained essentially intact (it remained so through the 1980s and the beginning of the 1990s, being politically, rather than academically, discredited only with the defeat of the communist rule under Yeltsin's administration).

this theme here.[18] What I would like to emphasize once again, however, is the discrepancy between the idea of history as certain continuity and cultural inheritance, and the task of the normative historical discourse to justify discontinuity and cultural autonomy. This discrepancy, which could be either avoided or purposefully appropriated into the rhetoric by theoreticians of Soviet ideology, came to constitute a problem of both conceptual and moral character for the intellectuals with all their cultural baggage or, as Bourdieu might call it, cultural capital in too many ways earned from the past. An attempt to establish an ideological discourse of a culturally autonomous present collided here with the predicament of modernity – that is, with intelligentsia's inherited unpreparedness to speak of the present in culturally autonomous terms, with its inherited uninterestedness in the present, and ultimately with the absence of spirit of modernity as such on the social scale in the society which in the course of some ten years managed to jump from one authoritarian regime into another. Inconsistencies in the way the dominant ideology itself treated the present contributed to the predicament. Paradoxically, the new timeless era of the Soviet present had to be subdivided and transformed into a transitional *moment* of the present on the way to the actual timeless era of the Soviet future; and the center of gravity in this subdivision was certainly laid upon the future, thus relieving the present of its actual value and importance. One may only recall Benjamin's insightful remark, "A historical materialist cannot do without the notion of a present which is not a transition".[19]

The result of the collision of the normative historical discourse with the issue of modernity was twofold. On the one hand, this discourse never

---

[18] For a fairly good discussion in English, see, for example: Alexander Dallin, "Soviet History," in *Soviet Scholarship Under Gorbachev*, ed. Alexander Dallin and Bertrand M. Patenaude (Stanford: Stanford University Press, 1988); William B. Husband, "History Education and Historiography in Soviet and Post-Soviet Russia," in *Education and Society in the New Russia*.

[19] Walter Benjamin, "Theses on the Philosophy of History," in *Illuminations* (New York: Schocken Books, 1969), p.262.

made its way into a sphere of broader intellectual conversation and gradually enclosed itself within the guild of bureaucratized academic historians. On the other, it pushed the intelligentsia into a historical quest of their own, which turned, in essence, into a melancholy Proustian *recherche du temps perdu* and step by step grew into an almost unconditional appropriation of the pre-revolutionary history, that same "anti-time B.C.," as a basic ethical and cultural point of reference. An array of various eighteenth and nineteenth century figures, from literary intelligentsia to artists and architects to representatives of political aristocracy were revoked one by one and informally legitimized in the intellectual discourse as founders and builders of the edifice of that "authentic" Russian culture which, thus, supposedly underlay the culture of the Soviet people, or at any rate remained its heritage and something of a moral conscience.

The growing persistence of this attitude gradually influenced not only the lay intellectual public but also the humanities, including even the guild of academic historians who, following the current of intellectual fashions, started to increasingly turn in their scholarly studies to the reassessment of the eighteenth-century and nineteenth-century history in a new moral and ethical light. A new discursive paradigm in the historical studies started to be formed: everything in the "Old Russia," except the political tsarist regime, was now to become a source of cultural value, cultural lessons, and cultural ideals. The tsars, together with their political administration and secret police, still remained the primary target for both historical and ethical criticism, having retained the role of "stranglers of culture and suppressers of progress." The rest of the society, however, from peasants to high aristocracy, were morally and historically elevated both as the real builders of culture and those who equally had to suffer under the injustice of the authoritarian social system. Peasants and working class, of course, were no unusual subject for historians, since they primarily occupied the focus of their attention in the framework of what we referred to as the normative discourse of history, but the nobility and aristocracy were undoubtedly brought into the pool of legitimate objects of historical investigation only with the tide of the intelligentsia's nostalgic recourse to the past, which began roughly in the 1960s, at the time of Khrushchev's "thaw," and has not ended as of the time of this writing.

The tendency toward the reappropriation (which in many instances was simply transplantation) of the old Russian aristocratic style of life as a cultural value became especially salient in the 1980s. (In fact, in the 1980s, we can speak already of the formed discourse of history of the new type, which was far away from the conventions of the normative historical discourse.) As a result of the general intellectualization of the topic and, therefore, of the intervention of various parties, such as literature, history of arts, cinema and theater, into the conversation, the role of aristocracy was more and more idealized and imperceptibly merged with the domain of "cultural heritage." It was still impossible, nor was it actually anybody's intention (save maybe for a few dissidents), to approve of tsarism and the old Russian political system as a whole, but it became possible to approve of good ethical and humanistic intentions of each particular representative of that system. The emphasis on humanistic intentions, as opposed to actions, acquired wide currency in the new discourse of history. Thus, in several cases of historical scholarship before the perestroika, even tsars were cautiously represented as positive figures. Tsar Alexander I was one of the earliest examples. In some historical studies, he began to be shown as an educated and intelligent person who *intended* to make some good changes to the political system, but was *unable* to make them because the system was full of reactionary bureaucrats and one tsar could not go against the corruption of the entire state. In other studies, he was shown as a merciful ruler who did not send as many participants of the Decembrists mutiny to Siberia as he actually could. Alexander I further earned some praise because he supposedly favorably treated Russian poet Pushkin, or at any rate put up with his provocative writings and behavior. Since Pushkin became a canonized figure in the Soviet culture, the tsar therefore could be, in a sense, forgiven. This is not to question the validity of such facts, many of which were probably based on careful archival investigations, but to point out a new paradigmatic trait of the new discourse of history – namely, its centeredness on the subject of aristocratic ethics and enlightenment as a foundation of Russian culture and social ideals. Under Gorbachev, with the loosening of the official ideological censorship, the penetration of the new discourse of history into the intellectual and broader cultural consciousness reached its utmost limits with the inclusion of the last prohibited area, that of the Russian Silver Age, into the domain of the legitimate. The Silver Age period of the end of the nineteenth century and the beginning of the twentieth century naturally remained the last restricted area of all Russian pre-revolutionary history because it was temporally too close to the socialist revolution and many of the Silver Age intellectuals were, as it is known, openly against the Bolshevik regime.

This paradigmatic shift in the discourse of history has not received much attention in scholarly works on Russia and the Soviet Union. A few authors do actually remark that in Russia of the 1980s, "an infatuation with topics of the tsarist past has significantly displaced post-1917 history as the center of public interest."[20] But the majority of scholars concerned with the subject until recently focused almost exclusively on the debates around Stalinist and, more broadly, Soviet past. While these debates indeed constituted one of the distinctive social topics of the perestroika years and there is no doubt that "for many in the Soviet Union, Stalin in particular was a quintessentially emotional subject,"[21] it is precisely these debates that could be defined by the term "infatuation," rather than those around the "tsarist past." The interest in the pre-revolutionary past did not really come as an infatuation that displaced Soviet history as a focus of attention at the end of the 1980s. It had come earlier, and it was already firmly built into

---

[20] William B. Husband, "History Education and Historiography in Soviet and Post-Soviet Russia," p.122.
[21] Alexander Dallin, "Soviet History," p.5.

the intellectual consciousness and the foundations of historical discourse at the moment when the infatuation with the immediate Soviet past started (being to a certain extent ideologically encouraged by Gorbachev himself) and temporarily overflowed, so to speak, the subject area of discourse. It has to be understood that the very intellectual attitude toward the Soviet past was radically different in nature from the attitude toward the pre-revolutionary Russian past, the former being of explicitly negative ethical character and the latter of explicitly positive one. The Soviet past was something that was sought to be eradicated, whereas the Russian past was something that was sought to be restored. The Russian pre-revolutionary past, no matter how idealized, was the culture that people *wanted* to identify with, and perhaps unconsciously *started* to identify with; while the Soviet past, on the contrary, was the source of that unwanted and forced but nevertheless real and conscious identity that people strove to get rid of.[22] It were monuments and landmarks of Soviet culture and history that were violently destroyed by the public in Moscow, St. Petersburg and other cities during perestroika on such scale that in the end frightened even the intelligentsia who more or less tended to think that cultural heritage was cultural heritage and some things just had to be preserved no matter how bad were the memories that they evoked. Needless to say, very few important monuments of the pre-revolutionary past were damaged during these years. Moreover, some of the old landmarks that had been destroyed during the first Soviet years were now restored (which was essentially a politi-

---

[22] A typical expression of the intellectual and, in a broader sense, cultural moods in the late 1980s and early 1990s is summarized in the following passage from an article by a St. Petersburg literary critic Konstantin Azadovskii: "We are settling scores with our history. We are hastening to rid ourselves of the burdensome legacy of the era of the Great Falsification. We are dividing our past into executioners and victims, prison guards and inmates ... We are infected with nostalgia for prerevolutionary Russia. We want to immerse ourselves in the age of 1910 as deeply as possible and to bring back – at least in part – the atmosphere and spirit of that era, to transport it to our troubled days." (Konstantin Azadovskii, "Russia's Silver Age, Yesterday and Today," in *Remaking Russia*, ed. Heyward Isham (Armonk, N.Y.: M. E. Sharpe, 1995), pp.86–9.

cal play on the interests of the public, that very *strategic* use of the historical discourse by the ruling power, and I will elaborate on it further in the section on architecture).

The debates over the Soviet past therefore constituted a topic – an important one, but still just a topic – in the intellectual discourse of history, whereas the domain of the pre-revolutionary Russian past was laid in the very foundation of that discourse as a new normative cultural point of reference, as an a priori point of departure in any historical judgment, and, more broadly, as a basic cultural protocol of ethics, morality, and humanism. One of the above-cited articles on history education in Russia quotes, though in a different sense and context, an interesting passage from an essay by some Russian teacher, or possibly professor of history, who says:

> The humanitarian science of history is a means for teaching elevated human qualities ... A new spirit in the teaching of history is more important to me than the distribution of hours among courses, methods of inquiry and the organization of work with textbooks.[23]

This type of statement, which has become common among the historians, is precisely one of the effects of the paradigmatic shift of historical discourse into the framework of ethics, morality and cultural heritage. And, of course, since the perestroika one could hardly teach elevated human qualities on the example of the Soviet history, unless one would like to go into another falsification and, even more problematically, go against the whole stream of negativity that flowed over this period of history. On the

---

[23] A. B. Sokolov, "Raskreposhchenie istorii," *Voprosy istorii* 9–10 (1991). English text quoted in: William B. Husband, "History Education and Historiography in Soviet and Post-Soviet Russia," p.119. Cf. what one history professor at Moscow State University told me in an interview in 1995: "All these years, we had history as a lifeless record of dates and events, that is as a purely mechanical form of knowledge. It was supposed to shape a certain type of personality. I don't think we need this type of personality anymore. History, therefore, should ultimately come to an ethical form of knowledge; it should inculcate the love for the past in the youth, because the past is that golden cultural fund on which they should learn to draw in their judgment."

contrary, the period of pre-revolutionary history makes an exceptional resource for this type of teaching, being already merged in the broader intellectual consciousness with an array of elevated themes, such as humanism and *culture* itself. The identification of *history* with *culture* is undoubtedly another profound effect of this clash of social discourses, although it might be again traced back to the traditions of the nineteenth-century Russian intelligentsia. Rilke's modernist statement that "history is another culture which is not and should not be ours" would therefore appear as something openly hostile to the spirit of the new intellectual discourse in Russia. According to the conventions of this discourse, history *is* culture. (In fact, one might go as far as to stress, without fear of falling into extreme overstatement, that there is no culture other than history. This statement might perhaps be a slight exaggeration, but it adequately describes the general contours of the new paradigm encompassing the discourse of history, as well as broader intellectual thinking to a large extent).

There is a curious colloquial expression in Russian, *prikosnut'sia k kul'ture*, which means "to touch culture," "to come into contact with culture," and its usage may be considered as just another illustration of this – all too common by now – social identification of history with culture. This expression is regularly used to describe the fact that someone went to one or another historically important place (be it an old town, a museum, or an archive) and experienced first-hand some remains from the past (be it an architecture, an old painting, or a dusty seventeenth-century book). What is implied in a sentence, like "I went to an old Russian town of Rostov and *prikosnulsia k kul'ture* [came into contact with culture]," is ultimately that one got out of the ordinary everyday surroundings of the contemporary and immersed oneself in the (supposedly intact and authentic) atmosphere of the past, which possessed, solely due to the fact of its historical value, a transcendent cultural significance. This expression would have been never applied to any place, no matter how interesting and intellectually or emotionally satisfying, if it was not related to cultural achievements of the more or less remote past. The realm of the contemporary lacks a cultural load. What makes objects in Russia *culturally* loaded is in the first instance their historical value.

The same attitude might be detected in virtually any sphere of Russian intellectual life. If we took theater, for example, which itself was traditionally seen by the intellectuals as a more culturally loaded and consistent genre than cinema with its immediate interests and, so to say, profane philosophy, we would find a no less salient obsession with historical themes, especially those of the nineteenth-century Russian intelligentsia and, more generally, aristocracy. A classic set of plays by such authors as Chekhov, Ostrovskii, Bulgakov, and a number of new ones, written in a similar historical-literary genre, constituted the most popular part of theatrical repertoire throughout the last quarter of the twentieth century. It is not to diminish the value of literary works by Chekhov or Bulgakov, since probably little as insightful as those has been created in Russia anyway, but to point out again that it was the historical reference that in most cases made these performances culturally valuable. Contemporary plays and performances, dealing with immediate realities of the Soviet society, did not enjoy popularity among the larger part of the theater public, which certainly included the intelligentsia, because the latter had little interest in the present realities and every right to suspect that such plays would contain nothing but ideological propaganda. In other words, here one can observe the same shift in intellectual interests toward the past as a culturally loaded and meaningful discursive zone. The contemporary was resisted both as a mundane realm of the everyday, and as a realm of ideological propaganda, while the historical was elevated to the transcendent level of pure *culture*, which thus came to establish itself as a condensed symbolic expression of social ideals of the intelligentsia. I am somewhat tempted to employ a Geertzian perspective and argue that history functioned in the late Soviet society (and in a sense continues to function in Russia today) as a distinctive "cultural system," that is, a powerful integral symbolic realm, capable of shaping individual experiences and identities in a transcendent way and putting them into a special meaningful framework which was not a part of everyday reality surrounding the individuals. Much like religion in some societies or dramatic arts of expression, such as *wajang*, in others, history in the late Soviet society became that significant symbolic domain which rendered "dramatization of individual subjective experience in terms at once moral and factual."[24] Furthermore, it acquired a certain function of intellectual counter-ideology that stood in opposition to the official ideology of the contemporary. Symbolic cultural systems, as Geertz noted, can be different in character and role. Some symbolic systems, like science, represent a diagnostic or critical dimension of culture; while others, like ideology, are much closer to a justificatory or apologetic dimension which refers "to that part of culture which is actively concerned with the establishment and defense of patterns of belief and value."[25] History in the late Soviet society, if we speak of it in terms of a distinctive cultural system, certainly had a justificatory and apologetic character – that is, it essentially played the role of a popular intellectual ideology. There was nothing diagnostic or critical to it, for it was *not* a sphere where things could be put to test, it was a sphere in which an unconditional "defense of patterns of belief and value" took place.

It did not matter much that many of those patterns of belief and value represented what seems to be clear instances of social romanticizing, nor did it matter that they contradicted the way the surrounding reality and social life itself was organized. What mattered was perhaps the meaningfulness with which they were able to fill the individual experience – the meaningfulness that could be no longer located in the official ideology of Soviet culture. Unfortunately, the persistence of this unconditional trust in

---

[24] Clifford Geertz, "Ethos, World View, and the Analysis of Sacred Symbols," in *The Interpretation of Cultures* (New York: Basic Books, 1973), p.138.
[25] Clifford Geertz, "Ideology as a Cultural System," in *The Interpretation of Cultures*, p.231.

the meaningfulness of the past still dwarfs the attempts of intelligentsia to think reflexively about their actual place in the actual moment of the contemporary and prolongs this particular discursive tradition within which the past again and again figures as a blamed and forgiven entity that gives one a license to a correct understanding of things. Interestingly, even in Russia of nowadays many intellectuals prove unable to reflexively reproach themselves for all their romantic attractions to the past. This could be shown, for example, in the brief excerpt from an essay, entitled "Who Are We?", by a well-known in Russia, and formerly in the Soviet Union, writer Fazil Iskander who says:

> Romanticizing the past is a false judgment about the past coupled with a false conclusion: life was more interesting and more harmonious then. Romanticism of the future is a false judgment about the future coupled with a false conclusion: life will be more interesting and harmonious. Despite its inaccuracy, romanticizing the past cannot do too much damage. A false estimate of the past is one that does not require us to pay a price. We will pay with our hides and those of our children, however, for a false calculation about the future. And we are already paying.[26]

Thus, even though romanticizing the past may be a false judgment, it does, as the author concludes, no harm as such. It is the future now that is to blame. Curiously, this whole statement is an inversion of the traditional Soviet intellectual motto "the past is to blame for our miscalculations about the future," and is undoubtedly a mere instance of situational logic, called upon to provide an excuse for the fact that "having invested so much effort in thinking about the past, the intellectual still managed to miscalculate the future." It is noteworthy that the category of the present is, as it always has been, omitted in these intellectual meditations on the subject of "who we are and what is to be done." Actually, to be punctual, the subject, as it were, is never "what is to be done." It is either "what was to be done" or

---

[26] Fazil Iskander, "Who Are We?", in *Remaking Russia*, p.42.

"what would have been done, if..." Issues are never posed directly, but are either mulled over *ex post facto* or addressed in the subjunctive future-in-the-past mode. So, in a sense, Lenin's disdain for the intelligentsia as an unable group that can neither pose, nor answer the question "what is to be done?" can be partly understood.

History, once again, assumed the function and role of universalistic meaningful framework that embraced and permeated the intellectual discourse in Russia of the last quarter of the twentieth century (structurally, in the same way as, for example, the category of modernity had assumed such function in the intellectual discourse in the US). While in the American culture the present strikingly functions as the ultimate judge, in the Russian culture the ultimate judge is history and one has to properly appeal to it, if one wishes to validate the present. This is where the issue inevitably becomes ideological, and we are going to turn now to the discussion of the discourse of architecture to see what kinds of practical applications and power manipulations this new historical paradigm in the intellectual consciousness has brought about.

II. Discourse of Architecture

If we speak of the disciplinary discourse of architecture, it has to be pointed out that its development was in many ways analogous to that of the disciplinary or, as we have labeled it, normative discourse of history. After the repression of the brief intellectual outburst, associated with the movement of Russian constructivism in the 1920s and 1930s, and with the beginning of the authoritarian era of the so-called monumental socialist style, the subject of architecture understandably disappears from the area of general intellectual conversation and does not enter the picture until the new historical paradigm in the intellectual consciousness begins to emerge. Within this paradigm, which increasingly begins to blur the distinction between history and culture and merge the themes of humanism, morality, cultural heritage, and cultural values, architecture logically acquires a new place and status – that of historical artifact, and therefore *cultural artifact*, which is ultimately something to be studied and preserved, rather than something to be designed and built. This regression of architectural discourse into the aesthetics of "preservation" or "conservation" from the aesthetics of "creation" (which had, for instance, unmistakably identified the constructivist intellectual discourse) represents essentially the same fundamental shift toward equating the zone of authentic culture with the pre-revolutionary past – the shift that came to constitute an informal ideology of the intellectual milieu in the Soviet Union and Russia of the last quarter of the twentieth century.

It is perhaps no surprise that it were departments of art history, rather than schools of architecture, that were responsible for the popularization of architecture in this new quality. Schools of architecture were preparing engineers with immediate objectives; departments of art history, now permeated with the new morality of history and humanism, were raising intellectuals who learned that the immediate objectives of architects–engineers threatened to destroy the precious heritage of Russian culture. Here, too, the contemporary became the subject of rejection and condemnation, as a wrong destructive path leading away from the authentic cultural roots. In this light, it should be rather clear why the movement of Russian constructivism, which attracted so much attention in the West, gained little popularity in the new Russian intellectual discourse. Apart from the obvious aspect that it was marked by a clear modernist spirit – a sentiment generally unpopular among Russian intellectuals – this movement, one of the major mottoes of which was "*not only construct but reconstruct*,"[27] was understood, in the framework of the new historical paradigm, as a violent attack on culture. As a matter of fact, constructivists, indeed, planned to rearrange

---

[27] El Lissitzky, "Russia: The Reconstruction of Architecture in the Soviet Union," in *The Tradition of Constructivism*, ed. Stephen Bann (New York: Viking, 1974), p.141.

and rebuild half of the historic center of the city of Moscow. Several of their projects, as it is known, required disassembling Kremlin walls to clear the space for new architectural ensembles (the idea of which, to an average Russian, would seem as barbarian, as the idea of demolishing the Westminster Abbey would probably seem to an Englishman, or the idea of destroying the Notre Dame – to a Frenchman). These grand projects, which were never realized in practice because of the financial problems of the Soviet state in the interwar period and for this reason came later to be known as the famous *paper projects*, somehow became imprinted in the consciousness of the Russian intelligentsia as the principal association with the ideals of constructivism. Constructivism therefore came to be seen in more ways as a movement of destruction, than a movement of creation. The fact that the phenomenon of constructivism took place during the Soviet period of time, that is *after* the revolution, not before it, certainly added to the negativity with which it was apprehended. If, hypothetically speaking, it could have taken place before the revolution, there would have been a good chance for it to be "forgiven" by contemporary Russian intellectuals. There were certainly a number of mediocre and untalented nineteenth-century architects, like Konstantin Ton, for example, who built tasteless buildings in the historic center of Moscow, having ruined older and perhaps nicer structures, and who nevertheless are never blamed by the intellectuals today (save for a few critically thinking art historians). What had been built before the revolution falls, according to the rules of the new intellectual discourse, into the category of *heritage of culture and history*. And the tendency certainly is: the deeper one goes into the history, the closer one gets to the authentic and culturally valuable. Art historians in Russia, for example, unquestionably praise the eighteenth-century architect Bazhenov who designed and constructed a number of famous royal palaces that surrounded St. Petersburg and Moscow and laid the foundation of the distinctive style that was later called *Russian baroque*. Perhaps Bazhenov fairly deserves the praise, but the interesting fact here is that his last and unfulfilled project, frequently mentioned by his biographers as his grand project, was that of demolishing the old medieval Kremlin wall and constructing a new gorgeous palace for Russian tsars on the banks of Moskva River. Needless to say, Bazhenov is certainly not reproached for his intentions in the way the constructivists are, and in his case the destruction of cultural and historical heritage is not an issue because, in a sense, he himself is already viewed as "culture" and "heritage," being a figure from the past, whereas the constructivists are still perceived as belonging to the contemporary with all its "uncultured" nature and malicious drives in regard to the past.

Architects of the twentieth century – or, more precisely, of the Soviet period of the twentieth century – are thus automatically out of favor, solely by the conventions of the new intellectual discourse; while those of the earlier centuries are automatically praised due to the nature of the same conventions. Interestingly enough, they are praised not only as *architects* per se, but also more generally as figures of national pride and significance, as thinkers and builders of *culture* and *history*, as representatives of what is thought to be that much spoken of Russian "organic intelligentsia."[28] A typical example manifesting the effect of such discursive conventions may be observed in the following passage from an essay by Dmitrii Likhachev, a St. Petersburg historian and philologist and prominent intellectual figure in the Soviet Union, who was and still is regarded by many as an exemplary scholar in the humanities. Trying to summarize high cultural points across the entire period of Russian/Soviet history, he comes up with a curious list:

---

[28] Incidentally, this raises an interesting point in respect to the notion of intelligentsia as it typically circulated in the Russian intellectual discourse. The status of *intelligentsia*, which on the one hand implied a rather high standard, not at all easily reachable, could on the other hand be easily granted to a person, regardless of the degree of conforming to such standard, on the merit of simply being born in the pre-revolutionary Russia. In other words, the general rule of the thumb seemed to be: if you wish to be counted as *intelligentsia*, you had better be born before the revolution of 1917.

Taking into account the entire thousand years of Russian culture, I would say that it is undoubtedly "higher than average." It suffices to mention a few names [further I quote the names only]: Mikhail Lomonosov, Nikolai Lobachevskii, Dmitrii Mendeleev, V. I. Vernadsky, Pyotr Ilich Tchaikovsky, Modest Mussorgsky, Mikhail Glinka, Aleksandr Scriabin, Sergei Rachmaninoff, Sergei Prokofiev, Dmitri Shostakovich, Gavrila Derzhavin, Aleksandr Pushkin, Nikolai Karamzin, Nikolai Gogol, Fyodor Dostoevsky, Leo Tolstoy, Anton Chekhov, Sergei Bulgakov, Aleksandr Blok, N. I. Voronikhin, V. I. Bazhenov, V. P. Stasov, I. E. Starov, A. I. Shtakenshneider, Petr Chaadaev, Nikolai Danilevskii, Nikolai Fedorov, Vladimir Solov'ev, Semen Frank, Nikolai Berdiaev.[29]

What is curious about this list in the first place is that it consists almost entirely of the nineteenth-century figures, with only three persons strictly belonging to the eighteenth century and a few who belonged in the Silver Age period and lived through the beginning of the twentieth century but none of whom was born after 1917. Considering the opening statement, "taking into account the entire thousand years of Russian culture," this list may indeed seem a little narrow and in a way even puzzling. However, there is really not much to be puzzled about, for what this list truly represents is not an "entire thousand years of Russian culture," but rather the new paradigm of intellectual discourse in the humanities as it formed in the last quarter of the twentieth century. "Culture," according to the conventions of this paradigm, moved back into the pre-revolutionary past, invisibly merged with "history," and became predominantly associated with the history of intellectual and aesthetic achievements of the nineteenth century. Although, in Likhachev's case, it does surprise me to a degree that such an erudite scholar should fail to mention at least a few obvious names from the twentieth century, like Bakhtin, for example, and a few from the earliest periods of history, it only indicates again and again how profoundly this

---

[29] Dmitrii Likhachev, "I Object: What Constitutes the Tragedy of Russian History," in *Remaking Russia*, p.59.

paradigm has penetrated the foundations of intellectual discourse in contemporary Russia.[30]

Along with writers, poets, composers, and other intellectuals in the list, Likhachev mentions five architects (Voronikhin, Bazhenov, Stasov, Starov, Shtakenshneider), all of whom were working in St. Petersburg in the eighteenth and nineteenth centuries. The choice is, again, too trivial both in the temporal and geographical sense, for he could have mentioned, even if for diversity sake only, one or two of the remarkable Moscow architects of the early twentieth century who designed numerous, often cited in architecture books, landmarks of the original style known as *Russian Modérn*. But even here, in the exclusion of these architects, his choice displays a telling influence of the same general paradigm of thinking. One of the distinctive features of the style *Modérn*, as it has been mentioned in passing in the previous chapter, was its employment of convoluted forms based on an elaborate engineering design. It is in many ways for this reason that the image of an architect at this point shifts away from the image of an "organic intellectual" or "creator of culture" (the image essential within the framework of historical discourse of the new type), and comes too close to the image of an engineer (a "technical worker" of sorts) and, so

---

[30] Bakhtin, as a matter of fact, must have been excluded from the list of cultural figures by the power of the same reasoning that separates the constructivists from Russian pre-revolutionary architects. In Likhachev's view, Bakhtin must be first of all an ordinary Soviet scholar, just like himself (hence belonging to the "contemporary," and therefore "secondary" to the original which is in any way the past before the Russian-Soviet divide), whose mission was not to construct but rather *reconstruct* and *interpret* the cultural foundation that had been created before. That is to say, Bakhtin must be viewed not as an original creator, but simply as a contemporary philologist and literary critic who studied and interpreted the original creations by *real* cultural figures, such as Dostoevsky or Rabelais. Furthermore, as Likhachev has been always known as one of the major proponents of the notorious "language cleansing," i.e. the idea of returning the "littered" language of nowadays to the "distilled" norms of the great old times, it is entirely conceivable that he should see in Bakhtin's own language, which abounds in neologisms and linguistic inventions, the same violent attack on culture that is generally seen by the new "humanistic" intelligentsia in the constructivist project.

to say, to the image of "pragmatician" of culture. Of course, the obvious connection with *modernism* probably plays a negative part too, insofar as it generally evokes a contradictory feeling that does not fit with the morality of the new intellectual discourse.

In a word, old Russian architects are ranked, in an aestheticized image of organic intellectuals, among the "timeless" nobility of culture, that is, all those great men – writers, poets, composers, artists, and others – who created that significant cultural space which is up to the present day supposed to constitute an authentic framework of national life and experience, and which therefore is to be by all means preserved and protected from the destructive influence of modernity. This is ultimately the way the subject of architecture was understood and taught in the humanities departments of major Russian universities in the 1980s–90s. At the Faculty of History of Moscow State University, for example, two courses, required for all students regardless of their area of specialization, were implemented in the mid-1980s. One was called "The Monuments of History and Culture," the other "High Points in Russian Culture."[31] About two thirds of the content of the courses was devoted to the discussion of the old Russian architecture in the general vein described above. Much of the discussion, in essence, was repeated in the introductory course on the history of Russian arts, which was also required for all students regardless of their majors. Furthermore, these courses were normally supplemented with actual excursions to places of architectural interest around the city, organized every semester, and even with annual bus trips to more distant places, such as small towns of the Russian North or historic Russian towns of the Golden Ring belt (Rostov, Yaroslavl', Vladimir, Suzdal', etc.), which preserved much of the old Russian architecture (albeit in a decaying state). These trips were certainly educating, as probably any travel is, and, as a matter of

---

[31] "*Pamiatniki istorii i kul'tury*," "*Shedevry i dostizheniia russkoi kul'tury*." The titles slightly varied in some years but the structure and the content of the courses remained essentially the same.

fact, students greatly enjoyed even the courses themselves because they were different from regular courses in many respects (they were visually oriented, slides were shown all the time, they constantly touched on some elevated cultural topics and appealed to sentiments of morality and humanism – that is, they were not academically boring, unlike many regular courses in history with their typical stress on the mechanical memorizing of facts and dates). But it is in many ways for this very reason that they were assimilated and digested much more successfully than other subjects. The cultivation of the new intellectual attitude, permeated with the spirit of humanism, history, and culture, was effectively accomplished through all these micro-venues in the system of education in the humanities, and architecture undoubtedly became an integral part of that system.

During the above-mentioned trips to old Russian towns, which allowed students, in that magic colloquial Russian phrase, to *come into contact with culture* (*"prikosnut'sia k kul'ture"*), students effectively learned that culture in its very essence was *history*, and that it was first of all subject to *preservation*. Students were encouraged to analyze the beauty of decaying constructions of the old ages, to interpret, substantiate, and often simply construe their cultural importance in the term papers that they wrote after such trips, as well as to publish their papers and, thus, to help preserve the heritage of Russian culture. In 1988, when I was myself a student in the Ethnography Department of Moscow State University, I went on a trip to Rybinsk, an old town in the north of Russia, with a group of other students from the Faculty of History. We were all permeated with the feeling of importance of the old culture, even with a certain feeling of responsibility for it. We wrote a passionate article for a local newspaper, in which we tried to point out the attention of municipal authorities to an old church in a deteriorating state, presumably built in the seventeenth or eighteenth century and presumably representing the last example of that particular architectural style in the Russian north. We heatedly argued that the authorities should by all means prevent the "tragedy of possible loss of such an important cultural monument." I do not know whether that article had any actual effect (although it is true that a word coming from the most prestigious university of the country to a small provincial town could not be left altogether unnoticed), but eventually we received a formal letter of acknowledgment from some municipal office of cultural affairs, together with five rubles for the publication, and that made us, to the extent that I remember it now, proud and happy.

Years later, I happened to get together with two other persons who had been on that student trip to Rybinsk and we got into some friendly disagreement about the old newspaper article as we recalled that funny event. One person, who had spent some time abroad in Hungary and just returned to Moscow, tended to remember that event indeed as a funny story from our student life and seconded my own thoughts. We laughed and wondered what on Earth had possessed us to so lose common sense as to seriously argue for the restoration of a mediocre construction which, if restored, would be absolutely dysfunctional today even as a church. More importantly, how could we argue for a totally unreasonable investment in such expensive restoration in the town that suffered from a dire lack of cafes, shops, and public places and where people had literally nowhere to go? The other person, who became an art historian, did not seem to share our thoughts and called us "westernized pragmaticians," saying that we lost the spirit and faith that we had once had.

The issue that arises from this story is central to the politics of intellectual "community" in Russia in two principal ways. First, the majority of people who have a background in the humanities typically have a wonderful sensibility toward the culture that no longer exists, but have no sense of the actual reality that surrounds them. Secondly, they uniformly talk in abstract terms of spirit and faith where one should talk in concrete terms of problems and decisions. And this is ultimately where the politics starts to learn from the intellectuals and discovers one of those Foucauldian *strategic* resources which open an advantageous space for power maneuvers.

Indeed, however unreasonable the intellectuals' claims and longings for the return of the destroyed past sometimes might seem to the ruling power, in the end they often prove cheaper to satisfy than pressing economic and social needs of the citizens. Furthermore, if handled in the right way, they often prove extraordinarily beneficial to the popular image of the authorities, for showing how they care about culture and history, the authorities achieve results that are both spectacular and immediate, unlike the results of social reforms that always come slow, if come at all, and usually do not stir up such public excitement. Restoring an old church is an act that involves substantially less money and efforts than the repairing of old deteriorating city roads, for example, and that paradoxically attracts more social attention and approval, for people normally tend to take for granted the duty of the government to perform public works or carry out social reforms. The strategy that the government has successfully learned to adopt under such circumstances is to invest a reasonable effort in the populist play on the elevated status of history and culture in the social discourse, and to ignore its taken-for-granted duties where possible.

An immediate example that comes to mind is the notorious restoration of the Church of Christ the Savior in Moscow in 1996–97, which received a truly immense coverage in the media and earned much glory to Moscow mayor Yuri Luzhkov, who managed to turn the process of architectural restoration into a national show that evoked the sentiment of faith, spirit, history, and culture so successfully as to even allow Luzhkov to collect some money for the restoration from the public itself. Newspapers and TV news from time to time conveyed touching stories about contributions that came to the restoration fund from the poor and old people. A popular Moscow newspaper *Moskovskii komsomolets*, for example, placed in one of its weekend editions an article entitled, "Muscovites donate their gold teeth for the sake of the Church."[32] It cannot be said with a positive degree of

---

[32] Tatiana Fedotkina, "Radi khrama moskvichi kladut zuby na polku," *Moskovskii komsomolets*, no.71 (13 April 1996): 8.

Church of Christ the Savior, finally restored to loom against the gloomy Moscow sky. (Photo by S. Mikhasenok, 1998)

certainty how much behind such stories was facts and how much an intention to promote the myth, but what is of interest to us here is a different issue. A truly interesting fact is that not long after the ceremonial opening of the newly restored Church of Christ the Savior, in the Spring of 1998 a major collapse of a city road occurred in the very center of Moscow, on Dmitrovka street, which had always been a busy pedestrian and city transportation way. The road collapsed more than fifteen feet underground, luckily having trapped only two vehicles and no pedestrians. The connection between the restoration of the Church of Christ the Savior and the Dmitrovka accident, indeed, may be said to be a direct one, representing priorities in municipal policy (especially considering the fact that there has been much talk in the past years about the necessity of inspecting the state of underground communications and soil depression in Moscow). I would like to stress that this incident is not an isolated one – it represents a trend, which is unambiguously reflected even on the pages of major Russian newspapers where columns praising the restoration of old churches periodically and, indeed, consistently alternate with columns reporting collapses of apartment complexes, city roads, and other instances of deterioration of vitally important constructions. In the year 2000, by which municipal authorities in major Russian cities promised their citizens to fix all serious problems related to the infrastructure, one could still see the same newspaper reports appearing under the same grim titles, like "Unlucky Island: Buildings Started to Sink Underground in the Center of Moscow," "Building on Bolotnaia Embankment Has Cracked," and so on.[33] For example, one of such articles reported, "In the very center of Moscow, next to the residence of the Duma, an apartment complex on Petrovka street 26/2 is collapsing. But nobody seems to pay attention to this. If somebody

---

[33] Yurii Kochergin and Sergei Samoilov, "Ostrov nevezeniia: V tsentre Moskvy nachali ukhodit' pod zemliu doma," *Moskovskii komsomolets*, no.114 (27 May 2000): 1; Adelaida Sigida, "Tresnul dom na Bolotnoi naberezhnoi," *Nezavisimaia gazeta*, no.96 (27 May 2000): 2.

is still surprised that buildings in Moscow suddenly collapse for no obvious reason, it is only out of naiveté. The whole system of municipal authority in the city rests on the principle: until the building has actually collapsed, an administrator won't give a damn ... Also, collapses without victims don't impress the administration."[34] Needless to mention, they generally do not impress the majority of the intellectuals either. What impresses the majority of the intellectuals is the process of the restoration of old churches and other landmarks of history that supposedly contain the magical spirit of Russian culture.

Another clear example of this ideological strategy in action is evident in Hedrick Smith's account of his encounter with Vladimir Galitsky, an architect and government administrator who was engaged in that same restoration of old Russian churches in the end of the 1980s. Hedrick Smith, interestingly, connects the rising interest in restoring old churches to the spread of Orthodox nationalist feeling in Gorbachev's Russia, but he does not analyze it in broader terms of power and the politics of intellectual discourse and, in my opinion, misses half of the issue. Galitsky tells Hedrick Smith a passionate story – which is, I would like to emphasize again, nothing but another typical manifestation of the new paradigm in the intelligentsia's thinking – about some eighteenth-century church, allegedly architecturally unique, which is falling into decay, hidden in the midst of regular Moscow housing blocks. He resorts in the end, as is usually the case, to a trivial argument of juxtaposing the beauty of the old church to the ugliness of socialist living quarters:

> Look at all those deformities, those ugly boxes ... I dislike them intensely ... It is important to me personally to restore such beauty, and to know that after our work is done, people can enjoy this beauty ... It is important to me because I love history – the history of the Russian people, of other nations. I feel great

---

[34] Irina Brichkalevich, "V raionnykh upravakh Moskvy sidiat potentsial'nye terroristy," *Moskovskii komsomolets*, no.137 (26 June 2000): 3.

respect for historic landmarks. So it was very important to me to help restore it. It was created by the people and the people need it back. This history will help people to be educated, to develop their morality, their culture.[35]

Clearly, what Galitsky fails to acknowledge as a real problem are the ugly living conditions for average people. That is to say, he acknowledges it in a way, but his solution is that of a typical Russian intellectual who reasons that the aesthetics of the past should somehow define the forms of the aesthetics of the future and magically cure all social problems. People who suffer should be given some abstract beauty from the old ages to contemplate, and that will fill their souls with harmony, educate them and make them happy. Ultimately, what students in the humanities learn at universities develops here into a conscious practical stance. Social issues are seen through the abstract prism of spirit and morality, and common sense appears to be absurdly lost. Indeed, who but a person working as a government administrator and architect can make a real difference and fix the problem of "all those deformities, those ugly boxes"? Why not design and build a new beautiful and aesthetically pleasing apartment complex, which would solve both the problem of beauty in the city and the problem of living conditions? It seems like an obvious thought, but this obvious thought, as I have been trying to show, contradicts not just the direction and ideals, but the very bases and founding rules of the intellectual discourse in contemporary Russia. It is a sad fact, but people like Galitsky, who have enough power and are actually in position to change things, almost always happen to be, due to the structure of education and employment, those most profoundly infected with the spirit of this intellectual discourse. They either fail to notice the needs of the contemporary moment, or consciously ignore them for ideological reasons.

The conservative ideological aspect of the intelligentsia's spreading attitude toward associating architecture with culture was noticed and en-

---

[35] Hedrick Smith, *The New Russians* (New York: Avon Books, 1991), p.397.

couraged by the Soviet authorities, in fact, before perestroika. The late 1970s and 1980s saw a gradual increase in the number of books written on the subject of historical architecture in a popularizing manner. In the beginning, most of these books were published by the major state publishing houses, but eventually the popularity of this genre successfully spread to smaller regional publishers, and one could hardly think of any city in Russia that would not have at least a couple of local publications on the landmarks of its historical architecture by the mid-1980s. Very often, the publishing of such books was sponsored directly by the municipal authorities and had to do with the activities of an organization, known as *VOOPIK*, which, strictly speaking, manifested a legalized administrative interest of the authorities in the matter. *VOOPIK* stood for the "All-Russian Society for the Preservation of Historical and Cultural Monuments," and the very fact of its formation and establishment on the national scale indicated that the authorities decided to place the new interests of the intelligentsia under control.

As a controlling institution, *VOOPIK* turned to be a success. It effectively bureaucratized the new humanistic discourse of the intelligentsia, having neutralized its critical dimension and having turned it essentially into a reactionary campaign for the conservation of culture. Some left-oriented Russian critics did comment on the conservative nature of *VOOPIK* in the 1980s, but, surprisingly, their criticisms often implied that the conservatism of *VOOPIK* somehow had to do with its failure to protect enough historical monuments. One may, again, only wonder at the level of penetration of the new historical paradigm into the intellectual consciousness. Boris Kagarlitsky, for example, writes that, "at the end of the Brezhnev era, right-wing Russian nationalists and anti-Semites secured complete control of this society ... [which was] more interested in combating Jews and freemasons than in preserving and restoring the heritage."[36]

---

[36] Boris Kagarlitsky, *The Thinking Reed: Intellectuals and the Soviet State from 1917 to the Present* (London: Verso, 1988), p.334.

He goes on further to counterpose to *VOOPIK* some progressive unofficial "movement for the defense of monuments which arose in the eighties" and which became "a real alternative to the official body." As an example of the real struggle for the preservation of culture, he describes the following "heroic" event:

> In 1986, when it was decided in Moscow to demolish the seventeenth-century Shcherbakov Palaces, a group of students and schoolchildren, led by Kirill Parfenov, occupied the building and held it for two months. As a result, not only were the Shcherbakov Palaces saved but they remained in the hands of the "invaders." Parfenov himself appeared on the TV programme *Twelfth Floor* and spoke of the need to carry on the struggle to preserve the capital's historic aspect.[37]

There are several interesting things that could be pointed out in this passage. One is certainly the involvement of schoolchildren and students in the action, which, on the one hand, was evidently just a political tool for Parfenov, but on the other, again, tells much about the education in the humanities and reproduction of cultural ideals. Another is the fact that the "invaders" managed to get hold of the building, which is presented as a positive development in the "heroic" context of the passage, but otherwise makes little sense, since it is very unclear what good practical use a group of students and intellectuals can make of an old dysfunctional building. Finally, the last issue, which should be actually put first, is that the Shcherbakov Palaces is in reality a mediocre and rather unremarkable building which aimlessly takes space in the busy district of Moscow, being totally useless and, indeed, dysfunctional within the context of the social life of contemporary metropolis.

The fact that *VOOPIK* was reluctant to protect this particular building, thus, does only certain credit to it, if the matter is to be considered seriously. However, this case has to be viewed as an exception to the rule, for

---

[37] Boris Kagarlitsky, *The Thinking Reed*, p.334.

Shcherbakov Palaces in the midst of never-ending reconstruction process. (Photo by the author, 2002)

both *VOOPIK* and the alternative movements in the end represent instances of essentially the same intellectual rejection of modernity on the social scale – rejection that constituted a dominant trend in the Russian culture of the last quarter of the twentieth century. The chairman of *VOOPIK*'s Moscow branch, Aleksandr Trofimov, interviewed by Hedrick Smith, says already familiar things:

> Destruction of the old architecture was a terrible thing ... Ancient Moscow cannot be restored ... This disturbs our people, and so masses of people have come to our organization, because there is a certain instinct for self-preservation in people ... If our national culture is alive, we can sleep peacefully. But if it is not, our nation will disappear. If the progress of our cultural restoration remains as

slow as it has been, we will risk, if not total disappearance, then the loss of our national cultural face.[38]

Thus, it is again the process of cultural *restoration* that is supposed to determine the progress of national life and advancement of national culture. The idea of *creation* as a moving force remains remarkably alien to the intellectual consciousness, for within the paradigm of thinking in which culture is fundamentally identified with history, *creation* unconditionally equates with *re-creation*, that is *reconstruction* – an unacceptable idea implying that something older, and therefore more historically valuable, must be destroyed to give way to something newer which, by definition, is going to be of lesser cultural value. The persistence of this axiomatic concept in the intellectual mentality and, to a large extent, in broader provinces of social thinking may be certainly identified as one of the major predicaments of the late Soviet and new Russian culture, for it actually spread far beyond the particular area of architecture, having saturated all areas of intellectual discourse to one or another degree. In the discourse of architecture it simply found an extreme expression, perhaps due to the specific tangible quality of the built environment and its dramatic involvement in the everyday. One has only to pick up a random issue of a Sunday metropolitan newspaper in Russia to locate an immediate trace of this omnipresent architectural discourse – there are all chances one would encounter either a nostalgic essay under a title, like "Everyday Charm of the Old Russian Aristocratic Estate,"[39] or a "critical" voice of a typical intellectual or scholar in the humanities: "This Terrifying Word *Reconstruction* – It Is under Its Cover That the Old Moscow Is Being Destroyed."[40]

The real issue that came to characterize the atmosphere of the 1990s, however, is that such "critical" statements seem to no longer represent any-

---

[38] Hedrick Smith, *The New Russians*, p.398.
[39] Liudmila Lunina, "Bytovoe obaianie russkoi usad'by," *Segodnia* (24 August 1996).
[40] Vadim Apenin, "Eto strashnoe slovo *rekonstruktsia* – imenno pod ego prikrytiiem unichtozhaetsia staraia Moskva," *Nezavisimaia gazeta*, no.151 (16 August 1996).

thing but the discourse itself, because in reality the Old Moscow is not being destroyed anymore. On the contrary, it is restored on such overwhelming scale that has never been the case before. If from 1965 to 1972 allocations to the restoration budget slowly grew from 2 to 4 million rubles, after 1976 they suddenly jumped to 15 million, and reached 25 million rubles already in 1984.[41] A pedestrian, walking about small streets in the historic center of Moscow, such as Arbat, Volkhonka, and others, may only look around and wonder at the amount of restoration work that is taking place these days. As a result of long and successful activity of organizations, like *VOOPIK*, thousands of pre-revolutionary buildings came to be marked under the category "monument of history and culture," which granted them an officially protected status and placed them in that magical area that was usually described in the Soviet ideolanguage as *vsenarodnoe dostoianiie* ["property and heritage of all people"].[42]

---

[41] Timothy J. Colton, *Moscow: Governing the Socialist Metropolis* (Cambridge, MA: Belknap Press, 1995), p.558.

[42] The phrase *vsenarodnoe dostoianiie*, like many others employed by the Soviet ideolanguage, is an interesting case. English dictionaries translate the word *dostoianiie* solely as "property," and that was indeed the original meaning of the word in the Russian language of the older centuries. In contemporary Russian, however, a substantial shift in the meaning of the word has occurred, caused most likely by the acceptance of another word, *sobstvennost'*, as a legal term for "property," and the wider social use of the latter in all situations. *Dostoianiie*, when used to imply "property" in its usual sense, sounds old-fashioned and a little awkward today. As is the frequent case with many old-fashioned words, it has acquired a figural and, to an extent, exalted sense, and it is casually used to refer to something in one's possession in an elevated manner, mostly to something that one is particularly proud of. For example, when a writer refers to her books as her *sobstvennost'*, it means only that *her books are her property*. When, on the other hand, she refers to them as her *dostoianiie*, it means that *her books are her spiritual heritage and ultimately something she is proud of*. The sense of "property" per se, thus, normally is lost in *dostoianiie*'s modern usage and replaced by the sense of "heritage," or an "object of pride." The choice of the old word *dostoianiie* by the Soviet authorities, therefore, was a subtle one. The category *vsenarodnoe dostoianiie* clearly meant that the old Russian architecture was "people's heritage," and that it was ultimately something people should be proud of, but at the same time it did not really imply that it was "people's property," since no one said it was *sobstvennost'* (i.e. "property" as such).

Just another old church is being restored in the midst of Moscow streets. (Photo by the author, 2000)

Of course, some of the buildings that came under the protected status were fairly considered as architectural masterpieces of the old epoch or important historic landmarks that deserved restoration. Too many of them, however, composed nothing but a dull mass of typical nineteenth-century or eighteenth-century constructions – inelegant, unattractive, and of no apparent architectural value – which were marked as "monuments of history and culture" solely because some important figure from the past, like Pushkin or Tolstoy, happened to dine there once as a guest. As one would expect, all buildings where Lenin or other heroes of the communist revolution set their foot were similarly counted as "monuments of history and culture" under the Soviet regime. Curiously, although the perestroika years dramatically changed the general attitude toward the Bolsheviks and many of the older Soviet memorial boards with inscriptions, like, "*V. I. Lenin gave a speech in this building in 1918. Monument of history and culture. Protected by law*," were removed during the late 1980s and 1990s, the buildings themselves apparently still remain under the protected status, since one might guess that it were not the boards themselves that actually protected the buildings but rather some bureaucratic municipal records – and, in the case of Russia, it is truly hard to imagine what might cause any change in the latter, except fire or flood. Most of such buildings are slowly decaying today, because the priorities of financing the process of restoration are often ideological and directed to those landmarks which have either an unmistakable architectural value or a significant symbolic importance in the eyes of the larger public (this was evidently the case with the mentioned Church of Christ the Savior, a rather mediocre construction in architectural terms, which nevertheless was for many reasons thought of as a historic landmark of paramount importance).

Without a doubt, today there are an increasing number of private investors who would like to purchase the spot of one or another of such decaying buildings, clear it up and construct a new properly equipped contemporary building that would attract growing businesses, but who are not allowed to do so simply because the decaying building is still in the roster of protected "monuments." In fact, disputes and squabbles over such structures have been continuously intensifying since the early 1990s. In 1991, Viktor Grishin, former head of the municipal administration of the city of Moscow, commented on the growing influence and interference of *VOOPIK* in all kinds of city management matters:

> It was practically impossible to do anything in Moscow with a structure that presented any sort of interest without incurring the active interference of the Society [*VOOPIK*]. I remember how on one street, Sadovaya-Karetnaya, a stone pedestal stood in the middle of the sidewalk. We thought that we had better tear it down – it was right in the center of the sidewalk, you see, and it was getting in the way. But no way, the Society [*VOOPIK*] got its dander up and claimed this was a valuable antiquity. And what do you think happened? We had to retreat.[43]

The intellectual fight for the preservation – in essence, conservation – of anything historic and the fear of "reconstruction," thus, assumed pathological dimensions and became both an obstacle to the normal growth of businesses and a general impediment in the city life. Most of the "historically" protected buildings are of no interest to a pedestrian, as they are neither aesthetically appealing nor functionally useful, in as much as they cannot effectively host even a café or a small shop. Nevertheless, they are preserved, despite the needs and interests of modern life, solely because the dominant paradigm in the intellectual discourse dictates that "we must preserve the smallest detail of the past we could be proud of." This paradigm dictates, with a surprising degree of authority, that it is only the past that can be an object of cultural pride. The present cannot become such an object because the contemporary has simply no cultural value. One cannot possibly build something to be proud of, for everything one can be proud of *has been already built*. Culture is *given* to people and the proper way to

---

[43] Timothy J. Colton, *Moscow*, p.559.

treat it is not to change it, not to develop or prolong it, but to *preserve* it. This principle is the core of the unwritten intellectual doctrine that shaped and framed the world view and cultural ideology of the Russian society in the last quarter of the twentieth century. It continues to exert powerful influence on this society today. Vladimir Papernyi in his earlier mentioned book *Kul'tura Dva* comes essentially to the same conclusion when he says, "Nobody creates in the culture-2 [late Soviet culture], because everybody is only trying to grope for a way to the already created and given. This explains the fervor of the negative attitude of the culture-2 toward individual creativity, authorship, and talent."[44]

The discourse of architecture in Russia essentially reflects the cultural struggle of tradition against modernity. It should be mentioned that, in fact, such type of discourse is not a specifically Russian phenomenon, but rather a mainstream aspect of cultural politics in many European states. This is undoubtedly one of the reasons why continental thinkers, such as Baudrillard, Foucault, and others, devote much attention to the subject of architecture. The case of the US is quite different, in the first instance because the architecture in the US almost in its entirety is a mirror of modernity. A critical discourse of architecture has only recently emerged as a distinctive phenomenon in the American intellectual milieu and this has been related largely to the apprehension of the coming postmodern age. One could agree, therefore, with a frequently made point that the discourse of architecture in the US reflects the struggle of modernity with postmodernity, which is a struggle of a different order than that of tradition with modernity (where by tradition a certain social primordialism or medievalism as an encompassing cultural attitude is implied).

Foucault on several occasions speaks explicitly against the traditional order of organized historical architecture, saying that the historical reference often appears today as one of the principal forms of oppression from

---

[44] Vladimir Papernyi, *Kul'tura Dva*, p.249.

which one has to constantly liberate oneself. This discourse of historicity, says Foucault, is aimed at provoking "an inclination to seek out some cheap form of archaism or some imaginary past forms of happiness that people did not, in fact, have at all."[45] This specific aspect of both the historical and architectural discourse is still another important area which attracts the attention and interests of the power, as a convenient strategic resource for ideological manipulations. In the Russian case, this resource has been perhaps more actively employed in the provinces than in the central metropolitan areas (St. Petersburg or Moscow), in which, as we have seen, the movement for the preservation of history and architecture essentially developed into a large-scale intellectual and administrative campaign. Smaller towns in the provinces usually did not have sufficient financial resources to support what could be properly called a restoration "campaign," nor did they have enough intellectual resources to organize a fight for such a campaign. Most of the old architectural landmarks in these towns, therefore, remained in a deteriorating condition. Yet they never ceased to be an object of close attention on the part of the local authorities who successfully learned the lessons – or perhaps simply followed the trend and example – of how the metropolitan authorities handled the issue of all these old architectural ruins and decaying churches. Being unable or for some reason reluctant to actually engage in restoring them, local authorities nonetheless invested enough attempts in popularizing them as some magically important vestiges of "the old Rome that once was." In colleges all across the country, courses and occasionally even departments of local history began to be introduced to cover this area of studies, which suddenly assumed unusual importance. Local historians, art critics, and journalists were encouraged to write fulsome articles and books about pre-revolutionary landmarks in their regions. Such books were usually marked by the naive provincial overvaluing, which metropolitan scholars often

---

[45] Michel Foucault, "Space, Knowledge, and Power," in *The Foucault Reader*, ed. Paul Rabinow (New York: Pantheon Books, 1984), p.248.

found comical and amusing.[46] But, however unreal or exaggerated those accounts might have been, from the authorities' point of view they served their purpose perfectly – and the purpose was, as Foucault aptly noted, to evoke a "cheap form of archaism or some imaginary past forms of happiness," as well as a patriotic feeling of pride that should arise in the town inhabitants solely owing to the presence of such sacred "Roman ruins" in a nearby neighborhood.

Indeed, it is hard to say why the dwellers of typical towns in central Russia, such as Rostov, Vladimir, Tula, or Yaroslavl', should be fond or proud of their hometowns, given the fact that their economy has been for long years in the state of profound depression and the living conditions there have been constantly worsening. But the effect of the ideological hypnosis of "history and culture" turns out to be so persuasive that, confronted with a question why they are proud of their towns, a great many of the dwellers will sincerely respond, "because of the unique old Russian architecture that we have here." A dweller of Rostov will unmistakably bring up the Rostov Kremlin which has preserved constructions "even older than some in the Moscow Kremlin"; and a dweller of Vladimir will typically point out to the *Pokrova na Nerli* church which is "the best in all of Russia." It is useless to ask how these constructions actually make their lives better. The fact is, they do not. But the answer one will be given will never acknowledge this fact – it will be either filled with already familiar words about cultural heritage and morality, or, in a more reflexive and sincere case, will state that the sense of cultural importance and presence of such beauty nearby makes them feel a little better and in a way compensates for the hardships of life.

---

[46] It is not that the metropolitan scholarship was free of cultural overvaluing – in fact, metropolitan scholars were as prone to it as their colleagues from the provinces. The difference was, however, that the metropolitan kind of overvaluing was traditionally based on a certain degree of sophistication and the complexity of argument, whereas the provincial kind was typically straightforward and the regular arguments involved in it were: "it is good because it is the best," or "this is unique because even Moscow does not have it."

The issue ultimately is that the imaginary compensation for hardship is an attractive idea for the government that is unable to compensate for such hardship in any practical way. In the cities and towns, where current economic and social conditions are frustrating and leaving little to be proud of, ideological discourses of history and architecture are increasingly exploited by the authorities as a means to establish and strengthen an imaginary spiritual bond between the citizens and their living environments. Such discourses are aimed at provoking a false feeling of pride and faith in some idealized facts of history, some bright and happy mythical past that presumably hides behind all these incredibly important architectural landmarks which are supposed to fill people with the sense of awe and beauty and compensate for their life in poverty and slums.

A picture below is an example of how these discourses typically circulate in the media. It is an advertisement page from the popular Russian magazine *Liza*, which by its content may be roughly equivalent to a magazine like *Good Housekeeping* in the US. *Liza* is heavily targeted at the small town population, rather than metropolitan audiences. The page draws the reader's attention to a small town of *Khot'kovo*, situated in the central region of Russia, and apparently invites everybody to visit the place. Everything is arranged in this advertisement according to the prescriptions of historical and architectural discourses. Two thirds of the description is a diligent explanation of Khot'kovo's historical importance, which presumably amounts to the fact that no pilgrim, going in the past from Moscow to Troitse-Sergieva Lavra (a famous monastery that had once played the role of an Orthodox "Mecca" in old Russia), could possibly avoid this place on their way. "In the past," the opening paragraph states, "Khot'kovo was allotted a very important role of a connecting link between Moscow and Troitse-Sergieva Lavra." The visual image takes on the architectural aspect. In the background of the larger picture, one can see a golden dome of some old Russian church, which has become an almost obligatory element within the new system of cultural representation. One of the smaller

"Khot'kovo: A Little Corner Dear to Your Heart." (Liza, no.28, July 1996)

pictures displays an old monastery wall and, upon a closer look, its decaying condition can be detected even without a magnifying glass (not in the black-and-white reproduction above, but surely in the color photo in the actual magazine). The picture next to it, oddly, shows a regular railroad bridge, which probably indicates that there was nothing else to show in the town. Finally, the sentimental title line of the page: *"Khot'kovo: A Little Corner Dear to Your Heart"* and the idyllic image of two little goats at the bottom crown the structure of representation in its entirety, for what they are supposed to accomplish is certainly that very task, pointed out by Foucault, of evoking in the mind of the reader some forms of cheap archaism, some imaginary forms of happiness, associated with the past, that are never the case in reality. Indeed, the reality of the present is not shown in the picture, for it ultimately consists in the fact that *Khot'kovo* is just a typical dirty central Russian village which suffers from the loss of active working population and is trying to attract the attention of investors by resorting to the appealing cultural trick of history and architecture.

Examples similar to the one described above are countless in the Russian press. The approach that they all demonstrate appears surprisingly unambiguous, once one starts analyzing it in terms of what we have referred to as the new historical paradigm in the intellectual discourse. The values of the past persist in the intellectual imaginary, even though the needs of the present seem to come into a substantial disagreement and contradiction with these values. When such contradiction is felt as troublesome, it is usually resolved in favor of the past to the detriment of the interests of the present. There certainly are some exceptions to this rule, but on the whole in the intellectual realm "modernists" continue to be significantly outnumbered by "traditionalists," and in most cultural litigations the past invariably turns out to be a plaintiff with a better attorney and the present traditionally ends up paying for damages.

III. Effects of the New Paradigm

The effects of the new intellectual paradigm and its strategic appropriation by the ruling authorities in Russia are transparent not only in the restoration of the old architectural landmarks but in the process of contemporary city construction as well. They are especially conspicuous in the case of the elite, but otherwise mediocre, Moscow architect Zurab Tsereteli who, being connected with the municipal authorities (or perhaps one should say, being *one* of the municipal authorities), has created an array of monuments in the city during the 1990s. The succession of these monuments displays an interesting retrograde temporal tendency running parallel to the rise of populist interest of the authorities in the restoration of "cultural heritage." In this case, the tendency points deeper and deeper into the past. First, Tsereteli takes part in the project of constructing a monument to General Zhukov (finally designed by Viacheslav Klykov), a hero of the World War II in the public memory. His next project falls two centuries back to the times of Peter the Great, whose figure he decides to immortalize on the banks of the Moskva River. Finally, after that he undertakes a journey into the "depths of national memory," into the archaic times of mythical folk figures, whose sculptures he meaningfully puts right in the Aleksandrovskii garden, next to Kremlin – that is, in the very center of the Russian empire.

Although some Western critics interpret these myth and fairy-tale sculpture figures, surrounding the territory of the Russian government, as a sign of the "infantilization" or "MacDonaldization" of Russian politics, while some Russian journalists, trying to be original, classify it as the "politics of surrealism,"[47] I would still argue that the phenomenon, properly seen within the Russian context, reflects the logical, and indeed hardly

---

[47] Sergei Dunaev, "Siurrealisty protiv realistov" ["Surrealists against Realists"], *Nezavisimaia Gazeta*, no.182 (27 September 1997), p.2.

Peter the Great once again immortalized on the banks of Moskva River. (Photo by S. Mikhasenok, 1998)

surprising, continuation of the same general move toward the ideological historicizing of culture that can be detected in many other phenomena occurring in the Russian society of nowadays.

If, incidentally, one should touch on the realm of political symbolism, one of the first examples to come to mind would be Yeltsin's decision to abolish the old Soviet coat of arms in 1993 and introduce the "new" one, which represented a medieval Russian (copied from the still older Byzantine) golden eagle with two heads and three crowns. In Kagarlitsky's subtle phrase, "The medieval bird was plucked out of three hundred years of oblivion because the country's coat of arms was supposed to be 'brought into accordance with the present-day conception of Russian statehood'."[48] Further, it became fashionable among the former communist *nomenklatura* and government authorities of lower ranks to dress in the outfit of old Russian nobility and wear all kinds of ancient regalia that made no sense in the present social environment and looked ridiculously comic and grotesque. This show was typically justified in terms of a necessity to return at last to the authentic national traditions repressed by the Soviets; but ironically it were the same former "Soviets" that had used to repress the traditions a decade earlier who now heatedly argued for their return. And, of course, the only trivial reason to all that was, as Kagarlitsky noted, that "the barbaric Russian official and the semi-criminal entrepreneur dreamed of at last securing their power and privilege with the help of the well-tried traditional symbols of Russian autocracy." The interest in all things aristocratic and historical that emerged by the mid-1980s as an intellectual infatuation, thus, was again strategically picked up by the ruling authorities at the appropriate moment:

> The whole point about tradition is its continuity. Understanding this, the nomenklatura sought assiduously to depict itself as the legitimate heir of the old

---

[48] Boris Kagarlitsky, *Restoration in Russia: Why Capitalism Failed* (London: Verso, 1995), p.24–5.

Display stand of the East-Side administrative district in Moscow with two medieval coats of arms, one (on the left) symbolizing the city of Moscow, the other (on the right) the local county. (Photo by the author, 2000)

ruling classes. "Councils of the nobility," "Cossack circles" and "unions of descendants of merchants" began appearing everywhere; here former Komsomol functionaries, local heads of administration and young careerists sat in state, pantomime actors in frock coats and old uniforms.[49]

The development of Russian business in the late 1980s and the 1990s manifested the same preoccupation with the historical themes. Private companies tried their best to demonstrate the pre-revolutionary origins of their enterprises, although in most cases the common sense alone should have been enough to disclose the absurd nature of their statements. At the risk of tiring out the reader with quotations, I would like to cite another paragraph from Kagarlitsky's account, because it presents what should be

---

[49] Boris Kagarlitsky, *Restoration in Russia*, p.25.

considered the most typical example of how new independent companies handled the issue of their origins:

> The Sviridoff company in its advertising clips reported with pride on its "five hundred years of prosperity." After the revolution the Sviridoff merchants had supposedly fled from Russia to Australia, had set up in business there, and were now repatriating their operations. And indeed, in Australia and the US there are firms with this name, though people there would be astonished to learn from Russian television broadcasts that the Sviridoff company was "a leader of the Australian financial market." In their newspaper advertisements the newly appeared Australians could not even manage the correct spelling for the city of "Melbourne." Moreover, the firm had been established not in the aftermath of the Russian revolution, but towards the end of perestroika. The family behind it was undoubtedly influential; however, it was not a family of old-time merchants, but of thoroughly modern Soviet industrial managers. One Sviridoff had been Minister of Heavy Machine Building of Ukraine, while the other had been the director of the Novokramotorskiy Metallurgical Combine.[50]

Other companies that could not forge a successful proof of their pre-revolutionary origins tried at least to invent a name for themselves that would sound reminiscent of the old Russia. Such was, for example, the case with the new Russian bank *Imperial* which was constantly advertised in TV and other media commercials through a series of historical "clips" evoking images of the old Russian empire. One of the gas and auto-repair stations in Moscow was named *Sorokin i K.*, which was a typical pre-revolutionary way of naming companies (it meant "Sorokin and company") and which came out of use during the years of the Soviet regime. Scrolling through popular magazines, one could come across even a web-designing company (one might think that younger people in the computer industry would not fall into the historical trap!) with the name *Kalita* – which is the name of the Russian tsar of medieval times, Ivan Kalita.[51]

---

[50] Boris Kagarlitsky, *Restoration in Russia*, p.26.
[51] *Kalita Web-Design* advertisement, in *Itogi*, no.37 (23 September 1997), p.81.

Many cafes and small shops changed their names in various ways, from usual contemporary *Chainaia* ("tea-room") to *Chaikhana* (same meaning, but with an old-fashioned exotic ring), or from *Kofeinaia* ("cafe") to *Kofeinia* (again, the same word but with the pre-revolutionary spelling), and so on.

As of this date, the strategic political investment in the past and history continues. Naturally, it will continue as long as the intellectual and broader social discourse remains locked within the history-as-culture framework. As might be expected, the authorities are interested not just in *using* this framework to their advantage, but also in *strengthening* it to a certain degree. The indications of that may be detected in various philanthropic campaigns of the government authorities, which are often loudly advertised as "humanitarian," but in reality rarely seem to serve other purposes than the strengthening of the ideological base of the social discourse and the authorities' own public image. For instance, in 1997 Moscow mayor Luzhkov decided to "give" 500 million rubles from the municipal budget to support the search for the allegedly lost library of Russian tsar Ivan the Terrible. The decision, to a little surprise, has been praised in the media as an exemplary humanitarian action. One curious thing about the coverage, though, was that it remained unclear to whom exactly Luzhkov gave the money; it was only said that it was given to a "search committee," which was also provided with an appropriate office space and equipment. But that aside, the main question that arises here is, why at the time when the city universities, especially their humanities departments, suffer from a dire lack of resources, computers, and office space, the mayor should allocate 500 million rubles, office space, and these much needed computers for the search of some fifteenth-century manuscripts that in the first instance have not been even proven to exist, and that, secondly, even if miraculously found, no historian would be able to study anyway for the lack of normal working conditions? This question was, unsurprisingly, avoided in the press, with the exception of one critical article that appeared in the *Itogi* magazine and commented on the suspicious nature of this "humanitarian action," pointing out that the search for the lost library looked actually more like a search for symbolic roots which could help legitimize the power in the eyes of the public.[52]

Questions like this are typically left unanswered in Russia. But how can one properly criticize the government for its reasoning that the lost library is more important than the needs of living people, if the same kind of reasoning paradoxically continues to permeate most of the educated intelligentsia who hold on to their humanistic conviction that the lost library is precisely what constitutes the needs of the people? When Professor Dmitrii Likhachev, already mentioned authority in the humanities in Russia, and his interviewer Sergei Bychkov discuss on the pages of a popular Moscow newspaper the issue of depressing living conditions in small towns of the Moscow region, they come to remarkably similar conclusions. They reason that the current depression in these towns is caused by the loss of intellectual culture that had been formerly, in the pre-revolutionary Russia, spread around by aristocratic estates located in or near these towns. They pick on one of such estates, *Muranovo*, and talk about its educational role. "Russian culture," says Likhachev, "was library-oriented. This had been inherited from the ancient ages of Russia when there had not been universities, but had been great monastery and church libraries. Russia was not just a literate country, but was a country that liked to read. Aristocratic estates were spreading religious culture, for there was a church at every estate, as was the case with Muranovo." Sergei Bychkov, the interviewer, concludes the thought, saying that unfortunately the building of the former church in Muranovo "still functions as a public storage today ... [and] the destiny of the richest Muranovo library remains unknown ... With the death of Muranovo, the neighboring population grows wilder too."[53]

---

[52] Sergei Ivanov, "Pod flagom Liberei," *Itogi*, no.39 (7 October 1997), p.53.
[53] Sergei Bychkov, "Akademik Likhachev," *Moskovskii komsomolets*, no.164 (31 August 1996), p.2.

So, the underlying theme, as is usually the case in most Russian intellectual speculations on the subject of history, is that the old aristocratic Russia embodied the ideal of enlightenment, education, and culture, and ever since then people have been growing wilder and wilder. The return to the ideals of the past, accordingly, is seen as the road to salvation. It might be interesting to note, though, that even the return to the ideals of the past as a cultural goal might be accomplished in different ways, and might imply different approaches. Thus, one might think about creating some new educational or cultural institutions in those small towns – institutions that could successfully take on the role, presumably successfully performed by the aristocratic estates in the past. In fact, this seems to be a reasonable approach. This approach, however, is not what the intelligentsia have in mind, for it probably involves too much dirty and boring bureaucratic work in the first instance, but, more importantly, does not resolve the issue as the intelligentsia see it. The issue, one should understand this, is not that "people grow wilder," but rather that church libraries are lost and ultimately that the old estates that had once belonged to the aristocratic intelligentsia of the past ages are no more in possession of the intelligentsia of nowadays. The fact that "people grow wilder" is just a side effect of the real issue, and it is usually brought up merely as an argument in support of the importance of restoring old estates and churches. This is clearly detectable in the above-cited Sergei Bychkov's interview in which the center of attention is naturally Muranovo, and in which the death of this estate maps onto the way in which "the neighboring population grows wilder." By and large, the intelligentsia are just pursuing their recurrent dream of getting hold of old aristocratic living quarters and spending their time there in relaxation and leisure, reading interesting books from a nearby church library and having pleasant evening tea on the porch – that is to say, pursuing what in their imagination constitutes a life of a good old enlightened intellectual. It is a curious episode, but the end of Bychkov's interview with Likhachev is indeed a moving sentimental description of how after the conversation they went to Likhachev's dacha and, in the company of some other intellectuals, had pleasant evening tea.

The problem of typical dreams and ideals of the intelligentsia is an interesting topic per se, and I will discuss it briefly in the following chapter, but here I would like to emphasize again that it appears culturally important because it is directly connected with the larger structures of the social discourse. The intelligentsia was responsible for the substantial transformation of the social discourse in Russia of the last quarter of the twentieth century in a way that reversed the ideological grounds of the traditional Soviet social discourse with its emphasis on the utopias of the future, and powerfully repositioned them around the utopias of the past. The conventional ideology of the Soviet social discourse, dictating that "the bright future will come as a redemption or atonement for the unclear past," gave way to the new cultural ideology, preaching that "the bright past will atone for the uncertainties of the future." Indeed, where but in the intellectual discourse of the late twentieth-century Russia can one encounter magazine headlines with such paradoxical titles as "The Majestic Russian Past Will Surpass the Most Daring Expectations in the Future".[54]

The efforts of the intellectuals have resulted in the formation of a specific discursive paradigm within which, in Foucault's words, history becomes not just one of the human sciences but rather a favorable environment, both privileged and dangerous, where other human sciences can exist. This historical environment is privileged insofar as it is empowered to impose its own regulations and determine "the cultural area in which [this or] that branch of knowledge can be recognized as having validity." It is dangerous because it "surrounds the sciences of man with a frontier that limits them and destroys, from the outset, their claim to validity."[55] The

---

[54] Nikita Sokolov, "Pravoslavie, samoderzhavie, elektorat: Velichestvennoe proshloe Rossii v budushchem prevzoidet samye smelye ozhidania," *Itogi*, no.37 (1997), p.66.
[55] Michel Foucault, *The Order of Things: An Archaeology of the Human Sciences* (New York: Random House, 1970), p.371.

effects of this development were apparent in that a number of disciplines in the humanities and social sciences in Russia fell in their academic and social status and became subordinate to the discipline of history. The connection with the moral quest for values and fight for cultural heritage turned to be the final factor which, in Michel de Certeau's phrase, put history "in the vanguard of the sciences as the present fiction of what they are only partially able to achieve."[56] The pedagogical superiority of history, thus established in the intellectual discourse, gradually influenced the direction of development and ideals of public education at all levels. The interaction with neighboring discourses of history of arts and architecture, among others, was instrumental in producing a fusion of categories "history," "culture," and "humanism," which constituted a core of the new influential paradigm of intellectual and in many ways broader social thinking. The strategic ideological appropriation of this paradigm by the ruling authorities has completed the establishment of a powerful ideological framework which, interestingly, is reminiscent of what three decades ago Karl Popper criticized as "the social order of moral historicism," that is, that kind of encompassing positivist cultural-historical morality which makes "a moral criticism of the existing state of affairs impossible, since this state itself determines the moral standard of things."[57] However different might have been the society at which he aimed his criticism, the Russian culture at the turn of the centuries, maybe in an inverse, strange, and paradoxical way, still subtly illustrates his theoretical insight.

---

[56] Michel de Certeau, "History: Science and Fiction," in *Heterologies: Discourse on the Other* (Minneapolis: University of Minnesota Press, 1986), p.220.
[57] Karl R. Popper, *The Open Society and Its Enemies*, vol.2 (Princeton: Princeton University Press, 1966), p.206.

Chapter 3
Power, Culture, and Changes in Values and Ideals

The subject of values and ideals, it should be perhaps noted from the outset, is too broad a topic to treat thoroughly within the format of a brief chapter for various reasons. First of all, in no modern developed society is there a single given set of values and ideals that could be unquestionably generalized, except maybe for the circle of so-called universal human values, but even that has been the subject of heated discussions in anthropology throughout the course of the twentieth century. There are values of different social classes and values of different ethnic groups, there are values of minorities and majorities, there are imaginary values and immediate practical ones, there are normative values imposed by ideologies and alternative ones that stand in opposition to them, and so forth. For this reason, I would like to stress that the discussion in this chapter will be specifically and purposefully limited to the cultural environment of the late Soviet/new Russian intelligentsia, and ultimately to what I believe constituted the *typical*, not universal or the only, set (or, using a rather discredited anthropological term, *pattern*) of values and ideals within that environment. Furthermore, I will limit myself to the discussion of the two major aspects of this pattern, which, in my opinion, constituted the core of value orientations of the intelligentsia as a hypothetical whole within the period under consideration. One of these aspects is the notorious relationship of the intelligentsia with power, which in itself is certainly not a novel subject. The other is the relationship between "culture" and the intelligentsia's lifestyle ideals, which has been a more peculiar theme in Russia of the last decade – theme not so frequently discussed and perhaps rarely approached or viewed from the right perspective.

* * *

If we speak of a society as a simplified and standardized whole for a moment, we may acknowledge the existence of two principal layers of social values: that of ideologically promoted normative values and that of actual mundane values pursued by and large. These layers may overlap to a degree, but they certainly do not coincide – otherwise, there would be obviously no need for anybody to promote anything in an ideological way. This incongruence, which is usually more or less apparent when values are considered at the national or state level, appears to be also the case, if only more or less inconspicuous, at smaller social levels, such as the intellectual milieu. One simple reason why it is inconspicuous in the latter case lies in the fact that the intelligentsia is not a political organization that has to deal with establishing clear-cut and written out social policies. It is a loose group that, on the contrary, generally holds on to the idea that no one should dictate its policies (although, for the sake of fairness, one might say that it is a group in which everyone likes to dictate policies, but no one likes to be dictated). Nevertheless, even this seemingly anarchic group habitually adopts certain "policies" which, though never pass through any formal process of ratification, become gradually legitimized through various practices in the intellectual discourse. The incongruence of values here consists in the fact that the policies, worked out within the framework of intellectual discourse, generally reflect the normative set of values (which in a sense might be considered as imposed on the individuals by the discourse, at least to a certain extent), while the set of actual life values or practical values remains largely outside the discourse. In particular instances, when such mundane values do make their way into the discourse, they are normally justified in terms of the prescribed normative values, so that the ideological contradiction is neutralized.

One of the notable manifestations of such discrepancy between normative values, pursued in the discourse, and actual values, pursued in real life, might be observed in the already discussed relationship of the intelligentsia with the bureaucracy. Within the intellectual discourse, as we have seen, it was an informally but firmly held idea that the connection with the state or bureaucracy was a mark of the corruption of one's conscience. In reality, the intelligentsia, with few exceptions, did not mind taking prestigious bureaucratic positions and even aspired to them. These real-life aspirations were not allowed to enter the intellectual discourse; in those rare cases when they did, they were characteristically camouflaged by something more or less agreeable to the discursive conventions. Thus, if an intellectual was appointed to a prominent bureaucratic position, the discursive policies required that she should at least cry all the way to the bank and pretend that she was not really happy about that appointment, or make some specious excuse, like: "I never aspired to that position, but they offered it to me and I reasoned that if I did not take it, some ignorant bureaucrat would instead."

In a word, if one was to judge the situation on the basis of the intellectual discourse alone, one would come to the clear conclusion that intellectuals were not interested in power. The persistence of this idea in the Soviet intellectual milieu is indeed known, as is now known the fact that the first years of perestroika revealed quite the opposite and the late 1980s witnessed literally an invasion of the intelligentsia into all kinds of government structures, which, to a little surprise, resulted in nothing but numerous political failures for all the same reasons that have been already discussed (e.g. the intelligentsia's centeredness on the themes of abstract moral order, inability to see concrete issues and make effective decisions, inherited disrespect for the present and "modernity" in general, and mere lack of competence in political and legal matters). The sudden outburst of the repressed desire of the intelligentsia for power shocked for a moment not only the intellectual community itself, a certain part of which was still permeated with the prescriptions of the conventional Soviet "anti-bureaucratic" discourse, but even some foreign observers, such as Jacques

Derrida who happened to visit Russia during the perestroika years. Derrida was greatly surprised to learn that a number of prominent scholars, like Academician Sakharov or Professor Averintsev, a recognized authority in religious and Byzantine studies, stood for election to the deputies of the Supreme Soviet of the USSR in 1989–90.[1]

Indeed, a rather unexpected appearance in the Supreme Soviet of the USSR of such people as Averintsev, who was regarded almost as a living saint of Russian culture in the intellectual circles, or Vyacheslav Ivanov, a popular writer, respected philologist and linguist, and public figure with a dissident image, left an unpleasant aftertaste in many of the intelligentsia, especially in the students in the humanities who just a year or two before enthusiastically crowded their immensely popular lectures at Moscow State University and listened to their critical anti-government speeches (at any rate, socially oppositional speeches, which may have been perceived as "anti-government"). Students felt that their intellectual heroes suddenly betrayed the ideals they preached. The feeling of disappointment soon intensified, when the intelligentsia's affair with the government ended in a fiasco and some of the participants in that affair simply left the country shortly after. Thus, Averintsev left for Vienna and Ivanov was invited to teach at the Slavic Department of the UCLA. Whatever their reasons for leaving were, from within the context of those turbulent years in Russia, to many it looked like they just fled from the scene of their embarrassment. All this undoubtedly did considerable harm to their image. In the beginning of the 1990s, for example, newly released and reprinted books by Averintsev were sitting on the shelves of the Moscow State University bookstore, without attracting a great deal of attention. This situation would have been absolutely unimaginable in the 1980s. Had the books been pub-

---

[1] Jacques Derrida, "Back from Moscow, in the USSR," in *Zhak Derrida v Moskve*, sost. M. Ryklin (Moscow: RIK "Kul'tura," 1993), p.28. One may ponder on the nature of Derrida's surprise, though; for the trajectory of his own interests through the 1990s seems to display a visible leaning toward politics as well.

lished at that time, the entire stock would have been swept out by students and professors probably in a matter of hours.[2]

The public disclosure of the intelligentsia's political aspirations and their subsequent inability to cope with bureaucratic matters significantly undermined the traditional Russian faith, invested in the nostalgic ideal of "organic" intelligentsia, and noticeably cooled down the interest in intellectual conversations on the part of many of the intellectuals themselves, who stopped buying and reading new publications and often refused to watch all the formerly popular TV debates, typically expressing their disappointment with words like, "I don't care what they have to say any more," "I've seen and heard enough of them lately," "it's probably nothing but another hypocrisy and lie." Although this feeling of dissatisfaction with the intellectual discourse somehow never came to be properly reflected in

---

[2] In the summer of 1995 or 1996, when I was conducting my research in Russia, I stopped by the Moscow State University bookstore and found two books by Averintsev on display. I was about to purchase them, but was upset to discover that I did not have enough cash with me, so I asked a salesperson if he would be so kind to keep the books for me for a couple of hours. He replied, "Don't worry, go get your money, these are not in big demand, and I got a bunch in stock anyway." I was truly surprised.

The reason why I was worried about the books would be obvious to perhaps any intellectual in Russia. Book publishing in Russia has always been one of the best examples of what they call the "economy of shortage" – a book is usually published in minimum quantities and never gets republished afterwards (save for *very* few exceptional cases); if it happens to be a good and popular book, you have all chances to never come across it, once you have missed it; for it is sold out in several days, after which it becomes a rarity and can be only found in the "black market," that is, in the suitcases of street-vendors, or so-called *lotoshniki* (people who often behave in a rude and offensive manner, look like recently released convicts, and do not remind one of book-lovers at all) who fill the central streets of Moscow in hope of cheating some foreigner or rich New Russian by charging them about twenty to thirty times the nominal value for the books they offer. Some of such vendors now legally rent spaces in Moscow universities, although it is quite difficult to imagine the profit they expect to make at the expense of Russian students, considering that their prices would be shocking even for a well-to-do professor from the West. For example, they charge $100 for a Russian edition of *Structural Anthropology* by Claude Lévi-Strauss, which was published at some 2 rubles in the mid-1980s (this could be roughly converted to an $8 worth within the present economy of life in Russia). The salary of an assistant professor in the humanities would amount, for comparison, to about $40 (per month).

the discourse itself (at least, in its official version represented by the media), toward the mid-1990s it became visibly widespread on the informal level – that is, in the realm of corridor talks. In private conversations, one could detect much discontent, sarcasm, and anger directed toward the subject of intelligentsia. Many simply did not want to talk on the subject, saying that they were fed up with it. Professor Alexei Nikishenkov, a popular figure in the humanities at Moscow State University, liked to joke, "I don't want to be associated with the intellectuals anymore. An intellectual of yesterday in Russia was a type perfectly shaved and occasionally drunk; whereas an intellectual of today is a type occasionally shaved and perfectly drunk."

Jokes about the falling moral and professional standards of the intelligentsia were indeed numerous. Aleksandr Saltykov, a former graduate and undergraduate student in history at Moscow State University, now working for a private Russian-American firm, told me in an interview in 1995, "I'd rather be associated with the New Russians today, than with the intellectuals; the former say little but at least get some work done, while the latter say much and do nothing. Besides, all they say is baloney anyway, so there is not even an aesthetic pleasure, a pure aesthetic profit that could be derived from their words. And by the way, you never know, tomorrow they might actually decide again to send the intelligentsia to Siberia, so you'd better stay the hell away from this weird group."[3]

---

[3] The comparison with the New Russians is, of course, more sarcastic than serious here, for the jokes about the stupidity of the New Russians perhaps outnumbered jokes on any other subject during the 1990s and the image of a "New Russian" had absorbed nearly all marks of cultural vulgarity there might be. The "Siberia" joke is also hardly accidental, for it evokes frequent public attacks "I'll send you all to Siberia!" by ultra-nationalist Vladimir Zhirinovsky, and several statements against the intelligentsia by Boris Yeltsin. Yeltsin's attitude, as a matter of fact, was reflected in a widely known in public joke: "One night when Yeltsin is asleep, Stalin comes to him in a dream and says, 'Well, comrade Yeltsin, I think it's time to send the intelligentsia to Siberia and paint the Kremlin walls green'. Yeltsin is bewildered, 'Paint Kremlin *what*? *Green*?..' Stalin answers, 'Very well, we can discuss that, but I am delighted that we did not have disagreements over the first issue'."

The negative feeling toward the intelligentsia might as well be detected in conversations taking place in various discussion groups, otherwise known as "newsgroups" or "Usenet groups," on the Internet, which started to rise in popularity since about the mid-1990s. For example, in the newsgroup "soc.culture.russian," which dealt exclusively with the topics related to Russia and the former Soviet Union, it was common to come across a message, like the one below, posted in August 1997, under a telling title "Intelligentsia is not the brain of the nation, but crap" (this phrase is commonly ascribed to Lenin):

> Newsgroups: soc.culture.russian
> Subject: "Intelligentsia - ne mozg nacii, a govno" (V.I.Lenin)
> Date: 25 Aug 1997 05:12:00
> Xref: rice soc.culture.russian:82384
>
> ... In fact, as the Russian sociologist Yuri Levada observed
> some time ago, the intelligentsia -- in the sense of an independent,
> free-thinking force defining itself in opposition to the country's
> rulers -- had vanished already before the birth of the Soviet Union.
> Of course not all were lured, either then or now, onto the slippery
> road to power, and some who embody the old pre-revolutionary
> values of the intelligentsia endure...

Yet, behind all that negativity, one could notice the beginnings of a positive development as well – that is, a process of forming a normal critical attitude toward the subject of intelligentsia. Today, an increasing number of scholars in the humanities, especially those of younger generations, seem to be very conscious of the need and importance of reaching such critical attitude. Olga Vainshtein, professor at the Russian State University for the Humanities, commented on this particular subject: "Our humanities people should finally abandon that idea, long cultivated in this society, of striving after the position of the genuine organic intelligentsia, some omnicompetent teachers of the nation, and just learn to pursue a normal critically oriented academic discourse. This complex of intelligentsia is an old Russian tradition that goes back to the nineteenth century, when Russian philosophers, such as Berdiaev, Soloviev, Chaadaev, or Rozanov, indeed occupied the informal position of teachers of the nation, of figures with an aura of knowledge and spirituality around them. This tradition, one must say, did persist throughout the twentieth century. Just think of such figures as Bakhtin or Averintsev – they actually were regarded as some spiritual genius of Russian scholarly thought. But now that Bakhtin is not with us and Averintsev has left for Vienna, many feel that the sacred place is vacant. And, surely, many would like to see themselves in that place. But, in my opinion, the major issue is: Do we need that place? How long can this state of things last when each historian or philologist will feel obliged to teach people how to live or explain to them how to distinguish between good and evil? I think that we are entering a different time now, when people can tell things apart very well and no longer need a sacred guidance of intelligentsia for that. What our time requires of an academic is not some universal moral empathy of an intellectual, but a critical reflexion of a scholar."[4]

Unfortunately, this view does not seem to be shared by the majority of the intellectuals, especially by those of older generations who were enjoying some official or unofficial recognition during the Soviet regime and who, having lost that recognition after perestroika, on the whole still manage to occupy prominent, if not dominant, positions in universities, research institutes, and other educational institutions, various organizations related to the humanities and arts, cultural institutions, like museums and creative unions, and so on. Typically, most of these intellectuals still pursue (even if they no longer believe in it) the old myth of "superior individuals" who were meant to play a unique social role, and continue to strive either after an informal position of "spiritual teachers of the people"

---

[4] Alexei Elfimov, "Academics and the Production of an Intellectual Discourse of Modernity in Russia," p.252.

or, when they feel that this particular goal is not attainable, after a formal position in the bureaucratic structure that would involve maximum amount of power and control. The combination of the two, obviously, would constitute an ultimate ideal of the intelligentsia. It is no surprise, then, that most of the intellectuals who rushed in the late 1980s into all kinds of governmental structures, eager to realize their newly developed or discovered ambitions of social and political managers, were those who had already gained some intellectual authority and recognition. Thus, among the deputies of the Supreme Soviet of the USSR at the time, we find above-mentioned academicians Averintsev, Sakharov, and Ivanov, much praised scholars and incredibly popular cultural figures in the late Soviet intellectual circles; several writers, such as Daniil Granin and Ales Adamovich, well known and also fairly popular (at least, before perestroika) figures; theater and movie actors Basilashvili and Lavrov, popular stars of the 1970s and 1980s. Another popular Soviet actor and theater director, Yuri Solomin, made it even farther and was elected the Head of the Ministry of Culture of the Russian Federation. Although his lack of expertise in managing cultural affairs on the national stage soon became evident and newspapers began criticizing him not just for "bad cultural policy" but rather for the lack of any policy to be criticized, his successor, Nikolai Gubenko, was recruited again from the same social milieu (furthermore, from the same professional milieu). He was a theater director working at the popular Taganka Theater in Moscow. Writer Chinghiz Aitmatov who gained popularity with the publication of his novels about the Stalinist past decided to complement his literary ambitions with a diplomatic career. A former political dissident Sergei Kovalev, who had been working for *samizdat* (underground press organizations) during the Soviet regime, in the 1990s ended up at the State Committee for Human Rights, an organization which was known and frequently criticized in Russia for its conservative policy, and which not only did not change its conservative orientation to any conspicuous degree with the advent of the intellectuals, but also, as some critics noted, benefited in its own way from the employment of such publicly renowned persons as Kovalev.[5]

The strivings of all these people to fulfill their bureaucratic ambitions and become popular social and political managers – and, thus, complete the imaginary process of transfiguration into the *organic* intelligentsia – unfortunately, or fortunately, resulted in a double failure. On the one hand, it was a failure to cope with power, which was noticed rather early both by the general public in Russia and some of the analysts in the West, such as, for instance, Ivan Szelenyi who stated in 1991, "The power of intellectuals may only be a transitory phenomenon – like their predecessors during the French Revolution, they may only lay the foundations of a new type of domination for a class other than their own."[6] On the other hand, it was a purely intellectual failure, which was reflected in the degradation of the elevated image of the intelligentsia in the eyes of the public, and which came in many ways as a result of that unsuccessful affair of the best representatives of the intelligentsia with power. Frequent cases of corruption and bribery, which started to be revealed in the 1990s almost on a regular basis, undoubtedly contributed to the deterioration of the intelligentsia's prestige. Such, for example, was the case with Sergei Stankevich, a young historian educated at Moscow State University, who was appointed to the Office of Moscow Mayor Gavriil Popov (as a candidate, he received solid,

---

[5] Kagarlitsky argues that people, like Kovalev, in fact, "have always supported the government in every way, calling on it to use 'the policy of the heavy hand', and as a result the authorities value them highly. It is very opportune for Russia's new rulers to have such human rights defenders, who speak out in favour of limiting the civil rights of people who do not share their views." (Boris Kagarlitsky, *Restoration in Russia*, p.11).

[6] George Konrad and Ivan Szelenyi, "Intellectuals and Domination in Post-Communist Societies," in *Social Theory for a Changing Society*, ed. Pierre Bourdieu and James S. Coleman (Boulder: Westview Press, 1991), p.338. It is interesting to note, though, that in another article, published simultaneously, Szelenyi did not want to take the risk of predicting the failure of the intelligentsia's affair with power. Having posed the question, "Is the newly won power of the intellectuals a lasting phenomenon or just a brief era of transition?", this time he chose to answer it, "I do not know." (Ivan Szelenyi, "The Intellectuals in Power?", in *After the Fall*, ed. Robin Blackburn [London: Verso, 1991], p.271.)

nearly wholehearted support from various people in the humanities as an honest person with progressive ideas). He further stood for election to a number of state and government committees, arguing in his public speeches that the old corrupted bureaucrats should be replaced with honest working people like himself. He succeeded in winning one of such elections and subsequently was appointed to serve as political adviser to president Yeltsin. A couple of years after his career success, however, he suddenly disappeared from the public view, and soon it was revealed that a major criminal lawsuit was instituted against him by government officials. According to some sources, he was accused of bribery that involved large amounts of money, presumably ten thousand dollars (by then standards in Russia, it was a truly immense bribe). Other sources stated that the money was actually stolen from the federal funds. Simultaneously, another story appeared in newspapers – namely, that Stankevich, who had been in charge of organizing a trip to Australia for the children of Chernobyl, had actually used the trip for his private purposes. Allegedly, knowing that the humanitarian mission would eliminate the problem of customs inspection, he himself joined the group of the children and their parents, although he evidently was not supposed to, and brought back from Australia computers and other pieces of consumer electronics for reselling them in Russia. This story disgusted many in Russia, but at that point Stankevich was nowhere to be found. According to unofficial information, he fled the country and settled down in California, but the actual attempts to locate him were unsuccessful. In the following years, many messages were posted on the Internet by Russians residing in the US, who were trying to help find Stankevich. Below is one of such messages, which expresses a common disappointment with the subject of "intellectuals and democracy" in Russia of the 1990s:

> From: adomrin <Johnson's Russia List>
> Subject: Where is Sergei Stankevich?
> Date: Wed, 23 Oct 1996 13:13:48 -0400 (EDT)

> I would like to ask multiple recipients of Johnson's Russia List:
> does any of you know anything about Sergei Stankevich and
> his whereabouts?
> ...
> According to a rumor circulating in Moscow in the last several
> months, Stankevich fled the country through Byelorussia and --
> settled down in California. I have a reason to believe that it's not
> just a rumor, but rather an inevitable end of yet another prominent
> Russian DEMOCRAD (a Russian neologism for a "democratic thief")
>
> Alexander
> Johnson's Russia List

This message fairly accurately summarizes a typical mood of the general Russian public in the mid-1990s, who were indeed no longer surprised at the failures of the intellectuals in power, and saw in cases, like that of Stankevich, nothing more but "an inevitable end of yet another prominent Russian" intellectual who had promised to bring democracy to the people.

The promise to bring democracy and, more specifically, the belief that, as enlightened individuals, intellectuals are actually *obliged* to bring democracy to the masses that are not capable of comprehending the complexities of social governance, thus, once again came to mark the mode of the intelligentsia's self-perception, with all its traditional recurrent themes of humanistic duty or debt to the people, that could be traced back to the Russian intelligentsia of the aristocratic age. It is true that until about the last quarter of the nineteenth century the aristocratic intelligentsia had remained virtually the only educated group in Russia, and the cultural gap between that group and the rest of the population had been at the time unbridgeable. The origins of the idea of moral duty to the people in the intelligentsia's consciousness are therefore understandable. But starting with the last decades of the nineteenth century, which witnessed the beginning of social modernization and emergence of various kinds of professionally educated lower middle-class groups in Russian cities, that gap began growing narrower. Paradoxically, the pattern of the intelligentsia's self-perception was only strengthened. The concept of moral debt to the people that had been developed in the aristocratic environment was then successfully transferred to the environment of emerging educated middle classes, or *raznochinskaia intelligentsia*.[7]

Absurdly enough, the concept survived even the socialist revolution and was inherited in its intact integrity by the deprived and proletarianized Soviet intelligentsia which, according to the logic of the new situation, should have perhaps reversed its judgment and started to reason that finally the time came when it was *the people* who were to assume the duty to the intelligentsia. After all, now it were the workers and the peasants who found themselves in a socially privileged position. It is certainly surprising that the social inversion that took place after the revolution did not affect the intelligentsia's understanding of the notion of "duty", notion that had originated under entirely different social circumstances. One might suppose, however, that a change in this particular idea would not be possible without a change in the entire model of the intelligentsia's self-perception, which had already acquired too much of a heroic and culturally prophetic quality to be too easily repudiated.

A curious inversion that did occur in the intelligentsia's thinking, however, is that the desire to preserve that particular self-image, which was torn out of the context of different reality and no longer corresponded to anything in the existing social order, added a new dimension to the ideals and strivings of the intellectuals. As the Soviet society was rapidly going through the process of industrialization, the concept of duty to the people was increasingly turning into the concept of duty to the disappearing tradi-

---

[7] The term *raznochinskaia intelligentsia* (literally meaning "intelligentsia from different ranks") came to signify a growing group of people in Russia of the second half of the nineteenth century, who got access to higher education but originated from gentrified classes. Most of these people did not move up the social ladder despite the education, for the social order in tsarist Russia was not flexible in that regard. Typically, such people had to work as freelance journalists, private tutors, and so on.

tionalism, and was in fact assuming a regressive, reactionary character. The ideal was no longer that of bringing education and enlightenment to the people, but rather that of saving the people from being deprived of what supposedly constituted their "true" cultural identity – namely, the old patriarchal traditional culture which came under destruction in the face of the twentieth-century modernization. Walter Benjamin, once again, had the unusual insight to capture this shift in the world view of the post-revolutionary intelligentsia as early as at the end of the 1920s. "It is typical of these [Russian] intellectuals," he wrote, "... that their positive function derives entirely from a feeling of obligation, not to the Revolution, but to traditional culture. Their collective achievement, as far as it is positive, approximates conservation."[8]

This conservative aspect of Soviet intelligentsia's understanding of the notion of "duty" or "debt" survived through the entire course of the twentieth century and was not affected even by the dissolution of the Soviet Union. On the contrary, it was further propelled by the spreading of state nationalism in new Russia and the formation of the new historical paradigm in the intellectual consciousness. It became also apparent in the debates over the subject and scope of humanities, which sprang in the air with the coming of perestroika and which will be discussed in the following chapter. It is no less apparent in intellectual discourses of nowadays and sometimes one can only wonder at the lack of cultural reflexivity that prominent Russian intellectual figures continue to display. For example, writer Daniil Granin, whose novels had been once assigned for reading in high schools, says in his nostalgic essay "The Russian Intelligentsia Is Leaving":

> The intelligentsia, famous Russian intelligentsia, is leaving ... Born with the Peter the Great, it became *incompatible* already in the nineteenth century and was cast from tsarist palaces. Since then, its *incompatibility* with power became

---

[8] Walter Benjamin, "Surrealism: The Last Snapshot of the European Intelligentsia," in *Reflections* (New York: Schocken Books, 1986), p.186.

its distinctive mark ... The intelligentsia had shouldered the cross of unpayable debt to the people well before the revolution. The communists turned that debt into yoke ... Our intelligentsia, both metropolitan and especially provincial, generation after generation, in spite of anything, held to its notions of honor, kindness, painstaking work, decency and, finally, honesty. Its spiritual merits in the face of history are beyond any doubt ... The intelligentsia was *incompatible* with power – and that's where its own power was ... Today, educated people, scientists, and scholars in the humanities have fallen in prestige. Other people have become elite; it is the notorious "new Russians" and bureaucracy. The winner place is taken by the cult of money and people who can make money.[9]

No special commentary is needed for the above passage, for it speaks well for itself. Every kind of intellectual self-idealization, from heroic "incompatibility" with power to the "cross of unpayable debt to the people" to "painstaking work, decency and honesty," is reflected in Granin's essay in its full measure. It is interesting to note the phrase, "the communists turned that debt into yoke," which is a typical rhetorical move that many intellectuals, especially writers, resort to these days. Instead of simply saying that the communists made the life of the intelligentsia a yoke, they prefer to speak in terms of the debt to the people, which somehow creates an impression that what really mattered was not the intelligentsia's personal life, but rather their *mission* (which is also evident in Granin's use of such metaphors as "cross of unpayable debt," for instance).

It is curious that even those intellectuals who have been in power under the socialist regime are not capable of thinking differently when it comes to the issue of the intelligentsia's social identity. Anatolii Grebnev, who was the head of the Union of Filmmakers under Gorbachev, effectively at the very top of cultural bureaucracy in the Soviet Union, said in a recent interview for the Moscow newspaper *Moskovskii komsomolets*, "The Russian intelligentsia should regain the understanding of its debt to

---

[9] Daniil Granin, "Russkii intelligent ukhodit," in *Russika-Izvestiia* electronic journal (November 5, 1997).

the people, which has been violated, and, through public enlightenment, press, culture, and arts, awaken positive sentiments in the people."[10]

One could go on with the examples like these (an enthusiast wishing to dig through dusty archives of Russian newspapers of the 1980s and 1990s will find that they are innumerable). The principal point behind all this, however, is that the pattern of the intelligentsia's social self-identification remained largely confined to the same model that had been developed in the aristocratic Russia of the nineteenth century and later insignificantly modified with the coming of the political regime of socialism. This pattern assumed a regressive and expressly conservative character, being centered around the idea of the intelligentsia's heroic mission – mission that could be maintained in the social conditions of modernity only at the expense of preserving traditionalism and, in a certain sense, cultural backwardness in the society. Ideals of social progress were largely discounted and gave way to abstract ideals of moral self-perception. The intellectual pedagogy became based on the same principle that had been vividly expressed at the end of the nineteenth century in the words of a populist Russian writer Mikhaylovsky who stated, "Freedom is a great and tempting thing, but we do not want freedom if, as happened in Europe, it will only increase our agelong debt to the people."[11] The fact that the intellectuals were not actually after freedom was painfully revealed, to much of a public disappointment, within the decade after perestroika which, in Kagarlitsky's words, resulted in the "total and final defeat of the dissidents," – that is, in the situation when the intellectuals, beginning to lose their imaginary authority and influence "under the onslaught of the old and new nomenklatura, willingly surrendered the role of a spiritual opposition."[12]

---

[10] Natalia Bobrova, "Anatolii Grebnev: 'Svoboda prikhodit liubaia'," *Moskovskii komsomolets*, no.149 (10 August 1996), p.2.

[11] N. K. Mikhaylovsky, *Sochineniya*, vol.IV (St. Petersburg, 1897). Quoted in: Leonard Schapiro, "The Pre-Revolutionary Intelligentsia and the Legal Order," in *The Russian Intelligentsia*, ed. Richard Pipes (New York: Columbia University Press, 1961), p.27.

[12] Boris Kagarlitsky, *Restoration in Russia*, p.11–13.

* * *

The second important aspect of the intelligentsia's value orientations, as it has formed in the last quarter of the twentieth century, is related to the issue of cultural lifestyle ideals and it stands, too, in close connection with the new historical paradigm in the intellectual discourse, to which I am pointing so much of attention in this work. As I have been trying to show, the major shift in the intellectual discourse that took place in the late Soviet and new Russian society was largely characterized by the nostalgic appropriation of pre-revolutionary aristocratic values and their rather unreflective transplantation into the normative dimension of contemporary social life. Everything in the present was routinely judged by the intelligentsia against the norms of the nineteenth-century aristocratic past, which thus became in their imagination the embodiment of the ideals of enlightenment and humanism, as well as the common-denominator reference point in intellectual conversations.

It would be pertinent to mention here that Foucault, discussing some recurrent topics in social discourses characterizing Western societies, made a distinction between the topic of enlightenment, as representative of the specific project of modernity, and the topic of humanism which, in his opinion, represented a different dimension in these social discourses. The idea of enlightenment became integral to the spirit of modernity because it constituted, says Foucault, "the mode of reflective relation to the present," while the idea of humanism constituted "a set of themes that have reappeared on several occasions, over time, in European societies," and have been equally picked up by Christianity and the critique of Christianity, by scientific humanism of the nineteenth century and anti-scientific humanism of the same century, by Marxism, existentialism, personalism, National Socialism, and Stalinism.[13]

---

[13] Michel Foucault, "What Is Enlightenment?" in *The Foucault Reader*, p.44.

This distinction may just as well characterize the intellectual discourse in Russia, for there is a pronounced tendency in this discourse, which is expressed in the fact that the themes of enlightenment and progress appear in it subordinate to, when not totally replaced by, the theme of humanism. It is precisely the constant stress on the humanistic inclinations of the pre-revolutionary intelligentsia that dominates the mode of reference and judgment within this discourse. The true nobility of the intelligentsia, according to the conventions of this discourse, derives from their humanism, not from their place in the social hierarchy. It is obvious that such emphasis is advantageous in multiple ways – it suggests a hypothetical solution to the predicament of class structure and social position, as well as to the issue of awkward relationship with power; however, perhaps more importantly, it puts Soviet and new Russian intellectuals on equal grounds with their pre-revolutionary ancestors.

Indeed, the interplay between the values, ideals, and moral standards of the nineteenth-century aristocratic and bourgeois intelligentsia and those of their proletarianized heirs of nowadays has been effectively employed within the framework of humanism as an apologetic and pedagogical tool. It was and still is very common of history or literature teachers in high schools to bring up some intellectual figures from the past as models of proper behavior and reproach pupils, saying things like, "Pushkin would never behave like that when he was a *litsei* student,"[14] or "Chekhov never treated his friends like that," and so on. Or, for instance, the typical attitude expressed toward Lev Tolstoy by teachers in literature classes was, "Yes, Tolstoy was a count and landlord with serfs and peasants working in his estate, but first of all he was a great humanist." Of course, in the discourse of grown up intellectuals the argument becomes more sophisticated, but

---

[14] *Litsei* stood for "college" in tsarist Russia. The name went out of use during the Soviet time, but again, as a consequence of the same trends of the last decade, it has been recalled and has come into fashion. A fairly large number of schools in Russian cities were actually renamed *litsei*.

still it is not unusual occasionally to come across a reference as trivial as those employed in school classrooms.

The point here is that themes and examples from the social scene of the past centuries – distinctly *different* social scene – are interpolated into the present environment without alterations and no reservations are made. Sometimes this leads, as might be expected, to rather odd developments. Since the early 1990s there has been a steady rise of interest in, and indeed attraction to, the idea of reviving aristocratic *salons*, poetic circles and various clubs of "nobility" as new fashionable centers of Russian culture and enlightenment. Indeed, numerous attempts have been made to revive such clubs and circles in the recent years, and many of them, unsurprisingly, have failed for different reasons. A great number of such projects were dispelled already at the inception stage because new Russian intellectuals "unexpectedly" came to face their own poverty – that is, the basic lack of resources necessary to maintain such clubs or simply rent an appropriate space for them. (Needless to mention, it is not *any* space that is considered by intellectuals as appropriate for their accommodations, but positively a fashionable place of residence of the old aristocracy, desirably in the historic city area; for the humanistic intelligentsia of nowadays become disappointed with the cultural ideals of enlightenment if they have to hold their meetings somewhere in the unsightly suburbs or at a friend's apartment.) Most of the old historic places and fashionable residencies of pre-revolutionary aristocracies, especially in capital cities, are undoubtedly so expensive to rent, that only new business elites and government authorities can afford them, unless, of course, a place is registered in the notorious roster of "monuments of history and culture." This, incidentally, explains the eagerness and dedication with which intellectuals sometimes rush to defend historic buildings, such as the aforementioned Shcherbakov Palaces, for the idea that somehow they might actually get hold of a prominent in the past aristocratic estate is precisely what appeals to their new humanistic ideals most.

The second scenario that the attempts to revive the "centers of culture and enlightenment" typically follow is a bit different. In some cases, intellectuals do manage to find a sponsor who agrees to pay the expenses. The catch here, however, is that such sponsors are usually found either among the infamous New Russians or among various rich but bored mafia-minded groups that Kagarlitsky aptly calls "lumpen-bourgeois sub-elite."[15] This is the kind of people who do not really have any ideals of promoting culture or enlightenment on their minds, but who are rather interested solely in entertaining themselves. (Their ideals of entertainment are also somewhat different from any notions the intellectuals might have on that subject.) The tradition of sponsorship and philanthropy which, one has to admit, had existed in pre-revolutionary Russia and played a very important role in advancing various arts and sciences, has been thoroughly erased from the social consciousness during the century of socialist regime with its unconditional rejection of private enterprises. A quintessential New Russian is a personality that reminds one of whimsical Dostoevsky's characters, morally devastated bourgeoisie who invest all their profit in gambling and drinking and do not care about tomorrow. The consequences of inviting such a sponsor are predictable. What is conceived as an intellectual or cultural *salon* very soon turns into a local mafia club with bouncers at the doors where the "organizers-intellectuals" end up serving as bartenders or at best accountants, if the club goes as far as to open a position of actual "accountant." That is all the enlightenment there is. In larger cities, such as Moscow and St. Petersburg, clubs of this type are now rather widespread, and very often they keep the name that might actually prompt one to think that there should be some intellectual activity afoot ("Artistic Café," "The Inspiration Club," "At Margarita's," and so on).[16] If one should decide to

---

[15] Boris Kagarlitsky, *Restoration in Russia*, p.19.
[16] Name "At Margarita's" is culturally loaded in the milieu of Moscow intelligentsia, for it is unmistakably associated with one of the main literary characters from an immensely popular in Russia novel by Mikhail Bulgakov "Master and Margarita."

enter a place like that, however, one would be most likely stopped by a doorman at the entrance and, sometimes politely sometimes not, inspected and asked about the purpose of the visit. The idea behind this customary inquiry is in most cases simply to figure out if a visitor has enough money to spend at their club or café. Thus, if you indicate that you only want to get a cup of coffee and have a quiet moment, you would not interest them as a potential customer, and you might not be let in on some grounds (for example, you might be told that all tables are taken and given a delicate hint that waiting is useless; or, if the doorman happens to be in a bad mood or simply a rude person, you could get a rather indelicate advice to find another place).[17]

Thus, not only have the intelligentsia's ideals of reviving old high-culture literary or artistic clubs failed, but even their more modest and quite reasonable strivings after such essentially democratic thing as a "French café" where people could sit with a newspaper or chat over a cup of coffee have been destined to failure. "Cafés" have quickly become the privilege of the new elite. Moreover, in too many cases, coffee and intellectual chat are the things that these cafés are the least meant for. Their purpose is to entertain the *nouveaux riches*, bored individuals with low intellectual

---

[17] In 1995, when I was conducting research in Moscow, I scheduled one of my interviews with two university students for a weekend. Since the university was closed and we could not meet there, we went to look for a quiet cafe. One place attracted our attention with an appealing name. At the door we were stopped by a yuppie looking young man, quite friendly though, who asked, "What do you guys have in mind?" We answered that we would like merely to have a conversation over coffee. The person estimated our student appearances with a meaningful glance and smiled, "If you are only going to order coffee, it will be five bucks per cup." We understood that it was not the place we were looking for and said, "Well, we think we'll find another place then, but thanks anyway." To which the door man, surprisingly, responded with some sympathy, "No problem – see, I spared you the trouble of going through the menu and awkwardness of having to leave immediately after that." (I ascribe the sympathy – indeed, somewhat unusual – to the fact that most likely the door man was one of the former intellectuals or those enthusiastic university students who once had dreamed about creating a culturally oriented coffee-place that would attract the intellectual public.)

demands who find it amusing and "cool" to waste hundreds of dollars a night on vodka and gambling.[18] Some cafés, especially those opened on popular tourist streets, like Arbat in Moscow, do actually offer coffee and cozy tables for conversation, but they are specifically meant to attract a foreign tourist who, for the lack of a choice, will have to pay offensive amounts of money for the cup of coffee that regular Russians from the intellectual strata, let alone students, could not possibly afford. Cheaper cafés, not large in numbers, occasionally open, but they usually try to attract public attention not by coffee or clean tables, but by alcohol (traditionally vodka) and cheap snacks or badly cooked food. Such cafés usually gather working class people who drink much during any time of the day, as it has always been the case in Russia. Both by their rude service and rather unpleasant environment, these cafés, again, cannot appeal not just to intellectuals, but to many people from all walks of life as well. Paradoxically, about the only place where intellectuals, students, and many others, under the circumstance, can and actually prefer to go is infamous McDonald's, which, since the moment of its introduction in Gorbachev's Russia, remains perhaps the most crowded public place in Moscow and some other cities. To a visitor from the West, it would appear strange to see neatly dressed people (often wearing suits and ties) standing in long lines at huge

---

[18] Incidentally, this touches upon one of the most problematic issues of Russian economy in the 1990s – namely, the lack of much needed financial investment, caused in many ways by the morals and habits of those who possess finances. So-called "businesses" of the new elite generally do not do much good to the economy, partly because a typical New Russian is not interested in investing his enormous profits in the growth of his enterprise but mainly interested in wasting them in a showing way. This is ultimately a matter of self-fashioning of the new elite, among whom prestige and respect – if only there is such thing as "respect" – are determined not by hard or successful work, but rather by the style of consumption which implies that spending much for nothing is "cool." The money they spend certainly might benefit the society under different circumstances, but a part of the problem is that they leave their profits at the clubs that they own themselves, so the financial circulation is purely internal, i.e. precisely that of a closed mafia structure. These cultural morals of the new Russian elite still stand as a serious impediment to the economic growth and general social improvement in the country.

Typical cafes attract their public not by coffee or cozy environments inviting for a chat, but by alcoholic drinks. Human size bottles of vodka and beer are prominently exposed at the entrance. The waiter (walking in between the tables) is characteristically dressed in a T-shirt and worn out sports slacks – a recognizable outfit of "young Russian entrepreneurs." (Photo by the author, 1996)

two-storey Moscow McDonald's buildings; but in the context of the discussion above one should understand that it may be (at least, may have been in the 1990s) about the only democratic and affordable type of "café" in Russia, which was free of alcoholics, heavy cigarette smoke, annoying New Russians, local mafias, and shocking prices. Today, things are beginning to change at a very slow pace; but until very recently, if you wanted to go out in Moscow and have an intellectual chat, all roads led to McDonald's. Such was the strange transformation of cultural values that the post-perestroika Russian society experienced.

Here is an example of a somewhat more "classy" type of entertainment. The commercial stand calls the attention of new Russian elites to "The First Vodka Restaurant." The advertisement, done in accordance with all the norms of new historical representation, features a nineteenth-century painting depicting a scene from the aristocratic life and the inscription "Petrov-Vodkin" spelled in the pre-revolutionary manner. (Photo by the author, 2000)

The failure of intellectuals to launch their own cultural *salons* or cafés, take possession of the prestigious property of old Russian aristocrats, and, more generally, establish an idealistic lifestyle of their dreams has been characteristically reflected in the intellectual discourse. Numerous articles discussing the appeal of lost life customs, aristocratic estates, art treasures, and other vestiges of the pre-revolutionary past, written in a peculiar nostalgic mode and at the same time defensive tone, began appearing on pages of various journals and newspapers, and kept growing in number throughout the last decade. The trend, for instance, could be easily traced on the example of half-scholarly half-popular journal *Nashe nasledie* [Our Heritage], which was initiated in the first years of perestroika, along with some other magazines of the sort. (The journal's title, of course, subtly registers the essence of the new paradigm that captured the intellectual discourse.) As a particular example here, however, I would like to discuss an article by Moscow art critic Liudmila Lunina, with a no less representative title "Everyday Charm of the Old Russian Aristocratic Estate." This article appeared as a full-page essay in the newspaper *Segodnia* in 1996, and it reflects the model of the intelligentsia's lifestyle ideals in a condensed form, displaying a variety of typical rhetorical devices that are used in the intellectual discourse and that are scattered through the majority of publications of this kind.[19]

The article, which was placed in a newspaper section under a telling rubric *Stil'* [Style], focuses on three of the most famous old Russian aristocratic estates, *Ostankino, Kuskovo*, and *Arkhangel'skoe*, which are located in what used to be fashionable residential suburbs of Moscow. In tsarist Russia, the estates belonged to the Sheremetiev (alternatively spelled in Western sources "Sheremeteff") family, one of the wealthiest and most renowned noble lineages. In the Soviet period, Ostankino and Kuskovo became state museums and the fate of Arkhangel'skoe remained somehow unclear (for years it was officially told that it was undergoing the process of architectural restoration, but it was informally known to be occupied by some bureaucratic structures. The history of these estates, as well as peculiarities of their architectural style, has been literally overstudied in Russia and the article by Lunina does not add anything interesting to the subject in this regard. Nor is it, in fact, her intention to add anything to the historical studies. It is rather to express the repressed ideals and broken dreams of the intelligentsia, the sorrows of their unfulfilled lifestyle, under the guise of what appears to be a historical study.

---

[19] Liudmila Lunina, "Bytovoe obaianie russkoi usad'by," *Segodnia*, no.153 (24 August 1996), p.7.

From the beginning to the end the article portrays an idealized reality of nice and cozy life at the aristocratic estate of the eighteenth-nineteenth centuries. It starts with an unambiguous rhetorical move, aimed at disguising the difference between the old Russian aristocrats and intellectuals of nowadays, and at equating the lifestyles of the former with those of the latter by appealing to the traditional archaic image of nature:

> [The Russian estate] has long been a universal scheme for spending summer leisure time in Moscow ... The high ideal of noble families and modest academics is by and large still the same: to get away from the noisy, dusty, and unbearable city, and create with whatever is available at hand a peasant's paradise; to merge with nature ... The style of Moscow summer life perhaps has lost its former dimensions, but in essence little has changed.

The hidden truth, of course, is that the style of life has changed substantially since the nineteenth century. What has changed little is ultimately the ideals of the intelligentsia. And the fact that these ideals cannot be fulfilled in any sense produces unpleasant aftertaste and sad feelings in the "modest academics" – which is, unsurprisingly, expressed in the immediately following paragraph:

> It is natural to write about the Russian estate at the end of the summer because sadness is already spread in the cold air ... And sadness is the necessary seasoning for all the talks about the Russian estate. Without nostalgia, it would not be a Russian estate at all, but rather a regular English one.

The comparison with the "regular" English estate seems to be rather absurd, especially considering that in the tradition of English literature nostalgic sentiment appears as a frequent attribute of all those misty fields and castles. But this is certainly not the point. The point is that the English have never lost their estates and they have nothing to be sad about, while the modest Russian intelligentsia of nowadays, naturally, can only be sad about what it never had. The arousal of all this mixed atmosphere of romance and sorrow points only to the deep inner dissatisfaction of the intelligentsia who try to soften with the nostalgic sentiment what cannot be softened with ownership. But since the real causes cannot be revealed, the sorrows are ascribed to the old and well-tried magic of "Russian soul":

> Grieving over the gone landscape of life at the Russian estate became one of the manifestations of the Russian soul, one of its most trivially obvious attributes.

It is thus, probably accidentally and unwillingly, acknowledged that the landscape is after all *gone*. But again, it is curious that the intelligentsia should ascribe its recurrent dreams to the "Russian soul," an old invention of its own. Everything in the above passage would be absolutely correct, if the words "Russian soul" were replaced with "Russian intelligentsia"; for those masses of people, that once were and still continue to be endowed by the indebted intelligentsia with this mysterious soul, have actually stopped grieving long time ago and are actively trying to find their way in the complex reality of the present by means that, true, may be sometimes mysterious but not in a romantic or nostalgic way. In fact, with the legalization of private property during perestroika, a great number of people from government officials to new businessmen and wealthier walks of the working class rushed to build suburban estates of their own, notorious *dachas*, all over Russia. This process, being part of a larger process of social privatization in Russia, was marked by much of an agony, rivalry, corruption and social manipulation, and the last thing that could ever come to people's minds in that situation was a "romanticism of the Russian soul" or some pathetic sorrows and nostalgia for the past. Everyone who had money and connections tried to make every effort to grab a piece of suburban land by honest or dishonest means, while the intellectuals were lost in meditations over the good old times and life forgotten. The process of redistribution of social wealth, therefore, has passed by the intellectuals once again. But if it were the Bolsheviks who were to blame for the original deprivation, now the object of the intelligentsia's anger has become associated primarily with the New Russians who apparently represent the most successful social stratum after perestroika. This anger is explicitly reflected in the concluding section of the essay, in which Lunina writes:

> Having completed another cycle, the end of this century has put us again in the position of barbarians mimicking the civilized way of life. Today, the suburbs of Moscow are crowded with vault-looking three-storey houses – a bizarre realization of the Russian idea of rich Western suburban estates.

What is unambiguously implied in this passage is that the intelligentsia, supposedly, would have brought a truly civilized way of life to the suburban estate, while New Russians only awkwardly imitate Western houses in their three-storey *dachas*, being nothing more than uncultured barbarians. Although it is true that the aesthetic style of the New Russians' *dachas* could be criticized on many points, it is equally true that the intelligentsia would be more than happy to get hold of those barbarian *dachas*, if only they had the opportunity. But since they do not, they try to hide their envy by exposing "barbarism" of those who do have opportunities and appealing to the nostalgic romance of the Russian soul and golden Russian past.

The inner psychological suppression that marks the narrative of the article is evident in the very title "Everyday Charm of the Old Russian Aristocratic Estate." A title of the kind would be indeed more appropriate for the discussion of something mundane in which charming qualities are usually unnoticed. For example, a title like "Everyday Charm of the Old Russian Peasant House" would make more sense, as it would prompt the reader to try to discover charm where it is normally neither seen, nor ever looked for. In the case of the aristocratic estate, the phrase becomes essentially nonsensical, for it instructs the reader to try to discover charm in that which is unquestionably charming without any second thought. In a word, it idealizes what does not have to be idealized at all – it idealizes the ideal itself. But there is another interesting move in the construction of this title.

The idealization, which is absolutely unneeded, is also oddly inverted in its logic. The ultimate ideal here is idealized in timid, downgraded terms of something "everyday," "mundane," because the object is indeed psychologically suppressed and the intelligentsia do not seem comfortable talking about their broken dreams openly. The stress on "everyday" is meant to create an impression of disinterestedness, an impression that the aristocratic estate is not really what the intelligentsia want and that they only see in it something endearing and charming in the "everyday" sense. The article's title, then, is artificially defensive (as would be a title like, "Gold and Diamonds, Such Boring Things, Turn Out to Have Their Own Charm") and once again indicative of what, in the beginning of this chapter, I mentioned as "incongruency of values" – that is, discrepancy between values pursued in the intellectual discourse and those pursued in real life. Values pursued in real life are nearly always camouflaged in some manner in the discourse or, if not camouflaged, justified in alternative terms, more or less suitable for the discursive conventions.

In Russia, this discrepancy may be said to be a particular cultural feature, for the intellectuals, both due to the system of their inherited idealistic philosophical ideals and due to their peculiar position within the Soviet social structure, were seen as a "class" that was not supposed to be interested in material privileges such as houses, estates, and other goods. The pursuit of the material, which constitutes a natural need, desire, and motivation in the lives of all people, became therefore a censured subject in intellectual conversations, and as such was expelled from the discourse. Obviously, it could not be expelled from the lives of actual people, so the two categories of values, material and ideal, started to diverge and eventually did diverge to a very substantial degree, having formed a dilemma of rather sensitive nature and rather serious dimensions.[20] A revelation in the public

---

[20] For an interesting discussion of the peculiarity of this relationship between Soviet intellectuals and material goods, see, for example: Svetlana Boym, "The Archeology of Banality: The Soviet Home," *Public Culture* 6, no.2 (1994): 263–92.

discourse that an intellectual, who, for example, was considered an advocate of humanistic values, acquired a fashionable apartment in a prestigious city district might damage his or her reputation among the intelligentsia (acquiring a fashionable apartment by honest means was known to be impossible and the picture of dishonest strivings after personal accommodations, of course, could not possibly fit the image of "advocate of humanistic values").

Several of the intellectuals whom I interviewed in 1995 and 1996 in Moscow displayed precisely this type of judgment. One of the academics in the humanities, for instance, spoke in a characteristically disapproving fashion of Soviet writers, who had dominated the intellectual scene for long decades:

> After perestroika, it all became too clear. For when one was allowed to openly say what one wanted, it became obvious, astonishingly obvious, that writers simply had nothing to say. Once, they were good at fooling people, playing the game of half-uttered words and pretending they were after the truth, while most of them really were after dachas in Peredelkino. But it was all unveiled in a matter of a few years.[21]

Thus, learning that someone who pretends to be after the sublime subject of "truth" is actually after a much more mundane subject, such as dacha, is taken almost as an offence. I have to repeat that it is not the striving for a fashionable suburban dacha itself that appears offensive, but rather that very discrepancy between value orientations in the discourse and in actual life. Intellectuals in many cases are normal people who want what other normal people want and do what others do, but who at the same time are often judged not according to the logic of everyday realities, but according to the logic of idealistic intellectual discourse, which has somewhat different rules and different regulations.

---

[21] Alexei Elfimov, "Academics and the Production of an Intellectual Discourse of Modernity in Russia," p.244.

Incidentally, speaking of Soviet writers and their dachas in Peredelkino, it may be noted that here, in fact, we have one of the few examples of the intelligentsia actually managing to get hold of a prestigious estate in Moscow suburbs. Writers did their best to incarnate in the Peredelkino estate their recurrent dream of "philosophical leisure in contemplation of nature and evening tea over relaxed conversation," – dream which is still transparent in such nostalgic and sentimental essay titles as "By Candlelight, Near My Beloved" that occasionally appear in various Russian publications.[22] What annoyed other intellectuals about the Peredelkino writers was precisely the fact that these writers had been posing as those performing the role – using their own vocabulary – of "spiritual conscience of the intelligentsia" (that is, those who should not be caring about such personal luxuries as dachas or philosophical leisure); while in reality, as it turned out, they had been easily selling out their "conscience," trading it with the communist bureaucracy for fashionable suburban properties. For instance, it was known that some of the popular movie actors or directors had fashionable apartments in Moscow or St. Petersburg, as well as prestigious dachas in the suburbs, but that fact did not seem to irritate other intellectuals because the actors usually did not pursue a discourse with excessive moral claims, in which they would pose as some "apostles of the pure truth"; accordingly, they were more often taken for who they were. Where there was no discrepancy between the self-fashioning in intellectual discourse and that in mundane realities of actual life, there seemed to be no internal intellectual censure.

In the reality of the 1990s, however, even Peredelkino – the last suburban citadel of the intelligentsia – has suffered both an economic and ideological decline, due to the intelligentsia's inability to practically maintain their dream of "aristocratic" lifestyle, which was so naively and unambiguously expressed in the discussed publication by Lunina and many

---

[22] Anatolii Pristavkin, "By Candlelight, Near My Beloved," in *Remaking Russia*, p.13–22.

other essays of that type. Writers were able to enjoy the pleasures of their utopian suburbia only for as long as the latter was directly supported and taken care of by the state. After perestroika, when the state monopoly over the real estate came to an end and much of Peredelkino became the property of several impoverished literary organizations, such as formerly famous *Litfond* (Literary Foundation), and of various individuals, the living conditions began to deteriorate and it became rather clear that the intelligentsia, having grown accustomed to the privilege of free state support, was neither willing nor able to fix arising problems on their own. In a sense, then, that much desired lifestyle in the imagination of the literary intelligentsia was indeed "aristocratic"; it was their understanding that philosophical meditations and tea parties should be their only business, while taking care of their own estates should be the business of someone else. Characteristically, contemporary journalist and writer Anna Kovaleva, commenting on the deterioration of Peredelkino, blames not the intelligentsia, but the infamous New Russians who have started to invade Peredelkino and build their luxurious dachas with pools and winter heat systems (that supposedly cause electricity surges and problems with water supply). In a typical nostalgic mode, quite similar to the one employed in Lunina's essay, Kovaleva tells the reader:

> Our little town [Peredelkino] is not quite ours now ... Roads, trees, houses and, more importantly, residents are completely different. But if the roads are simply damaged and trees and houses dilapidated, the "residents" are new. New Russians, so much "loved" by people, have started to settle in the old literary dacha town ... We have been told that with the appearance of [their] houses, for the first time in its history the town has begun to experience problems with electricity and water ... However, the issue is not that there is no electricity or water and the quality of the roads is far from being civilized. After all, people have learned to put up with that during the long years of Soviet rule. The issue is that the charm of the town disappears because of the *nouveaux riches* who are attracted here by this very charm ... People who were the heart and personality of the town, as well as its pride, are gradually leaving, taking with them the charm

of intellectualism and the life that once was: evening tea meetings, walks and talks, in which something more than kitchen tiles or another million bucks was discussed.[23]

It is truly amazing how illogical sometimes such intellectual statements are. They begin with complaints about the worsening life conditions and end with absurd arguments that what really matters is not living conditions, with which people somehow have learned to "put up," but "the life that once was," some imaginary lost lifestyle, nostalgic landscape of the things gone. In the changing social world at the turn of the century, with all its turbulence and creative potentialities, the intelligentsia still do not want to let go their old imaginaries and cultural ideals. Even when given a real chance to start, so to say, a brand new life, most of them keep on dreaming about the old lost life and exhibit no excitement about the possibilities that the world of modernity, however imperfect, opens to an enthusiastic intellectual mind. The figure of the enthusiast of modernity remains firmly associated with a kind of immoral uncultured business undertaker[24] whose image is often traced back to Ivan Lopakhin, one of the main characters of Chekhov's classic play "The Cherry Orchard." In the play, Lopakhin buys and cuts down that very orchard (the symbol of nostalgic aristocratic ideals) together with the old mismanaged Russian aristocratic estate, thus embodying the coming of the new capitalist bourgeoisie to the Russian society. The character of Lopakhin has always been a target of criticism and, at the same time, an awkward predicament in the Soviet literary discourse because Chekhov himself did not portray Lopakhin as an entirely negative or immoral figure. In the perception of the late Soviet and new Russian

---

[23] Anna Kovaleva, "Nash gorodok," *Moskovskii komsomolets*, no.150 (13 August 1996), p.3.
[24] The Russian word *predprinimatel'* ("one who undertakes a business," "one who starts an enterprise," "undertaker," "entrepreneur") has traditionally had a negative connotation in the intellectual milieu. To say that someone was a *predprinimatel'* meant in most cases to deny that person any intellectuality.

intelligentsia, however, it remained as such. As Anatolii Grebnev, head of the Union of Filmmakers under Gorbachev, exclaimed in his interview, "The New Russian – he is the same old Lopakhin!"[25]

To sum up, the ideals of the intelligentsia at the turn of the centuries remain by and large marked by the fear of the process of social modernization, and by the aesthetics of cultural conservation which often finds its key expression in the recurrent concept of "debt to the people" – that is, in the reactionary desire to preserve cultural traditionalism in order for the intelligentsia to sustain or secure its imaginary role of a heroic group with a prophetic enlightening mission. The persistence of these ideals heavily influenced and continues to influence the academic discourse in the humanities, which is going to be the subject of the following chapter, where we will see on particular examples how the understanding of the object of humanities has shifted toward the primordial social themes in the last quarter of the twentieth century.

---

[25] Natalia Bobrova, "Anatolii Grebnev," p.2.

Chapter 4
Restoring the Humanities

Since the beginning of perestroika it has been frequently declared in the Russian media and especially in various academic and quasi-academic publications that the humanities in Russia are undergoing the rapid process of revitalization.[1] Although it is true that the late 1980s and the 1990s were marked by the continuous series of attempts at reforming the shape of the humanities both at the level of institutional bureaucracy and that of intellectual content, today a growing number of people are inclined to acknowledge that the reforms at the bureaucratic level have failed as such, while the reformation at the level of intellectual or scholarly content, though has taken place, has gone somewhat awry.

This uneasy feeling is not unfounded. Ever since the end of communist censorship over the process of education in the humanities, there has been a growing divergence between the interests of academic research and teaching and the manner in which bureaucratic changes in academic organizations were implemented. With a very few exceptions (the earliest of which, and perhaps the most successful of which, was represented by the newly organized Russian State University for the Humanities in Moscow), the "revival" of the humanities proved to be more of a talk show than a successful reform in any sense. One of the major causes behind this, which during the 1990s was frequently covered up in the official discourse that tended to ascribe all failures to technical problems (such as the lack of financing or side effects of the transition period), is well understood today

---

[1] For a representative article in English, discussing this "revitalization," see, for example, an essay by Yuri Afanasiev, rector of the Russian State University for the Humanities, "Reviving the Humanities in Modern Russia," in *Remaking Russia*, p.255–70.

by too many scholars and students in Russia: the bureaucracy has never changed. Nearly all important positions in university administration (as well as in administrative offices of research institutes and other academic organizations) are still largely occupied by the very same personnel who composed the conservative body of communist *nomenklatura* before perestroika. These people are reluctant to change, unwilling to listen, and they continue to resist the implementation of new flexible educational mechanisms that would be appropriate to the changing reality of the present day world.

The idea of expelling the old bureaucracy from the educational system in the humanities was actually seen by democratic-minded people in the early 1990s as a natural prerequisite for a good start in the building of a new liberal edifice of education and knowledge. However, President Yeltsin somehow found it too radical and disapproved of it. Some analysts suggested that "in rejecting the proposal for a purge of the *apparatchiks* and *nomenklatura* from the educational establishment, Yeltsin agreed to preserve the national territorial integrity of the Federation and to orchestrate a peaceful transition to a democratic form of government and education."[2] As the course of the last decade has shown, the indicated transition did not turn out to be entirely peaceful, nor did it result in any acceptable democratic form of social management. The sphere of education, just like the rest of major state sectors, has essentially turned into a terrain, endlessly contested between weaker democratic and stronger reactionary forces. Eduard Dneprov, one of the defenders of democratic reforms, who was appointed Minister of Education under Yeltsin, spent many years trying to implement a progressive educational system and a new state legislation on education, but in the end he was not even given a chance to complete his reforms, which were successfully blocked by the conservative opposition. Since Dneprov was in a position to properly see all the obsta-

---

[2] Brian Holmes, Gerald H. Read, and Natalya Voskresenskaya, *Russian Education: Tradition and Transition* (New York: Garland Publishing, 1995), p.297.

cles created by the presence of the old bureaucracy in administrative structures, he chose to follow a political strategy of isolating, as much as possible, "those who stood in the way of overcoming the remnants of totalitarian structures and practices."[3] This strategy caused a particularly strong negative reaction among the opposition who united their efforts to provoke a scandal and eventually remove Dneprov from the office.

The old Soviet bureaucracy, thus, continues to play a very influential role in the debates over the destiny of the humanities (or perhaps, more precisely, in determining the practical outcome of these debates). Today, this is distinctly felt by an increasing number of academics who recognize the need for the adoption of new scholarly practices, both in the sense of establishing a more flexible system of teaching and research at universities, and in the sense of reaching a more critical and reflexive level of scholarly discourse in general. Many of the scholars whom I interviewed in 1995–96 and later in 1999–2000 commented on this as the most important and painful problem of the current state of the humanities and social sciences in Russia. Olga Vainshtein, professor of the Russian State University for the Humanities, said:

> Institutionally, we are clearly lagging behind. It seems to me that we still follow that nineteenth-century institutional model aimed at the classic disciplinary accumulation of data, where one is supposed to read and examine *everything* that has been ever written within a given discipline and then, having done with it, to add another little brick of data to the top of the pile. It is this model of academic inquiry that still characterizes both the system of teaching and the system of research in this country. I know, for example, that our brilliant art historian Raisa Kirsanova, who has recently finished her new interdisciplinary study of public clothing as reflected in art and literature, is experiencing problems with the academic bureaucracy. This work was supposed to be her post-doctoral thesis, necessary for her tenure, but *VAK* [State Tenure Committee] say there is no discipline in terms of which the work could be properly registered in their

---

[3] Brian Holmes, Gerald H. Read, and Natalya Voskresenskaya, *Russian Education: Tradition and Transition*, p.298.

rosters. Similarly, Elena Novik, who is going to defend her doctoral dissertation on Siberian folklore at the university where I work, has suddenly come to face the problem of finding a proper committee for her defense, because she studied folklore as a complex interdisciplinary genre that involved ethnographic data, rituals, historical texts, studies of symbolisms of material culture, and other components.

The issue of outdated bureaucratic norms and regulations in the humanities and social sciences in the face of actually changing interests and practices of scholarship, pointed out by Vainshtein, was literally seconded by professors from different institutions and different disciplines. For example, Sergei Sokolovski, scholar at the Institute of Ethnology and Anthropology, Russian Academy of Sciences, said in his interview the following:

> Contemporary science is organized around *issues* rather than around disciplines. It is only the structure of university education, together with the system of tenure to some extent, that reproduces old disciplinary barriers ... If one should try to find something specific in our disciplines and name it a "paradigm," then that would certainly be the degenerate romanticism that came to us through Marx and Hegel, having been propelled in its own day by the ideas of enlightenment and positive knowledge ... But what is interesting is that a positivistic science is admittedly supposed to reconstruct the whole from the fragments. We have not even followed this model. What we have is surprisingly parcelled out, because of the typical idea that every scholar should get hold of a little piece, should bring a small brick, and that's how the wall of knowledge will be composed. In fact, this wall of knowledge, the vision of the whole, always remains virtual. This is some sort of *virtual holism*.[4]

Another prominent Russian scholar, Alexei Nikishenkov of the History Faculty of Moscow State University, says things that are surprisingly similar:

---

[4] Alexei Elfimov, "The State of the Discipline in Russia: Interviews with Russian Anthropologists," *American Anthropologist* 99, no.4 (1997): 776, 779.

Sadly, I have to state that our academy has a complex hierarchical structure and is highly compartmentalized. The disciplinary partitions are very strong, and this affects everything. This is an obvious case at the university where I work. Every single soul is attached to some department, like a serf. One may be personally interested in a variety of subjects, but in the end, one remains formally bound to the courses taught in one's own department. The idea of letting students register for classes outside their departments has been talked about much but has never come true ... If you look for institutionalized mechanisms that would allow for a broad interdisciplinary education, there are none ... Further, a specific disease of this educational system is the fact that it is monologic in character, it is based on the old German and in some ways old Eastern canon. It is typical to have a professor talk endlessly while students just listen along. In the end, students lose the habit of speaking. But they should be active ... It is important that ... students be able to *do* something, act independently, and articulate their point of view all the time. [5]

It has to be noted that despite the fact that there was widespread dissatisfaction with the state of the humanities in the 1990s, critical assessments or self-conscious reflections on the practice of teaching and research, such as those in the interviews above, were very rare. They are still far from being common. Most of the professors, especially those of older generations who enjoyed some prestige under the socialist regime, remain more apologetic than critical and continue to insist on, as well as to carry out in their own practices, the conservative dogmatic pattern of educational process, which no longer appeals to the students. This state of affairs makes students increasingly indifferent, for they feel that the knowledge offered to them is outdated and has little value in the reality of social life that they are about to enter. Ekaterina Yagafova, professor in the humanities at a research institute in Samara, who had studied at Moscow State University in the late 1980s, observed, "When I came back to the university ten years later, I was stunned to see that nothing had changed. My department was a

---

[5] Alexei Elfimov, "Razmyshlenia o sud'bakh nauki," *Etnograficheskoe obozrenie*, no.5 (1996): 9, 13.

disaster. Students did not attend lectures and professors did not care. I did not notice any new courses; it was just the same old stuff taught by the same old people. There was really a surprising apathy all around."[6]

Alexei Nikishenkov also commented on the persistence of the conservative philosophy of teaching in the humanities as one of the primary flaws of the current university education system, which induces apathy in students: "[Most professors] instinctively fear and try to avoid by all means possible troublemaking words and concepts ... This *has* to be overcome. We *have* to make students active, thinking, reflective. We *have* to respect what is troubling or interesting to them, instead of trying to form their intellectual baggage without asking them ... I was trying to introduce a more lively style in my own seminars, but as for what came out of it, it is not my place to judge."[7]

Furthermore, it appears that the indifference toward learning in the humanities, which students seem to have absorbed during the 1990s as a result of such teaching policies and practices, is not so easy to cure. Sergei Sokolovski remarks that the persistence of the conservative attitude, which has been traditionally associated in the Russian discourse with the nationalistic Slavophile trend, has in fact deeply hurt the young generation of scholars and students:

> They have not been encouraged to study the disciplinary achievements of the West, and they have not been excited by the study of those at home. They have a consumer attitude: "So what? Nothing Works. The postmodern debate is said

---

[6] The role of the "old guard" in producing indifference among the students has been frequently commented upon by other authors. Cf., for example: "An unusual phenomenon compared to other countries' experience is that, during profound social transformation in the countries of the former USSR, the teenage and student community to a large extent is inactive and invisible ... [because] during the first stages of post-totalitarianism, certain state structures are renewed, but only at the top, while underneath, bureaucracies are preserved. Political apathy is encouraged by the old structures and residual *nomenklatura*." (Igor V. Kitaev, "The Labor Market and Education in the Post-Soviet Era," in *Education and Society in the New Russia*, p.317–318.)

[7] Alexei Elfimov, "The State of the Discipline in Russia," p.781.

to have failed. Now give us the next theory to consider. What else do you have to say?" I ask them, "Just what do you mean, *What else?*" It is *you* who should have something else to say! What do you mean, "The debate has failed?" All theories fail one day; that's not the point. The point is you have to learn something from them.[8]

For comparison, I found it interesting to interview several graduate students in the humanities to hear what their own opinion of the issue was. The responses were by and large predictable in that they manifested the same feeling that the course material offered to them was outdated and boring. Students typically complained that professors were "imposing the ideals of the 1970s on the new generation" without respect to the radically changed nature of political and social reality surrounding people. Some said that they indeed felt indifferent toward the subjects they studied and wanted just to get the degree so that they could go on with their lives. The mainstream attitude, however, was best of all summarized in the response given by Aleksandr Saltykov, another graduate of Moscow State University who shortly after the graduation in the beginning of the 1990s left the academy and went to work for a private joint Russian-American firm: "You ask me why I quit the academy? Basically, for two reasons. First, I am married now and have to take care of my family, which would be a rather utopian project with that $30 per month that my assistant professorship provided me with (it is, if you need this comparison, three times less than the salary my wife has as a secretary and probably about fifteen times less than what a poorly qualified bus driver makes these days). Secondly, I think I had the same reason as many other intellectually curious scholars who have recently left the university walls ... It is a telling tendency, indeed quite obvious, if you are not completely blind, that every creative person should sooner or later quit the academy, because our academy is an outstandingly boring and terribly bureaucratized place. It is a gathering of the

---

[8] Alexei Elfimov, "The State of the Discipline in Russia," p.783–84.

most uncreative and unexciting people who engage in thoughtless compilations and have an inflated opinion of themselves – well, like all small bureaucrats do. They are very inert, afraid of any change, and usually try to avoid far-reaching proposals at all costs. Besides, they always expect something from the government and also want to gain some glory by silently sticking to their little spots. It is a dream of every bureaucrat, isn't it? Maybe I am too harsh. I know their life is not very easy these days, as the academy is breaking apart. It is, of course, a shame that academic salaries have gone so miserable lately (there is no excuse for that); but, on the other hand, I can understand why the state does not want to pay academics more. Why pay them at all? These people are totally useless. What they do is of no benefit to anybody. Well, as a result, creative people have to leave both because they are bored in that environment *and* because that environment tends to reject them as aliens. I can name literally three or four, no more, broadly educated, intelligent, and creative professors among the entire staff of the faculties in the humanities departments at Moscow State University. The rest are just sitting there and enjoying the opportunity to exercise power over students, because that is the only place on earth where they could show any power and influence. And outside the classroom, who cares about them?"

Saltykov's response, indeed, raises many questions. It is apparent that those whom he identifies as a "gathering of the most uncreative and unexciting people who engage in thoughtless compilations and have an inflated opinion of themselves" are precisely the representatives of the old conservative guard who are worried more about their own authority, which they feel has been shaken, than about the interests of the students or new areas of research. One of the particular problems that marked the style of teaching in the humanities at the time when students like Saltykov were taking classes (the late 1980s and early 1990s) was indeed the preponderance of outdated themes and research projects, offered by professors, and the fear of new approaches. The readings that were assigned in classes – typically, old books by those very professors – had not only lost their appeal among the majority of more or less curious students, but were at that time largely ignored by these students altogether. Many students consciously refused to read those books, trying to learn the information required for tests and examinations from other sources, even though they unambiguously risked getting lower grades. Indeed, cases, when students ended up getting lower grades in such manner, were not uncommon. On the one hand, professors never hesitated to lower the grade if they detected that students had not read an assigned book, even when examination answers were excellent and displayed enough knowledge for an "A". On the other hand, students who took such risks perfectly understood that the purpose of many examinations was precisely to detect whether one particular book had been read, not really to examine the actual knowledge of studied material. That situation symbolically devalued both the meaning of the grade as such and the sanctity of examination ritual, which was therefore seen merely as an indecent game with no fair outcome.

In his earlier works on education, Pierre Bourdieu paid much attention to the institute of examination, which he saw as an element of paramount importance in the system of university education, because its function was a special ritual that legitimized knowledge and converted it from a profane form to a sacred one. "The examination," reasoned Bourdieu, "is not only the clearest expression of academic values and of the educational system's implicit choices: in imposing as worthy of university sanction a social definition of knowledge and the way to show it, it provides one of the most efficacious tools for the enterprise of inculcating the dominant culture and the value of that culture."[9] Among the most unfortunate consequences of the conservative pattern of teaching and prejudiced practices of professors in Russian universities of the 1980s–90s were the de-facto desacralization of the examination ritual and destabilization of the general authority of the

---

[9] Pierre Bourdieu and Jean-Claude Passeron, *Reproduction in Education, Society and Culture* (London, Beverly Hills: Sage, 1977), p.142.

system. The examination was no longer felt by most of the intelligent students as an important rite of passage in any sense, and it essentially failed to function as an efficient tool of imposing the true definition of knowledge (or simply as an efficient test tool). A strange and indeed socially painful situation (which in fact had begun to form long before perestroika) ensued. Many of the best students kept getting lower grades, while less able and less intellectually curious students who continued scrupulously to learn from the required textbooks were generously awarded by the insecure teachers the highest ones. This unfairness unquestionably added to the social and moral apathy that was forming in the student milieu.

A typical case of such practices might be exemplified with personal stories told to me by Liubomir Zekhirev and Julia Stepanova, who graduated in the early 1990s from Moscow State University, majoring at the Department of American History. Despite the formal defeat of the communist bureaucracy and several years of "perestroika cleansing" (which, it may be pointed out again, has not proved to be very successful in the case of institutions of higher learning), the body of the department at the time remained largely composed of the same professors who had been associated before perestroika both with the higher levels of communist party *nomenklatura* and with the most dogmatic and conservative version of Soviet-style Marxist scholarship. The chair of the department, Professor Yazkov, who also was the author of a textbook required for a number of courses taught at the department, became one of the most unpopular figures among the students. Many of the students felt that Yazkov's policies were an obstacle to studying the American history from a new fresh perspective, free of the Cold War mentality, and that they continued to confine them to the old socialist style of formalized and politicized history. As a result, the situation at the department turned out to be very similar to what has been described above, since many students refused to read Yazkov's textbook and preferred to learn the material from alternative sources. Examinations at the department, as Julia recalled, "were depressing and frustrating."

Julia, who was writing her thesis in twentieth-century American history, had a good command of English, and she was fortunate to be invited for a year of research and studies at a US university (within the framework of the first study-abroad programs opened up by perestroika). During that year, she managed to collect interesting information and, naturally, to gain familiarity with a number of different concepts and alternative points of views in regard to her project. Upon her return, she completed her thesis, having framed it theoretically in terms of the new concepts she learned in the US. Both at the thesis defense and at the final examination she was deliberately overscrutinized by the departmental committee, chaired by Yazkov, and given a "B" ("4" in the Russian grade system) on a charge of "not having sufficient understanding of some basic concepts that were clearly explicated in the required textbook." "Even though friends of mine warned me that something like this could easily happen," Julia told me, "I somehow did not believe they would have a nerve to do such an obvious foul thing. You know, they did not ask me even a single question about the concepts I was trying to develop or interpretations I was trying to test. All their questions were centered on that darn textbook, as if it were an ultimate authority on all matters. Of course, it's true that I did not read it too closely – but who could take much of that old garbage without going nuts?.." It certainly appeared offensive to the students that neither their actual work, nor certain ideals of knowledge and scholarship as such should be taken into consideration, and the judgment instead should be pronounced on the basis of some ridiculous and irrelevant personal obsessions of professors, who had lost all their authority and prestige. "When I left the exam," Julia remembered, "I really wanted to cry. But next day, I calmed down. You know, who cares? Then again, when later at the graduation I got my diploma with the inscription "Good," and the other guy who based his whole thesis on Yazkov's textbook alone and did not read a single monograph in English got his with the "Excellent," I felt somehow offended. But, you know, I was not the only one who felt that way."

Liubomir's story was a little different in formal details but very much similar in content and conclusion. He was writing his thesis on the problems of American Civil War. Having a good knowledge of English, he also invested much time in reading original sources. Not many of them were available in Moscow libraries but, being enthusiastic about his project, he managed to acquire several books, published in the US, through rarity bookstores and informal book retailers, having spent a good fortune on them, for such editions were always extremely expensive and difficult to get in Russia. He also corresponded with a number of US scholars, who kindly provided him with articles and essays relevant to his project. In a word, Liubomir's thesis was advancing successfully and the faculty at the department were aware of that. Professor Yazkov, however, disliked Liubomir, since they had already met at term examinations, which apparently had revealed some incompatibilities in their worldview and scholarly interests. The fact that Liubomir's thesis was advancing now with success and beyond the scope of the traditional added to that dislike. "Already from the way they informally treated me," says Liubomir, "I could tell that the thesis defense was not going to be fun. I mean, I expected a low blow of some kind." The low blow came three months before the defense and caught him off guard, despite all his expectations. One of Liubomir's committee members asked him to bring his thesis draft for the final reviewing. Liubomir brought his manuscript, which was the only copy he had. (The early 1990s had not yet made computers or xerox machines available to students in Russia – furthermore, not many students could afford even a typewriter because of its cost, and often they worked on their theses in a handwritten manner, typing them only prior to the defense. In any case, a student normally did not and could not have more than one copy of his or her draft work.)

The process of reviewing took a surprisingly long turn. After some three weeks, Liubomir decided to inquire about his manuscript, but the professor who took it was now out of town. When after another week he returned, he told Liubomir that he did not have the thesis and that he had left it at the department before he left town. At the department, strangely, nobody saw the manuscript. Liubomir started to worry and informed his committee about the incident. "Nobody reacted as if they were surprised," recalls Liubomir, "They said that two months would be enough to recover the lost draft, can you believe it." It was never revealed whether the loss of the manuscript was an accident or intended trick, but the fact is that Liubomir had to hastily compose another paper from some pieces that he managed to put together within the two months remaining before the defense, and the defense brought him a "C" ("3" in the Russian grade system, and the lowest passing grade there). "The unfairness was just too blatant," says Liubomir, "Personally, I am sure it was one hundred percent intentional." He decided that the matter was worth the trouble and appealed to the dean. The grade, to his surprise and satisfaction, was changed to a "B" ("4") after some deliberation. Upon his graduation, Liubomir tried to apply to an American Studies program at a US university, but had no success, for it is entirely conceivable that the recommendations given to him by his former committee members might have been not of the best kind. Today he works at the Moscow branch of the Siemens Corporation.

It is easy to see that the process of "exclusion and selection," of which Bourdieu likes to speak as an inherent mechanism of the university system, assumed a rather regressive dimension in the humanities departments of the post-perestroika Russia. In too many cases, it were not the best students who were encouraged and given the right of way. The best students, on the contrary, typically encountered continuous problems, so that by the graduation time many of them felt tired of obstacles and indifferent to the academic career. The repulsive forces therefore arose on both sides of the divide. As Saltykov mentions, "creative people have to leave both because they are bored in that environment *and* because that environment tends to reject them as aliens." If we should add to this flaw in the functioning of the system the financial humiliation of the Russian academy, which proved to be especially hard on younger scholars, we shall have the basic set of causes that has been turning younger intellectual generations away from the academy since the late 1980s. By the end of the 1990s, this trend resulted in a certain intellectual vacuum, which was keenly felt by critically minded scholars. Sergei Sokolovski, seconding opinions of several other scholars, at once connected the crisis in the humanities with the issue of discontinuity in reproduction of intellectual resources. "There seem to be serious generational problems," Sokolovski observed, "I believe we have lost the active generation of scholars who quit the academy during the perestroika years. The intellectual resources of those who used to rule the disciplines have expired. Meanwhile, the younger generation has not been able, or has not been given the chance, to stand on its own two feet."[10]

This state of things may explain much about the conservative dogmatism that prevailed in the discussions over the humanities in the 1990s. Well educated people in large numbers were thrown out to other sectors of the society, mainly business and commerce,[11] while the mediocre residue that was left in the academy continued to debate the fate of the humanities. It is no surprise then that the character and direction these debates assumed were defensive rather than progressive. The defensiveness was salient both in publications and in actual academic behavior, which can be illustrated by the following case.

In May 1995 I was present at a conference on the "State of Research and Knowledge in the Humanities," held in the framework of encompass-

---

[10] Alexei Elfimov, "The State of the Discipline in Russia," p.785.

[11] This social tendency cannot be considered as an entirely negative phenomenon, even though it apparently constituted a certain tragedy for the humanities as well as a personal tragedy for many individuals, for the influx of educated social strata into such spheres as business, politics, or commerce, which have been lacking intelligent management for a long time, should indeed be seen as a positive phenomenon. In the new Russian society where the rationalization of professional recruitment, which Max Weber saw as a major trait of developed modern bureaucracies, is only beginning to take shape, new corporate structures often do not mind hiring persons with a background in the humanities, presuming that they will learn and be able to acquire necessary qualifications fast.

ing debates on like issues at the Russian State University for the Humanities. The keynote lecture of the day, devoted to the subject of power, knowledge, and truth in the humanities, was delivered by Georgii Knabe, a senior historian who had been considered a respected scholar in the Soviet time. In the discussion part, Olga Vainshtein, who was also a speaker and discussant at the conference, remarked that the name of Michel Foucault was for some reason never brought up in the talk and asked why Foucault's works, being so pertinent to the subject, were altogether dismissed in the lecture. Knabe did not answer the question, and the remark all of a sudden made him so angry that he expressly raised his voice and asked Vainshtein to "call off her irrelevant attacks." Vainshtein shrugged and dropped the question.

Knabe's irritation was a typical reaction of a scholar of the "old guard." The question about Foucault was very much relevant to the discussion, and it was least of all an "attack," but it was perceived as such since Knabe probably took it as a personal reproach concerning his ignorance of Foucault, whom he apparently did not read but was not able to admit that fact in front of the audience. The insecurity of conservative professors in the face of new areas and interests of inquiry makes them perceive these areas as a personal threat, which they rarely separate from a global threat to the Russian humanities.

It is typical that most of such professors are often extremely afraid of new scholarly terms and concepts that have emerged in the theoretical debates within the past two decades in Europe and America and, in a way, have already spread beyond particular national traditions and been adopted into the international vocabulary of the humanities and social sciences. For example, describing the situation in the Russian anthropological community, Alexei Nikishenkov mentions that words like "paradigm" or "episteme" are still seen by many as awkward and troublemaking.[12] Instances of

---

[12] Alexei Elfimov, "The State of the Discipline in Russia," p.781.

hostility toward new terms and words actually abound, and some of them may appear truly ludicrous to a normal intelligent scholar. In one of his latest articles, senior Russian anthropologist V. N. Basilov of the Russian Academy of Sciences openly reproaches younger ethnographers for their use of the word *discourse*, suggesting that that jargon term "should be replaced by some normal phrase, like *scholarly conversation* or *exchange of ideas*." As if illustrating Nikishenkov's remark, he further writes that the word *paradigm* does not convey any new meaning, and so it is not needed at all. (He even goes as far as to lay the blame for introducing this word into the academic vocabulary on Mikhail Gorbachev.) Curiously, he fails to come up with a "normal" word or phrase that would express the "old" meaning that he sees as unnaturally communicated by the term *paradigm*. Finally, he protests against quoting terms or phrases in a foreign language, claiming that it is a "presumptuous practice" of less intelligent scholars or immature students who want to show off.[13] These instances reflect nothing but the emerging fears of the entrenched sector of the academy, for in fact terms *discourse* and *paradigm* have been in use among Russian scholars in many different disciplines for some time by now, while quoting in a foreign language has always been a regular practice and it was not censured as such even under the Soviet regime.[14]

---

[13] V. N. Basilov, "Traditsii otechestvennoi etnografii," *Etnograficheskoe obozrenie*, no.2 (1998): 21.

[14] Olga Vainshtein commented in her interview on the issue of "foreign language as a threat," linking it closely to the general issue of rapid informational change at the end of the twentieth century: "Now that the iron curtain between the West and the East has broken and a flood of information has suddenly rushed into our society, scholars have got to face the challenge of navigating the new informational space. Many senior scholars who often do not have an adequate proficiency in foreign languages feel isolated in this situation since they cannot respond to this challenge, which, at the same time, can be more and more often taken up by an increasing number of students who have gone through practical training or graduate studies in the West and who can easily correspond in a foreign language or have a basic experience with e-mail, computers, etc. Older scholars, being unable to catch up with this development, naturally take it as a threat that comes from the West and tend to adopt an oppositional stance toward it."

The rise of fears and insecurity feelings among the conservative group of scholars, which finds expression in their hostility toward new ideas (very frequently, toward all kinds of unimportant details rather than the essence of such ideas), is also closely related to the traditional Russian split between the so-called *Slavophiles* and *Westernizers*. This split had been a particular feature of Russian intellectual life in the nineteenth century, with its heated debates over the issue whether Russian social institutions should follow the Western way or their own "native" way. With the coming of the socialist regime and subsequent political suppression of socially meaningful intellectual debates, the fight between Slavophiles and Westernizers ended as such, for the way the country was to follow was chosen to be neither Western nor Slavic, but Soviet, and it could no longer be disputed above all. With the demise of the socialist political machine in the early 1990s, the question of the "path" sprang up again, and this time it essentially separated radically or liberally minded social reformers from the former communist *nomenklatura*. The scheme of subsequent divide within the humanities and social sciences was in many ways the same as it was within the political realm. Most people who had enjoyed academic prestige and privileges in any form under the Soviet system (and, granted, some who did not enjoyed them, too) now resisted the prospects of perestroika and adopted a conservative stance appealing to "native" Russian feelings and evoking a primordial sentiment of traditionalism. They were quickly identified as Slavophiles. People who saw in their position an impediment to cultural and social development, in contrast, were generally ascribed to Westernizers. It is important to note that in many cases these newer "Westernizers" might not necessarily proclaim "Western" values per se, and so the logical line of distinction between the camps perhaps was not as subtle as it had been in the debates of the nineteenth century. Yet the existence of two more or less identifiable patterns in the social worldview, closely resembling those of the older "Slavophiles" and "Westernizers", was generally acknowledged as an apparent fact in Russia of the 1990s. Professor

Sergei Cheshko of the Russian Academy of Sciences, responding to my interview question regarding the matter, said:

> We have both Slavophile and Westernizing trends in the academy, but they are, of course, informal. They are related to the ideological demarcation among scholars as well as among politicians and other people in society, since science essentially reflects what is going on in society. The demarcation started at some point in the late 1980s. But this divide is certainly not total. Most scholars hold on to a neutral or more or less balanced position.[15]

Sergei Sokolovski of the Institute of Ethnology and Anthropology makes a similar statement:

> Both tendencies are present. Which is prevailing today, I do not know. But ... since the beginning of perestroika, when the doors opened a little and major publications from the West became accessible, it was a Westernizing trend, rather than Slavophile, that spread among scholars. They were able to place local knowledge in a more global context, the result of which was an immediate reevaluation of knowledge. Then the Slavophile trend began to emerge as a reaction to reevaluation, as a reaction to the influx of books and people from the West ... This trend involved mostly conservative scholars, those who openly opposed everything but Marxism prior to perestroika ... Their orthodox feelings were being hurt. In my mind, their reaction was a purely political rather than scientific affair. All the constructions they were trying to sell as theoretical were in fact ideological.[16]

Professor Alexei Nikishenkov of Moscow State University makes a more extended comment on the matter:

> There is a tendency, typical for all acculturation processes, which is called, I suppose after Ralph Linton, "nativism". Such is the case here. Very often, it is hard to figure out who is a Slavophile and who is a Westernizer. It is a mess, like any acculturation process. Tables turn every day, and all kinds of inver-

---

[15] Alexei Elfimov, "The State of the Discipline in Russia," p.784.
[16] Alexei Elfimov, "Razmyshlenia o sud'bakh nauki," p.20–21.

sions take place where you would least expect them. In retrospect, however, one might delineate a certain order in which these trends have flourished for the past ten years. First, there was an intense interest, inflated to a degree, in all things Western. Books became more or less available, trips abroad became more or less available. Every month there would be a guest scholar from the West giving a talk at the Russian Academy of Sciences, and there was great excitement. Then came a period of indifference, as if people had gotten fed up with that. And recently I have observed the coming of a Slavophile trend and the strengthening of an entrenched group within the academy. Within this group, you would now see many of the same people who had been actively attending the talks of the guest scholars. It goes without saying that there are hardly any academic issues involved in the matter; it is all ideologically charged.[17]

The ideological ingredient that penetrated the humanities and social sciences in the form of Slavophile sentiment had, of course, much to do with the new historical paradigm in the intellectual consciousness, which proved to be an ideal environment for the Slavophile discourse to grow within. One of the major tropes employed in the language of the Slavophile discourse became that of "revival." While those loosely associated with the Westernizing trend were usually looking for (and were generally speaking in terms of) "new forms," the followers of the Slavophile path were stressing the importance of "reviving" something that had once existed. The debate over the fate of the humanities, in this regard, was no exception. Progressively minded scholars and students were interested in new models of education, free of dogmas both of the socialist authoritarianism and of the more general scholarly positivism that largely characterized the first three quarters of the twentieth century worldwide. In a word, their desire was for something appropriate for the new moment. The rhetoric of the Slavophile wing, on the contrary, stressed not so much the uniqueness or needs of the new moment as the necessity of reviving the classical humanities that Russia once had had. Strangely enough, even Yuri Afanasiev, the

---

[17] Alexei Elfimov, "The State of the Discipline in Russia," p.784.

founder and rector of the Russian State University for the Humanities, who managed to successfully turn his former reputation of a party official into that of a radical reformer, proved unable or unwilling to avoid the rhetoric of revival, which gained wide currency solely due to the power of encompassing social infatuation with history and cultural heritage. This rhetoric is reflected not only in the title of his recent article, but also in its very content which represents a typical attempt at idealizing the humanities of the old Russia, which, according to Afanasiev, "were formed as a comprehensive family of studies, not as an individual science or branch of knowledge, developing fruitfully and achieving visible results." Furthermore, giving praise (no matter how well deserved it might be) to a variety of Russian scholars and philosophers of the nineteenth century and the pre-revolutionary Silver Age, Afanasiev concludes, "Naturally, it cannot be said that the development of thought in Russia and the West moved in the same direction."[18]

It is certainly not clear why the common direction of scholarly developments in Russia and the West should be denied "naturally." In fact, with the exception of that particular kind of late Russian aristocratic philosophy, scholarly developments in the late nineteenth and early twentieth centuries could be seen as essentially moving in the same direction in all developed countries; indeed, contacts between Russian and European scholars, as well as the increasing role of exchange of opinion between them, were known to be the case at that time.[19] The notion of common destiny and common path, however, cannot be said to fit nicely into the new particularistic intellectual framework, in which history and cultural heritage reign supreme, so Afanasiev chooses to reaffirm the sentiment that appeals to the Slavophiles, even though he himself and his institutional reforms at the

---

[18] Iurii Afanas'ev, "Reviving the Humanities in Modern Russia," p.266.

[19] In a sense, one could argue that it was rather during the Soviet period, when the freedom of international contacts and exchange of opinion was limited, that the scholarly development in Russia went its own "distinctive" way. (But even that could be contested.)

Russian State University for the Humanities in the strict sense can hardly be attributed to the Slavophile (or Westernizing, for that matter) current.

Part of the problem is that the Slavophile trend, as Alexei Nikishenkov and Sergei Sokolovski noted in their interviews, is in its many aspects an ideological matter rather than a theoretical scholarly position. The case with Afanasiev should be perhaps interpreted from this point of view. Being the rector of one of the major universities of the country at the time when allocations to the educational budget hopelessly decrease with every year (at least, did so until very recently) unquestionably requires some political insight and ideological maneuvering. It is therefore understandable that in the situation, when nativist feelings prevail among those who hold much of the political and administrative power, an appeal to such feelings can gain much more than the pursuit of some truth of the day.[20] But, of course, the cultural paradox is such that the situational logic of ideological maneuvering gradually becomes the actual logic of life, and the appeal to nativist feelings becomes in effect the truth of the day. There is a curious old Russian saying, still widely used in Russia today, that subtly expresses the commonsensical basis of the transformational power of practice: "If you are called a pig one hundred times, the one hundred and first time will make you grunt."

The dissemination and strengthening of the Slavophile attitude, for this reason, appears to be a fairly complex process, maintained by a variety of conscious efforts and ideological practices on the one hand, and propelled, on the other, by peripheral support of those who unreflectively and sometimes naively see in the immediate effects of such efforts and practices the real truth of the day. It is characteristic that many of those who unreflec-

---

[20] In fact, it is known that at the time of the general economic turmoil in Russia the Russian State University for the Humanities was one of the most financially secure institutions. Although the wages of the faculty and staff were only barely meeting the lowest living standards, they were still kept at the top level compared to other universities in the country. There were no delays with compensation, and so on.

tively identify the essence of the moment with the Slavophile social moods often conceive of that moment as of something romantic, if not heroic, and easily subscribe to the rhetoric of revival in its any form. In the humanities and social sciences this seems to be especially the case, for the Popperian spirit of moral historicism that continues to dominate the mainstream pattern of disciplinary inquiry comes highly conducive to a form of naive emotional excitement about the things long gone and forgotten. Sergei Cheshko commented on the proliferation of romantic revivalist moods in Russian anthropology in the 1990s:

> The idea of "ethnic renaissance"... has been in the air during all these turbulent years. Many ... got romantic about it and started speaking and writing in defense of the rebirth of traditional culture, of ethnic revival, and so on. I was always curious about what it was they wanted to revive. Bast shoes? Samovars? Wagons on the roads? For some reason, this mythic idea of a rebirth as a return to the old is appealing to anthropologists. I do not really understand this. Culture is a continuity, and the only sense we can apply to a "rebirth" is that of producing a new entity. But today this romantic trend is fairly strong in the anthropological community.[21]

Similarly, Alexei Nikishenkov remarks that the romanticism about the traditional objects of study in the humanities and social sciences has suddenly sprung in the air, and "too many ... have decided that their heyday has come, and they can finally apply their theories to practice." He further makes a good observation, adding that in many cases this infatuation "has been, in essence, just another bluff, although some scholars must have been sincere in their belief."[22]

In a word, levels of comprehending the phenomenon of new Russian Slavophilism and levels of participating in it were different and are still different today, both inside and outside the academy. Thus, if depart-

---

[21] Alexei Elfimov, "The State of the Discipline in Russia," p.784.
[22] Ibid., p.778.

mental curricula at Moscow State University have been kept traditional and ideologically conservative because of the politically conservative nature of the institution, which, in the Russian society, has always played a technical role comparable to that of Harvard in the US society; at other (less politically important) universities, the Slavophile make-up of curricula could be explained by the sincere romantic belief in the importance of reviving old traditions. For example, at the Department of Sociology of the recently established Moscow University for Business and Management, a substantial part of the readings assigned to students represents the long abandoned tradition of Russian formalist sociology of the late nineteenth and early twentieth centuries. Furthermore, the department for some reason finds it necessary to invest much time, effort, and money in publishing a large thick two-volume textbook of readings in sociology, the entire first volume of which is devoted to the Russian sociology of the nineteenth century and contains hundreds of pages of outdated scholastic debates, more philosophical than sociological in character and having no significant relevance to the changed social reality of nowadays.[23] The fact should seem especially puzzling if one considers that at such institutions as Moscow University for Business and Management the academic priorities are hardly focused on the scrutinizing of some philosophical scholasticism of the earlier ages, but rather on preparing students to effectively cope with the social complexities of the present moment. As a matter of fact, the de-

---

[23] The volume contains essays by many mediocre and uninfluential nineteenth-century Russian sociologists and social philosophers, such as B. Kistiakovskii, V. Ivanovskii, K. Takhtarev, V. Khvostov, N. Korkunov, V. Chernov, and others, who mainly discussed not sociological questions per se, but rather those typical for the atmosphere of the late nineteenth century philosophical ideas of Comte, Spencer, and many minor figures. Among such ideas, for example, were issues of the individual and the crowd, class struggle, social progress, and so on. These issues, of course, can be considered as still relevant and important, if viewed from the right angle, but it is hard to imagine how the readings, confined to a rather dull and positivistic nineteenth-century Russian view of the matter, could provoke any active interest in the subject in a student who has to live in the reality frequently described as the postmodern age.

scription of the sociology program in the general announcement catalog of the university clearly indicates that "the department trains sociologists in the area of business and management, according to the accepted standards of sociological education worldwide ... The program and its courses have been developed in consultation with the teaching experience of the leading universities of Russia, the US, Canada, and Europe. The entire course of study is based on the latest scholarly publications in Russian and foreign languages."[24]

Publications may be certainly the latest in the formal sense, but the information they contain is too often the oldest. It is interesting to note that the advertising puts an explicit emphasis on the criterion of being in line with contemporary scholarly developments in the West ("worldwide standards," "experience of leading universities of the US, Canada, and Europe," "publications in foreign languages"). It is therefore technically understood and acknowledged that the interest in the latest scholarly developments in the world (again, particularly in the West) is what to a large extent constitutes the disposition of the younger generation and, therefore, the marketable matter at the present moment. But in practice, which very often has little to do with this understanding, oddly enough, the idea of humanities and social sciences continues to be dominated by the Slavophile (at any rate, "Slavophilish," or pseudo-Slavophile) romantic "nativism" and general philosophy of "revival."

It is not very difficult to make a connection between the revivalist trend in the academy and the fever of architectural restoration discussed earlier. What is concealed in both phenomena is essentially the same interplay between the concrete political or ideological interest of the power and the abstract humanistic romanticism of the intelligentsia. The impact of the humanities and social sciences, in this regard, may not be as immediate as that of spectacular urban restoration campaigns, especially considering the

---

[24] *Mezhdunarodnyi Universitet Biznesa I Upravleniia* (Moscow, 1997), p.13.

financial crisis in the academy and the steady decline of interest in the humanities among the youth,[25] but its pervasiveness is nevertheless felt. For example, almost every educational program on public television during the 1990s was not just permeated, but in fact heavily loaded with the idea of revival and "return to the cultural roots." Evidently, many of such programs were created by (or, at least, with the assistance of) the same scholars in the humanities, the majority of whom consciously or unconsciously subscribed to the concept of historical restoration. During the course of the year 1996, for instance, the *ORT* network (Russian Public Television) was broadcasting a series of weekend programs created by research scholars from the State Historical Museum. One of the distinctive episodes of the series (broadcast on June 29, 1996), characteristically entitled "In Search of the Lost Unity," was devoted to the discussion of the old Russian peasant household. A long tedious display of old wooden peasant utensils and hand-made household tools was accompanied by a nostalgic story about the many strengths of the human spirit, and the ultimate message of the story was that a peasant of the old days had possessed the unity of the soul. It was implied that such unity was lost in the modern society and the result of that loss was to account for many misfortunes of nowadays. In the narrative of the story, one could unmistakably detect a clear reaffirmation of a particular traditional value – that of the old rural household as a building cell and source of the social stability. This is a common example of how the intellectual production of the humanities merges with the ideological agenda of the Slavophile political game.

---

[25] The admissions statistics at the most prestigious institutions in the humanities, such as Moscow State University, for example, indicates that the average rate of competition in the late 1980s (10–14 applicants competing for 1 position) gradually fell during the 1990s to 2–3 students for 1 position. In many of the social sciences, with the notable exception of economics, the situation was nearly identical. For instance, the number of persons applying (again, for 1 position) to the Department of Sociology at Moscow State University from 1990 to 1995 was as follows: 14 (1990), 5 (1991), 3 (1992), 3 (1993), 3.7 (1994), 3 (1995), 3 (1996). (Source of information: the official 1997 admissions bulletin board at Moscow State University.)

The Slavophile politics of cultural revival or restoration, without any doubt, became the dominant ideology in the Russian humanities and social sciences at the turn of the century. What is remarkable, though, is that this fact is surprisingly rarely acknowledged by the majority of Russian academics. Most scholars, especially those associated or sympathetic with the Slavophile trend, assert that the academic discourse itself and their own practices are politically neutral and essentially non-ideological. Some of them even emphasize the need of designing a proper ideology for the "new" humanities. Philosophy professor Eduard Mirskii, for example, says that since the beginning of perestroika the principal task of the humanities was to rid themselves of the communist ideology and "depoliticize" academic scholarship. Now, reasons Mirskii, when the task has been accomplished, there has emerged an ideological vacuum in the humanities which has to be filled with a proper alternative.[26]

Such views, if they are sincere, can only be blindly naive. The idea that the humanities were nicely "depoliticized" and cleared of unwanted ideological content upon someone's decision, and thus became somewhat of a clean blank territory that could be now appropriately filled with the desired ideological content, is nothing but merely imperceptive. Communist ideology, in the first place, was never successfully swept out from the academic territory, as I have mentioned earlier. It was discredited and broken apart as a powerful unity, but it survived and adapted to the new situation, having transformed itself into various oppositional currents. Secondly, according to the Russian proverb "the sacred spot can never be vacant," as soon as that communist ideology started to retire to rear positions, other ideological forces began taking over the terrain of the humanities and establishing their hegemony. It was evident already in the early 1990s that the ideology of "Russian revival" was violently pushing not only the weakened communist doctrine, but also those new progressive intellectual

---

[26] E. M. Mirskii, "Zametki o gumanitarnom obrazovanii," *Chelovek*, no.6 (1995): 158.

forces that might be loosely identified with the Westernizing trend (certainly, not all Westernizers could be described as progressive) and that held on to the idea of developing an open internationalized and modernized society. The strengthening of the Slavophile ideology, which manifested its conservative aspect rather early, subsequently attracted many of the former adherents of the communist doctrine, who thus joined the Slavophile bloc in the academia under different guises and began to contribute to its well-being. The process of "clearing the humanities of the ideological content" which, according to professor Mirskii, was a success that ended in a miraculous "depoliticization," was therefore only a process of imposing another powerful ideology over the weakened one.

It is appropriate to note another fact here – namely, that the concept of "depoliticization" of the humanities itself assumed wide currency among the Slavophile and other conservative academics. It came, strictly speaking, as an extension of the rhetoric of "scientific objectivity" that had been long practiced under the socialist regime and left recognizable traces in the tradition of contemporary Russian scholarship. Olga Vainshtein provided an interesting comment on this issue:

> The humanities people here certainly have a leaning toward political conservatism, although it is traditionally camouflaged by the we-are-beyond-the-politics posture. This posture is in many ways a product of the Soviet political system and has been developed over the long decades of our history. That is to say, many Russian intellectuals still have that reflex of steadfastly resisting any kind of politicized forms of knowledge. I know that Western scholars have often found this striking, but, well, that's the reality we live in. I do not think it is going to change soon. It seems unlikely that Russian intellectuals will ever be able to develop that left-wing complex of Western humanities (I mean all those things related to the PC debates, critique of the right government, and the like). Stories about political correctness that sneak into the Russian press, and specifically into the newspaper *Segodnia* [Today], which most of our intellectuals seem to read these days, are perceived here with much irony. They appear under titles like "I Don't Want to Be a Noblewoman, but Want to Be a Black Lesbian" (clearly, what is meant is, to get a job in the U.S., the best strategic

device is to belong to several minorities simultaneously). So, as I say, we have a somewhat different view of things here, which is an outcome of our history.

The guise of ideological neutrality, thus, appears to be a safer mode of self-presentation among the majority of Russian scholars who still often believe that taking an ideological or political side would undermine their academic (or, as they prefer to say, "scientific") authority and simultaneously expose them to the critique of the other side. The influence of this anti-ideological principle in the humanities is so persistent that, curiously enough, even some scholars who recognize its false nature are not always able or willing to expel it from their thinking. For example, Sergei Cheshko of the Russian Academy of Sciences, answering my interview question, readily admitted that "the slogan of a 'pure science not involved in politics', frequently heard in past years, is obviously nothing but a naive and unfeasible ideal." Minutes later, however, when I asked him to identify his own ideological standing, he came up with the following statement, somewhat different in character:

> Just how could science be conservative or liberal? It may be science or non-science. A considerable number of scholars today start working for the governmental sphere and pursue political issues rather than scientific ones. Some of them tend to the liberal side of the divide, some to the conservative, but what they do is *not* science ... Regarding the relationship between science and the political regime, a certain distance must be kept there.[27]

The resistance to the test of ideological identification is a phenomenon common not only among the Slavophile and conservative intellectuals, but indeed very frequently even among the Westernizers, liberals, and radicals. Professor Cheshko, as a matter of fact, can hardly be said to be a Slavophile or conservative in any sense. His academic views are rather those of a critical-minded scholar interested in contemporary disciplinary develop-

---

[27] Alexei Elfimov, "The State of the Discipline in Russia," p.782–83.

ments, fresh approaches, and new directions of research. His recent book, "The Dissolution of the Soviet Union," was in some ways even radical in its argument, and was sharply criticized by conservative anthropologists and political scientists in Russia.[28] The more so, the awkwardness of the idea of ideological positioning in the academy and the tradition of dismissing the ideological nature of scholarship in the humanities appear to be a striking feature of Russian academic life. It is no surprise that such books as *Writing Culture*,[29] in which the issue of ideological and political situatedness of scholars and their work was specifically posed, met with a largely negative reaction among Russian academics and were quickly ascribed to the sins of "unscientific" postmodernism.[30]

Another thoughtful perspective on the issue of ideological "neutrality" in the contemporary Russian humanities was given by Alexei Nikishenkov, who admitted that conservative tendencies, masked as "scholarly neutrality," were prevailing in Russia of the 1990s, but noted that the latter were in many ways a specific result of the general disappointment with liberal promises of perestroika and the outcome of many years of extreme social and personal confusion and frustration, brought about by political and cultural instability of the 1980s and 1990s:

> You know what the intelligentsia is all about. A revolutionary yesterday is a conservative today and will probably become a religious fanatic tomorrow. Intellectuals are evolving in very strange ways ... Everyone was a liberal during the early perestroika years. But then all that gradually changed, maybe because of the constant drop in salaries, maybe because of psychological tiredness,

---

[28] Sergei Cheshko, *Raspad Sovetskogo Soiuza: Etnopoliticheskii analiz* (Moscow: RAN IEA, 1996).

[29] James Clifford and George E. Marcus, eds. *Writing Culture: The Politics and Poetics of Ethnography* (Berkeley: University of California Press, 1986).

[30] See, for example: V. R. Rokitianskii, "Chego zhdat' ot postmodernistskoi etnografii?" ["What to expect from postmodern ethnography?"], in *Etnometodologiia*, vol.1 (Moscow, 1994); Yu. I. Semenov, "Predmet etnografii (etnologii) i osnovnye sostavliayushchie eio nauchnye distsipliny," *Etnograficheskoe obozrenie*, no.2 (1998).

maybe because of disenchantment in something. Or perhaps for all these reasons ... I am not sure which tendency really dominates, left or right. I would rather say neither. Perhaps it is really some kind of unsettled center. What I mean by "unsettled" is that that centrism is not a self-consciously adopted stance. It is by and large an accidental attitude caused by a state of deep perplexity and frustration. What lies at the core of this, in my opinion, is an *illness of language*. These days people experience an utter lack in ability to *verbalize* their moods. They do not know *how* to speak; they do not know what *name* their moods have. The fact that many people tend to express an extreme political judgment does not mean they are firmly convinced of what they say. Quite the contrary, in most cases it is just an easier way of expressing emotional states.[31]

In a later interview, in response to my specific question about the negative reaction to critical publications, such as *Writing Culture*, and the dismissal of issues raised in them, he added: "The entire question of whether the anthropological community is liberal or conservative is not as relevant here as, for instance, it might be in the West. Western anthropology, ever since it was born, has been socially charged with an air of Rousseau's morality, meaning that two things have been always present in the game: a certain affection for the native and a certain observance of the ethical code in respect to one's own society. This has never been the case here. First of all, anthropology has never played an important role in society or, for that matter, in the academy. It has never risen to the same level of academic enterprise as in the West. What we used to have here was simple: the native was just an object, and the relationship with the establishment of one's own society was absolutely unquestioned."

In fact, what Nikishenkov says specifically about anthropology is essentially true for other disciplines in the humanities and social sciences in Russia, regardless of their particularity or social weight. The object of study is just an object of study and it has nothing to do with the relationship between the researcher and his or her social environment. In turn, this

---

[31] Alexei Elfimov, "Razmyshlenia o sud'bakh nauki," p.19.

relationship between the researcher and his or her social environment is rarely questioned as such, for it is assumed that it brings no influence to bear on the study of that abstract object which is presumed to be securely separated from the inquirer. Furthermore, the questioning of this relationship is often merely thought to impede the objectivity of research. It has to be admitted that there are, undoubtedly, an increasing number of Russian scholars who break with this sort of understanding of things and try to promote ideals of reflective scholarship in the humanities and social sciences, but at this point they are far from being a majority or even an influential group in any sense. The overall paradigm of understanding and practicing social research in the last decade by and large rested on the premises and habits described above.

On the positive side, within the last decade, several attempts have been made to establish new and more efficient institutional structures in the humanities, such as interdisciplinary research centers at universities, local collaborative networks, various working groups and sections at research institutes, and so on. These experimental structures were meant (not in every case, but still, I believe, in many cases) to free academic scholarship from the unchanging rigid constraints imposed on professors and students by the dogmas of disciplinary bureaucratism. Some of such attempts paralleled – most, in fact, simply followed – the example of interdisciplinary developments in the Western humanities in the 1980s and 1990s. Due to the lack of financing, or simply proper organization or enthusiasm, not many of these interdisciplinary ventures have managed to survive, but nevertheless some have been successful. For instance, the Marc Bloch Center for Historical Anthropology, established at the Russian State University for the Humanities, from the very beginning proved to be an effective interdepartmental structure that stimulated research both on the part of professors and that of graduate students.

Perhaps the most notable of these developments, however, has been the institutionalization of the new discipline in the humanities, so-called *culturology* [*kul'turologiia*], which has loosely approximated the model of Cultural Studies in the US. Initially, culturology was conceived precisely as an academic discipline that was supposed to liberate research in the humanities and social sciences from the narrow disciplinary constraints by allowing for a unified holistic approach to the study of social phenomena. At the time when culturology was on the eve of its formal disciplinary institutionalization, and perhaps for some time after it, there was a due excitement around it and many scholars were in anticipation of some novelty and invigoration in research trends. However, very soon it became rather obvious that the intellectual production coming out of culturology departments was clearly falling short of expectations. The promised, or at any rate anticipated, disciplinary synthesis was not occurring in culturological works, the social sciences as such were absent from culturology's field of vision, and the discussion was primarily centered on philosophical issues of various kinds. Having hardly impressed scholars both of conservative and liberal orientations, culturology did not permanently settle in many schools of humanities and social sciences at universities, and instead was implemented largely in what was called "pedagogical institutes,"[32] as well as in some of the schools of natural sciences, where it was read as a foundation course.

Despite the specific manner of its institutionalization, culturology nevertheless succeeded in drawing surprisingly solid support from the government and various foundations. During the 1990s, publications in culturology were proliferating with a substantial degree of success (at least, in terms of the number of copies published, if not copies sold), although some

---

[32] Pedagogical institutes [*pedagogicheskii institut*] were a widespread kind of higher-education institution in the Soviet Union, and they were intended basically for preparing high school teachers, unlike universities which implied higher standards of education and therefore were meant to provide intellectual forces for advanced levels of the academy. During the 1990s, almost all pedagogical institutes in Russia were renamed "pedagogical universities" for prestige purposes, but the sense of the pedagogical university being secondary to the "original" academic university by and large remained.

scholars skeptically remarked that, "books in which the word *culturology* appears in the title or subtitle are normally those you would not want to read."[33] It is true that, in practice, culturology very soon abandoned the ideal of discovering new forms and strategies of inquiry and found a more or less comfortable canonical genre of its own, so that most of the works published in the field around the mid-1990s looked already essentially the same. In 1996, Sergei Sokolovski described the state of culturology in the following way:

> I would not really translate the practice of culturology into what has been known in the West as "cultural studies." In this country, culturology is some kind of cheap philosophy of culture. It is very indistinct, but at the same time terribly systematized and structured. It is one of those echoes of the Hegelian tradition. Recently we have had an odd reaction to Marxism: a rejection of everything related to the issue of class but a complete digestion of the systems approach. It is, if you wish, "total functionalism." All is intended for something; everything determines everything. All we have to do is analyze some parts of the system and reconstruct what is missing. Culturology is an adapted version of Parsons, seasoned with various philosophical exercises that often start with an analysis of the notions of morality, elevated to a global scope, and going back as far as the time of anthropogenesis.[34]

One of the main reasons why culturology was successfully proliferating, despite its growing unpopularity as a scholarly or intellectual endeavor, had to do with the specific category of people who gradually took over the discipline. In most cases, these were former nomenclature academics – that is, rather mediocre scholars with no suitable academic background, but with strong bureaucratic connections both inside and outside the academy. Alexei Nikishenkov, who had happened to teach at one of the culturology departments in the beginning of the 1990s and got a more

---

[33] Alexei Elfimov, "The State of the Discipline in Russia," p.781.
[34] Ibid., p.781.

intimate knowledge of the inside organization of culturology as a discipline, later reflected:

> Culturology was conceived and created by a group of philosophers who were lagging behind all the time and who, I suppose, dreamed about a disciplinary sovereignty of their own. Now, since almost anything could be instituted during perestroika, from universities to academies, they set up a discipline and registered it through all the corridors of academic power. They got tenure-track positions, a tenure council of their own, and so on. It was only long after this discipline was institutionalized from above that people started questioning its status. I did not like the whole thing because, from the very beginning, the process displayed its negative side. Culturology was settling down with great success into the places made vacant by sweeping out Marxist philosophy, scientific communism, the history of the Communist Party, and other such disciplines. The armies of people who used to be related to these disciplines were suddenly renamed "culturologists." They were, in fact, forced to requalify to fit some tracks previously unknown to them. So there was much window dressing involved in the appearance of culturology on the academic stage.[35]

Intellectual failures of culturology that followed its official institutionalization eventually turned the attention of many thinking scholars away from it, and this resulted in a noticeable withdrawal of intellectual resources from the newly established field which lacked such resources, as a matter of fact, from the very beginning. The same professor Nikishenkov, who in the late 1980s had been still enthusiastic about a possibility of taking interdisciplinary perspectives, opened up by culturology, into anthropological research, some five years later stated with regret: "I would not like to identify anthropology with culturology now. Nor would I like to see anthropology going in the direction of culturology anymore. Yes, I had once thought anthropology should go in the direction of cultural studies. I thought it was *culture* that was primarily deserving of the anthropologist's attention, for Soviet anthropology had long been superfluously centered on

---

[35] Alexei Elfimov, "Razmyshlenia o sud'bakh nauki," p.5.

the *ethnos* concept. This preoccupation constricted the intellectual development of the discipline, and so I held on to the idea that anthropology should take cultural studies as its model. But when culturology was officially established as a formal discipline in the late 1980s, supposedly to cover the domain of cultural studies, I began changing my mind."

One of the most commonly heard, and perhaps most sound, criticisms directed toward the field of culturology is that the disciplinary practices of the latter became enclosed within a kind of superfluous holistic genre which made the object of study (that is, "culture") a vague philosophical territory removed from any concrete reality of social life. Viktor Karlov, professor in the School of Humanities at Moscow State University, for example, clearly expressed this disappointment, saying that it was no wonder why culturology was "mainly introduced today at schools for education retraining, or just read as a foundation course." "I saw their curriculum," remarked Karlov, "and must say there are a few interesting things. What they definitely lack is a good knowledge of facts and history. Their courses are very abstract and too general, more like philosophical speculations. To make something interesting out of culturology, one would have to rely on actual facts."[36] Professor Sergei Polyakov, his colleague and co-worker, seconded his thoughts, "Culturology may make spectacular theoretical claims but in fact it does not have a platform of its own. It makes no discoveries of its own and lives as a parasite on the findings of history, sociology, philosophy, and other disciplines. " Sergei Cheshko, similarly, pointed out that culturology had no specific disciplinary vision of its own, despite its claims, and could at best provide a researcher with some insights of general methodological character. "It is mostly philosophers," said Cheshko, "who are fond of cultural studies here and who are trying to present culturology as some sort of superdiscipline. Maybe it is, I do not know. As for me, I would rather regard cultural studies not as a discipline

---

[36] Alexei Elfimov, "The State of the Discipline in Russia," p.781.

but as an approach or strategy that may be employed by any discipline in order to study various phenomena of culture, in the broadest sense of the term. You know that there are many notions of what culture is and that culture is studied by a variety of disciplines, including anthropology, history, sociology, and others. So it seems to me that an attempt to establish culturology as just another discipline is quite meaningless."[37]

Opinions of this sort are generally shared today by many scholars in the humanities and social sciences. In any case, it is clear that culturology, being successfully institutionalized as an independent discipline, did not fulfill its intellectual promise as an interdisciplinary research program. Yet, it should be acknowledged that culturology, as a general educational program delivered in the form of foundation courses to college students, perhaps represents a positive development on a broader social scale. Leading scholars usually have rather high demands and therefore tend to focus their attention on matters of advanced research, often disregarding general education matters. At the same time, as Mikhail Epstein, noted Russian literary critic and one of the early promoters of culturology (now living and teaching in the US) points out, "culturology long remained a blank spot on the map of the Russian humanities. What was termed the 'theory of culture' in the Soviet Union was taught to future librarians and club workers: the theory of political management of cultural affairs and the administrative organization of its institutions."[38] The replacement of that utilitarian administrative approach to the subject of culture in the area of general education with a more interesting approach offered by culturology can be perhaps seen as a long needed step forward.

Epstein himself certainly represents one of the few prominent Russian scholars who remain romantic (in a good sense) about culturology and conceive of it as somewhat of an unrealized potential in the Russian hu-

---

[37] Alexei Elfimov, "Razmyshlenia o sud'bakh nauki," p.14.
[38] Mikhail N. Epstein, *After the Future* (Amherst: University of Massachusetts Press, 1995), p.284.

manities. He extends the area of culturology to include the work of such Russian and Soviet thinkers as Mikhail Bakhtin, Yuri Lotman, Alexei Losev and Sergei Averintsev, who in their different ways started, in Geertz's expression, to "blur genres" of research. In other words, the foundations for culturology as a particular field of inquiry, in Epstein's opinion, were laid as early as in the times of the Soviet Union, but it could not be formally established as an academic discipline at the time because of the reactionary nature of the encompassing social and cultural attitude. "The fact that culturology could not exert a tangible influence on the development of 'Soviet culture'," writes Epstein, "reflected the latter's arrogance and one-dimensionality. Official culture resisted intimate scrutiny or comparison with other cultures, claiming for itself a kind of superhistorical and supercultural status. It failed to develop the need or capacity for self-reflection, and it is precisely this that constitutes culturology."[39] Although Epstein's diagnosis in regard to "Soviet culture" seems to be certainly perceptive, his views about what is to constitute culturology as a discipline and field at the present moment remain rather idealistic, for culturology has already happened as a discipline and field, and it has been constituted according to different practices and ideas.

Perhaps the only idea, among from those envisaged by Epstein as vital for culturology, that has been actually whole-heartedly adopted by culturology but strangely led to its growing unpopularity, is the already mentioned universalistic or holistic framework of the discipline. Culturology, unlike the field of Cultural Studies in the West, argued Epstein, is an "indivisible discipline that cannot be reduced to a number of special studies." Its object of study is ultimately "culture as the *integral* system of various cultures." "This integral area," reasoned Epstein, "requires specialization in its initial stages, but at the present point in time, we must have *specialists in the universal*."[40] The intuition about the needs of the present moment per-

---

[39] Mikhail N. Epstein, *After the Future*, p.285.
[40] Ibid., p.284–85.

haps failed Epstein this time, for what he proclaimed as a "must-have" was in fact already had in abundance – namely, specialists in the universal without any knowledge of the particular, who actually made culturology so unpopular among many professors and students in the humanities in Russia during the 1990s. Indeed, how could such specialists provide a "reflective comparison with other cultures" – an essential constituent, and in fact basis, for a true culturology, in Epstein's reasonable opinion – if other cultures were not even known, leave alone their own culture which was known not much better? What was needed for such purpose was a critical anthropological eye that could register and expose images from actual lives of "others" and "ourselves," and thus provide effective grounds for cultural juxtaposition and comparison. Culturologists, the infamous "specialists in the universal," on the contrary, learned only to speak of "culture" as an abstract unified whole that did not refer to any culture in particular. Most of the comparisons that culturologists would typically draw were those between national literary and philosophical traditions of the nineteenth century, with rare excursions into the realm of social sciences of the early twentieth century.

If one should take as an example a seminal text *Kul'turologiia* [Culturology], which was written by Pavel Gurevich, Russian academician with many distinctions, and published by *Znanie* [Knowledge], one of the biggest Russian (and formerly Soviet) scholarly publishing houses, one will be indeed surprised at the virtual absence of anything related to the second half of the twentieth century.[41] With the exception of three briefly cited works by Claude Lévi-Strauss, Daniel Bell, and Peter Berger, which appeared in the early 1960s, the entire text is based on the comparison of Russian and European literary and philosophical traditions of the nineteenth and the beginning of the twentieth centuries. The issue of "contemporary culture," for instance, is discussed through the comparison of

---

[41] P. S. Gurevich, *Kul'turologiia* (Moscow: Znanie, 1996).

Daniel Bell's views with the views of nineteenth-century German philosopher Windelband. The issue of nationalism, strangely enough, is demonstrated through the comparison of ideas of Nikolai Berdiaev, Russian nineteenth-century philosopher, with those of Erich Fromm. Other names, scattered throughout the book and called upon to exemplify various problems of culture, include again mostly nineteenth-century Russian and European philosophers, such as Soloviev, Chaadaev, Spengler, Toynbee, Cassirer, Taine, etc.

The understanding of "culture" within the genre of culturology therefore typically rests on the so-called great literary canons of the Victorian age. Very often, though, even these great literary canons are poorly understood and largely misrepresented in culturological works. Any more or less intelligent reader, for instance, would be puzzled to learn from the opening passages of Gurevich's text that culture is a phenomenon that nobody has even ever inquired into:

> What is culture? This question should have since long time ago troubled the humankind, which considers itself a cultured humankind. Strangely enough, in the world literature nobody posed this question or, as a matter of fact, tried to answer it.[42]

In view of such statements, one should not be surprised after all by the unflattering labels frequently attached to culturology by critically minded scholars, who say that "books in which the word *culturology* appears in the title or subtitle are normally those you would not want to read." It may be also noticed that sometimes even those who work and write in the general genre of culturology prefer to avoid the word because of its ambiguous popularity and connotations, and replace it instead with an alternative term. For example, philosophy professor Leonid Yonin, who published what may be considered a typical textbook in culturology, chose to entitle the

---

[42] P. S. Gurevich, *Kul'turologiia*, p.21.

book "The Sociology of Culture."[43] (What is more, he even took the trouble to define the scope of "sociology of culture" as distinct from culturology's.) Although the book is a more knowledgeable and somewhat better researched account than the above mentioned work by Gurevich, it manifests the same preoccupation with the philosophical traditions of the nineteenth century and delivers very little information on the actual issues of contemporary culture.

Thus, even in the genre of culturology, which is (or, at any rate, was) thought of as liberating academic scholarship from the rigid disciplinary constraints of the traditional system of Soviet/Russian humanities, one can observe clear traces of the same encompassing paradigm of "history and culture" that has so powerfully influenced the framing of the contemporary intellectual discourse in Russia. "Culture" as an object of the humanities is, again and again, predominantly associated with the intellectual achievement of the past epochs, not with an actual variety of forms of social life in the present world. At the time when the issue of cultural diversity is becoming increasingly significant and problematic in the landscape of Russian politics and social order, it still attracts surprisingly little intellectual attention, which keeps on wandering in the enchanted spiritual lands of the past.

The fact that even younger scholars who wish to keep in touch with the latest developments in the Western humanities often fall into the same intellectual trap of the past is also in some ways explained by the dire lack of translations and publications of contemporary scholarship and critical literature in the humanities and social sciences. Access to original foreign language publications remains extremely limited in Russia. Such publications, which during the Soviet time were received by few libraries and generally were a subject to restricted use, turned out to be too expensive for libraries to handle when they were cut short of financial support as a

---

[43] L. G. Yonin, *Sotsiologia kul'tury* (Moscow: Logos, 1996).

result of the infamous privatization program in the early 1990s. In fact, most academic libraries stopped ordering not just foreign editions, but many important domestic publications as well. Furthermore, they started to sell off their own collections – sometimes officially, sometimes "under the table" – in order to support their staff.[44] Interlibrary loans, too, ceased functioning as such and were eventually closed in many libraries during the 1990s because of the same insufficient financial support and the general unreliability of Russian postal services. By the mid-1990s, for instance, the humanities library of Moscow State University was no longer accepting interlibrary loan requests and, as a matter of fact, was open just for some five hours a day during the weekdays only.

Acquaintances with the developments in the Western humanities, thus, were mostly occurring through some random books and journals brought from abroad by scholars who had a chance to attend a conference in the West or travel to another country for other academic or non-academic reasons. Sergei Sokolovski recalled:

> Last time, when I was fortunate to attend a conference in Seattle, I brought back with me two sacks of books. They were so heavy that I had to pay an overweight charge. But what can you do? You cannot order these books from Russia. Even if you could, the chances they would reach you are still remote, for everything valuable somehow tends to get lost in our mail.

Olga Vainshtein, similarly, points out that the lack of translated works, as well as the unavailability of original ones, makes teaching in the humanities a task both difficult and unproductive because the professor, under the circumstance, basically takes on the role of an interpreter and students have to rely solely on her word as they have no access to any sources of information themselves. "I was reading a course on recent theoretical debates and new directions of study in the humanities," says Vainshtein,

---

[44] See, for example: M. M. Samokhina, "Gumanitarizatsia obrazovania: vzgliad iz biblioteki," *Chelovek*, no.4 (1996).

"and I had to base it, for example, on the book *Redrawing the Boundaries*, edited by Stephen Greenblatt. Of course, I knew that many other books of the kind existed, but I just happened to have this one. In what I did, therefore, one could see is a simple mission of a cultural interpreter, for in a sense I was merely popularizing some Western ideas and delivering them to the students in an understandable form, trying to provide as much useful context as I could."

Alexei Nikishenkov, who has been reading for a decade courses on the history of Western anthropology, says, "Current works in anthropology are not translated, nor are available to the students in the original language (very often to the faculty either), so the professor has to play the role of a storyteller. This role does not appeal to me personally because it evokes the old canonical practice of teaching that makes a student a passive listener. But, I think, fortunately for my course, we have at least a few translations of the older works by Boas, Lévi-Strauss, Evans-Pritchard and Victor Turner, otherwise I would have had no readings to assign in my class."

During the 1990s, there were random attempts to translate some of the older works by major European philosophers; and by the very end of the decade, a number of more coherent initiatives were undertaken to launch specialized series of scholarly translations. The result, however, was somewhat mixed and in some ways even discouraging, as Olga Vainshtein observed, because "most of what was translated were not major works but minor essays and review articles," and because the "quality of translations, with few exceptions, was very poor." She commented:

> It is wonderful that *Gnosis* publishers recently came up with a collection of Lacan's essays in Russian. However, I do not understand why none of the major essays was included in the book. Same with Jacques Derrida's work. Several minor articles have been translated, while seminal works, such as *Of Grammatology* or *Writing and Difference*, remain unavailable, many years after they were published in the West. As for the recent collection of Bataille's essays, it provoked a harsh review which demonstrated that the editor–translator was not even familiar with some of the major Bataille's writings. This situation

has a rather bizarre effect in that all these names, Foucault, Lacan, Derrida, and others, in the absence of actual works translated, turn into a kind of unreflexive and superficial academic slang which becomes increasingly fashionable among the students.

It should be acknowledged that, within the past few years, the situation with translations has somewhat improved, and some of the landmarks of scholarly thought of the last quarter of the twentieth century, such as Derrida's mentioned *Of Grammatology* and *Writing and Difference*, have been recently translated. Several of the series launched at the end of the 1990s continue to develop (albeit not as dynamically as one might wish). However, there is still a complaint, frequently heard from the scholars who happened to read such works in the original language, that the quality of translations leaves much to be desired and often does not withstand any criticism (that is, theoretical or conceptual terms are often rendered in a distorted way, stylistic features are ignored to the extent that the translated work looks like a book written in a genre different from the original, and so on). This, of course, has to do not only with translators' skills, but also with the already discussed "language conservatism" in the academy – that is, the hostile attitude toward the new conceptual vocabulary that emerged in the humanities and social sciences within the last quarter of the twentieth century. Due to particularities of employment trends, the editorial staff at academic publishing houses in many cases remains composed of those intellectuals (typically with a background in Russian philology) who are profoundly permeated with this attitude.

However, even if we leave translations flaws aside and recognize an increase – indeed, a welcome increase – in the number of important works translated and published, we still have to pinpoint an unfortunate tendency that has for long time distinguished the scholarly publishing business in Russia and the Soviet Union (especially in the humanities and social sciences). Works that are being currently translated and published are usually already thirty or more years old. Scholars, thus, are invited to participate in a discourse that is, in a way, considered passé. As a Russian proverb has it, "a spoon is brought to the table when the dinner is over." Works that are being discussed in the West today remain again largely an unknown territory.

Svetlana Levit, editor of one of the most interesting and successful series of translations in the humanities, says, "What is taking place today is the process of catching up. We are currently publishing the literature that should have been published thirty years ago. The lag is obvious. Look what we are releasing: Erich Auerbach in literary criticism, Malinowski in anthropology, Raymond Aron in philosophy, and I do not even want to mention Dilthey or Cassirer. These are great and important works, but it seems that, if we continue at the same pace, we will get to publishing works of the 1990s at best by the year 2020. Actually, we are very much interested in translating contemporary works, but part of the problem is that Western publishers usually set for such works copyright fees that turn out absolutely prohibitive for us." Svetlana Anikeeva, director of the *Vostochnaia Literatura* academic publishers in Moscow, expresses a very similar view, "We prefer – actually, we simply *have* – to deal with works written in the 1970s or earlier. Fees for the translation of such works are reasonable. If it is anything more recent, publishers tend to set terms that are unacceptable to us." Alexei Moiseev, editor of the *Akademicheskii Proekt* publishers, says essentially the same, "Copyright fees are unreasonable. We are not a high-profit corporation and book prices are different here too. Had we to pay their fee, we would have to price a book at $30 or so, to recover the expense. But who could buy such a book if academic wages in Russia are $50 per month?"

In a word, for a variety of reasons, the pattern of publishing outdated literature in the humanities is somehow reproduced in Russia, and most of the works that are currently in the focus of intellectual attention in the West remain unknown or at any rate unavailable to Russian scholars. Unfortunately, this is true in respect not only to the works that are *currently* in the focus of intellectual attention, but very often also to the works that were in the focus of attention yesterday. The discourse of humanities and social sciences in Russia for the most part refers to the works that had been in the center of attention in the West the day before yesterday. This situation – the time lag and highly irregular character of access to, and therefore familiarity with, the contemporary developments in the Western humanities and social sciences – has had a harmful effect on the intercultural circulation of ideas. This, in turn, has become a channel of many academic misunderstandings in Russia. As Bourdieu argued in his *Homo Academicus*, the international circulation of academic ideas is always characterized to one or another extent by the specific pattern, "where texts are transmitted without the context of their production and use, and count on receiving a so-called 'internal' reading which universalizes and eternalizes them while derealizing them by constantly relating them to the sole context of their reception."[45] In the Russian academic environment of the 1980s–90s, this pattern of judging foreign texts on purely internal domestic criteria, without any regard to the context of their production, was magnified and, being coupled with the Slavophile moods, led to the proliferation of a hostile and essentially uncritical attitude toward the contemporary Western scholarship. The multiplying instances of misrepresentation of the latter distinctively marked discourses in virtually all disciplines in the Russian humanities and social sciences of the period. In the discourse of anthropology and sociology, for example, it became a standard practice to speak of the Western disciplinary tradition as being under the negative influence of "postmodern methodology," although none of the authors who criticized what they understood by the "postmodern" were able to provide a remotely consistent account of the subject or even name proper works or authors that might be related to it. For instance, Professor S. A. Shandybin in his long essay entitled "Postmodern Anthropology and the Realm of Applicability

---

[45] Pierre Bourdieu, *Homo Academicus* (Stanford: Stanford University Press, 1988): xv.

of Its Cultural Model" typically brings up for discussion an odd mixture of very different, and indeed having little to do with "postmodern anthropology" per se, Western authors, such as philosophers Zygmunt Bauman and Richard Rorty, French sociologist Pierre Bourdieu, and anthropologists Stephen Gudeman and Allan Hanson.[46]

Another prominent senior Russian anthropologist, Yuri Semenov, who censures all contemporary anthropology in the West as totally permeated with postmodernism, cannot name but a single work to support his criticism, which in the end unfortunately happens to be the book that has already become a standard target for all kinds of academic allegations – that is, *Writing Culture*. "The proliferation of postmodernist concepts in the Western anthropology," says Semenov, "is the manifestation of the crisis it is undergoing. The essence of the postmodernist approach consists in denying the objectivity of facts and objective truth and, therefore, science as such ... All these concepts found their expression in the most salient form in the collection of essays, characteristically entitled *Writing Culture*."[47] Another Russian scholar, V. R. Rokitianskii, in his article "What Is to Be Expected From Postmodern Ethnography?" similarly bases all his criticism of the idea of postmodernism on the discussion of the same volume *Writing Culture*, torn out of the context, largely misunderstood, and judged against the reality of Russian cultural problems.[48]

New areas of study and research approaches, which in the 1990s found their way into the humanities and social sciences in Russia with extreme difficulties, are still often treated as half-welcome in many disciplines and institutions. Undoubtedly, there are isolated scholars who are actually interested in raising the standards of scholarship to the level meeting the needs of the present moment, but they can be considered an excep-

---

[46] S. A. Shandybin, "Postmodernistskaia antropologiia i sfera primenimosti eio kul'turnoi modeli," *Etnograficheskoe obozrenie*, no.1 (1998).

[47] Y. I. Semenov, "Predmet etnografii (etnologii) i osnovnye sostavliayushchie eio nauchnye distsipliny," p.14.

tion rather than the rule. The general pattern of social and cultural studies, as well as the institutional infrastructure of the academy in Russia, remains dominated by the inflexibility, inertia, and traditionalism which impede the development of research trends. The situation is very often perfectly understood by younger scholars who keenly feel both the discursive and bureaucratic limitations that are imposed on the actual dimensions of scholarly research. Aleksandr Saltykov was very clear on the subject in his interview: "If clever people come to the Ministry of Education (which is highly unlikely), loosen up our terribly centralized educational system, and remove that bureaucratic excrescence from all our academic institutions so that creative people, rather than all these old nannies, could be welcome there, then we can expect a certain change in the intellectual discourse. But as long as it goes the way it goes, nothing will change. I mean, there will be no discourse as such. What discourse? Scholars from neighboring universities in this country never talk to each other, nor even about each other, except in disparaging terms. Discussion, you know, is an event that is not specifically particular to our academic climate. So, the academic community here can hardly make what you call critical intelligentsia. It is not even a "community," for that matter, it is just a conglomerate of separate individuals who do not want to deal with each other. I really wish this could be different. I hope it will be in due course, when the entrenched group of academics finally retire and a younger generation of scholars come to set their own rules. But, you see, the problem is, younger people somehow tend to leave the academy, and those who leave are not particularly excited about returning. So, I guess, there is not much hope to put on the younger generation either."[49]

Some of the more insightful professors in the humanities would actually second Saltykov's opinion, despite its seemingly extreme negativity

---

[48] V. R. Rokitianskii, "Chego zhdat' ot postmodernistskoi etnografii?", pp.73–93.
[49] Alexei Elfimov, "Academics and the Production of an Intellectual Discourse of Modernity in Russia," p.250.

toward the professorial staff of the academy. Alexei Nikishenkov, for example, in a similar way connected the stagnant state of the humanities to the general paradigm of uncritical scholarship, by and large maintained in the Russian academy. "This paradigm," stated Nikishenkov, "does not let young scholars grow. They like to undertake ventures into new and unusual terrains and it is understandable that the first results of their attempts may be not always perfect – that's why they need encouragement and support from us, professors. What they get instead is usually censure and disapproval, which induce frustrated feelings and often make them lose their interest in the matter." Nikishenkov continued:

> I remember that when a former graduate student of mine, Lena Miskova, proposed a field study of a Siberian people, based on conceptual premises of Western interpretive anthropology, her dissertation project immediately aroused strong skepticism among the faculty and the chair of the department even told her that it was not worth going to the field for that kind of research. Fortunately, she was not discouraged enough and still decided to pursue the project. But many people do get discouraged. Another graduate student in our department, who studied the impact of feminist movement on anthropology, was advised to change her dissertation topic to something more traditional and acceptable, which she eventually did. Or take as an example still another former graduate of ours, Siberian ethnographer Golovnev who has recently published a study of the peoples of the North, in which he has employed a defamiliarization strategy, borrowed from the recent Western anthropological works. He has been immediately censured by our ethnographic authorities as "postmodernist," although I detect nothing particularly postmodern in his work – he just tried to employ a proper technique to understand and represent another culture.

Sergei Sokolovski, in the same vein, recalled, "They branded me as a postmodernist every time I made a positive comment about contemporary Western anthropology, even though I thought I often wrote pretty standard things that were commonsensical in nature. Besides, I certainly do not like everything about Western anthropology. All the same, one of my previous essays, in which I compared ethnographic practices at home and abroad, had been rejected for nearly five years by the editorial board of the Institute of Ethnology and Anthropology at the Academy of Sciences, before they finally published it."[50]

In a word, one of the most distinctive traits that characterized the academic community in the humanities in Russia of the past decade was the unwillingness to acknowledge the emergence of new cultural realities and to legalize new intellectual interests stemming from those realities and spreading among a growing number of scholars and students. Very unfortunately, this trait is still the case today. It continues to constrict the intellectual potential of the humanities; and, as Nikishenkov points out, it also makes them closed to the issue of reproduction of cultural values, which for some reason appears to the larger community of academics as an insoluble predicament or a threat of some coming crisis. Nikishenkov elaborates: "This issue is now discussed everywhere, to the point that it has become commonplace. If you want to ask me what the humanities do in regard to the issue, I will answer, 'Nothing.' The humanities are simply not ready to handle it. They can only talk about it in the same manner that millenarian prophets talk about the end of the world. This might be of some healthy apocalyptic importance; I am not denying that. But it is silly to think that the priest could actually *cause* the rain; at best he might *guess* when the rain was about to start. Cultural values *are* constantly reproduced, and *new* cultural values constantly come into existence. The humanities would really do their best if they attempted to track this process and verbalize what is going on instead of plunging into eschatology. New values and new meanings are already out there, but we are still not ready to perceive them, having stuck to the old language. I think this is the most important task academics should attend to.[51]

---

[50] Sokolovski refers to his essay, "Etnograficheskie issledovaniia: ideal i deistvitel'nost'" [Ethnographic Research: Ideals and Practice], *Etnograficheskoe obozrenie*, no.3 (1993).

[51] Alexei Elfimov, "Academics and the Production of an Intellectual Discourse of Modernity in Russia," p.251.

The view that the humanities should follow the development of cultural reality, adapting their language to new conditions, however, remains largely unpopular among the majority of academics who are accustomed to seeing in the humanities a kind of exact analytical science which transcends cultural reality and exists independently of it. The underlying assumption that the sort of cultural reality that does not fit into the analytical framework of the humanities simply does not exist is in fact rather widespread in the academic thinking. An idea that the object of study might alter the analytical framework of a discipline is often seen as absolutely unacceptable. The choice of the object of study, therefore, remains in many instances heavily influenced by particular disciplinary dogmas; consequently, those objects that are considered as inappropriate for the humanities to analyze are typically filtered out and rejected as "not scientifically relevant." Sokolovski, reflecting on the issue as it stood in Russian anthropology, observed:

> Ethnic space is literally conceived as physical or geographical (we have all these manifold ethnic maps of peoples distribution). Since scholars are accustomed to thinking of ethnic space in this way, they believe that to get immersed in ethnography, one simply has to move physically over a certain distance. "Now I am going to take a plane, land in Chechnya, and there I am in the field!" In other words, one cannot walk to a Moscow bazaar market and find oneself in the field. This is not appropriate. One cannot describe the "New Russians" as an ethnographic group. This is not appropriate either. One cannot go study the businessmen. No, one should fly across the country to get to the Yukaghirs.[52]

The object of study that threatens to alter the analytical framework of a discipline is frequently understood simply as a potential danger. Yuri Semenov, already mentioned distinguished scholar at the Russian Academy of Sciences, openly declares in one of his latest articles, published in the

---

[52] Alexei Elfimov, "Razmyshlenia o sud'bakh nauki," p.9.

main Russian anthropological journal *Etnograficheskoe obozrenie*, that the proliferation of "alternative" objects of study in the research area of contemporary anthropology makes the discipline essentially "unscientific." "Western social anthropologists," writes Semenov, "have started to deal with all kinds of exotic groups of people, including homosexuals and lesbians. This trend, which could be called Western social neo-anthropology, is becoming increasingly dominant. The noted degradation that marks many Western anthropological periodicals today has to do with this as well ... It is precisely this Western social neo-anthropology (not necessarily in its postmodern version) that has become an object of adoration among many of our countrymen who think of themselves as scientists, but who in reality are far from any authentic science, especially ethnology."[53]

The fear that new objects of study could disturb an authoritative "authentic" canon of science is a common phenomenon in the Russian academy of nowadays. The status of the humanities as such continues to be anxiously equated with that of exact sciences, despite half a century of critique of such position, labeled by Evans-Pritchard as early as in the 1960s as "academic snobbery." Attempts to rethink academic practices in a cardinal way are still rare and not potent enough to bring influence to bear on larger strata of the academic profession in the humanities, especially at the time when the general interest in the humanities as such has been declining on the broader social scale. Nevertheless, as the worst oddities of the transition period seem to be slowly receding into the past, a growing number of scholars – who, unfortunately, until now have been in the minority – are beginning to think that the situation shows certain signs of improvement, and to hold to optimistic positions. The essence of such positions has been succinctly summarized by Olga Vainshtein: "I have no doubt that after a while all things will fall into their places. Despite a variety of negative things that could be said about the present state of our humanities, there are

---

[53] Y. I. Semenov, "Predmet etnografii (etnologii) i osnovnye sostavliayushchie eio nauchnye distsipliny." p.14.

signs that indicate a positive tendency as well. New interdisciplinary areas of knowledge find their way to our universities – and this is natural, for it is felt by many that traditional disciplines, like history, philology, or anthropology, are tired of their own subject. Cross-disciplinary cooperation and exchange of knowledge are now seen by an increasing number of scholars as perhaps the most interesting potential the humanities can take advantage of ... And so, speaking about the task of academics, I think it is one of critically rethinking the new cultural and informational space, in which we found ourselves in the nineties, and establishing new rules for the humanities that would allow for an intelligent scholarly dialogue. This would involve many things, like the training of a new generation of teachers in the humanities, not just students, who could competently navigate the cultural space of modernity, being proficient in languages and computer technologies, as well as the reforming of the old institutional structure of the humanities. Which is, I guess, more than enough to cope with."[54]

---

[54] Alexei Elfimov, "Academics and the Production of an Intellectual Discourse of Modernity in Russia," p.251–52.

Conclusion

Russian intellectual culture, as I have tried to argue in the preceding chapters, has been for long time obsessed with the subject of the past. The particularities of social development in the late Soviet Union and post-perestroika Russia pushed this obsession to the limits that could be called without much of an exaggeration extreme. The necessity of reference to the past as a zone of cultural ideals, cultural values, and cultural identification assumed utmost importance in the intellectual thinking. Moreover, it constituted a distinctive paradigm in the intellectual consciousness, which gradually spread its influence over a wide range of social discourses and sectors, from the academic discourse and general education in the humanities and social sciences to politics, city planning, and even business. I am certain that it is impossible to render a correct view of the intellectual atmosphere in Russia of the last quarter of the twentieth century without specifically focusing on this general paradigm in intellectual thinking and on what, in broader terms, I tried to describe as the cultural predicament of modernity.

The main goal that I was trying to accomplish in this account consisted in delineating the basic contours of that cultural paradigm, in demonstrating it as a distinctive and important issue, and in suggesting it as a useful conceptual framework for the discussion of late Soviet and contemporary Russian intellectual culture. Up to date, indeed, there have been very few works in which this issue has been raised or reflected upon in a more or less consistent manner. Some of the more insightful scholars, such as, for example, Viacheslav Ivanov or Boris Kagarlitsky, touch on the issue in passing in the essays that have been quoted in the preceding chapters; but, on the whole, authors dealing with the subject of academic and intellectual culture in post-perestroika Russia tend to dismiss the issue. If many Western authors usually simply pass by the issue, attaching no special conceptual importance to it, many Russian authors typically do not notice its presence for reasons of a different nature. That is to say, the noted paradigm of cultural consciousness escapes from their view by and large because many intellectuals continue to be dominated by it, or perhaps because in one's own culture some things are just taken for granted. A particular feature (whether unfortunate or fortunate) of Russian intellectual life, it has to be mentioned, is that those few reflexively thinking scholars who have a deeper understanding of cultural environment around them mostly do not write books.

"We do not necessarily proclaim loudly the most important thing we have to say," said once Walter Benjamin. This kind of principle is precisely what, for better or worse, many Russian intellectuals hold to. For a researcher who undertakes an inquiry into particularities of the intellectual discourse in such cultural milieu, this situation poses a problem, which is both methodological and interpretive in character, because the most important things that people have to say often remain unsaid or omitted in the official discourse. This is why, as I mentioned in the introduction, the anthropological involvement in the everyday appears to be a more effective method for analyzing such essentially "unanthropological" subject as intellectual discourse.

The arguments that I made in the course of the present work, therefore, are in many ways based on the interpretation of a variety of "important things" that are not pronounced loudly but nevertheless shared, so to speak, on a sub-discursive level among many intellectuals. I believe, furthermore (at any rate, hope), that my conclusions would be shared by many interesting people with whom I had a chance to work in Russia. Some of the ideas that I pursue are actually part of everyday knowledge among these scholars and intellectuals, but the problem is exactly that that everyday knowledge is rarely explicated or conceptualized in academic works.

Still, a number of academics in Russia would probably object to my view of the development and predicaments of intellectual discourse in the late Soviet and contemporary Russian society. This is inevitable because the ideals of the intelligentsia remain by and large marked by the fear of the process of social modernization and by the aesthetics of cultural conservation, which have been analyzed in the course of this work. Every month in Russia of nowadays brings new examples that support the main statements made in the preceding chapters. For instance, just a few years ago, a group of Russian academics decided to submit to the Duma (infamous Russian parliament) a draft of a federal law that would legalize the notorious language cleansing (which had been traditionally a dream of many conservative Soviet/Russian intellectuals) and establish the rules of using "pure Russian," with the aim of cleaning the language of the litter of modern jargon and bringing it back to the classic nineteenth-century norms. As the English newspaper *The Times* commented, "Taking a stand against the Americanisation of the language of Tolstoy, Chekhov and Turgenev, the proposed law will limit the use of the unnecessary foreign words which arrived in Russia with the first 'Beeg Mac i fraiz' and have increasingly infected the language ever since."[1] "At the Marina Tsvetayeva museum this week," the article continued, "a photograph of the poet looked sadly down on the assembled Russian literature lovers whose society had brought them together to discuss the desperate state of their language." It is needless to repeat at this point that the state of the language is seen as "desperate" by these intellectuals precisely because the language has made a certain progress, has adapted to the new social reality, and has become too modern to their taste – the taste which is still determined by the encompassing cultural paradigm of the past, history, and moral heritage. (That particular attempt to institute "language cleansing" failed, but another one has been recently made again – fortunately, to no success.)

---

[1] Anna Blundy, "Russia Battles To Purge Language of Foreign Invaders," *The Times* (November 7, 1998).

Infatuation with an array of themes pertaining to "old aristocracy," "bourgeoisie," "nobility," which on some level are still necessarily equated with "old architecture," "estates," "salons," and other traditional objects of intellectual daydreaming, continues to mark the moment in various social spheres from the artistic milieu and the humanities to politics and business. In November 2000, for example, St. Petersburg media announce the opening of a new intellectual elite club "Bourgeoisie" (*Burzhuaziia*) – just another "pseudo-intellectual salon" with a sadly predictable name, which in essence is a poor attempt at self-fashioning by a group of unsuccessful poets, journalists and painters – that is, those intellectuals who are anything but bourgeoisie in Russia of the twenty first century, but who, uninterestingly and trivially, keep desperately pursuing this self-image. Of course, it is not remembered anymore that progressively minded avant-garde artists of the old Russia were consciously anti-bourgeois in their worldview. The intellectuals of the new Russia do not want to be social critics, they want to be bourgeoisie. Scholars in the humanities, as has been pointed out before, are frequently no exception. Unlike their more straightforward colleagues from the artistic milieu, however, they tend to camouflage their ambitions and imaginaries and keep them disguised under the veil of "neutral" academic discourse. The tradition, criticized by one of my interlocutors as a hypocritical game of the intellectuals pretending to be after the truth but in fact striving after dachas in Peredelkino, did not end with the perestroika period. The campaign after the fashionable suburban estate still manifests itself in the emergence of such organizations as *OIRU* (Society for the Study of the Russian Aristocratic Estate). *OIRU* was created (again, allegedly, it was *restored* 70 years after it had been discontinued by the Soviet regime) in 1993 as a scholarly organization with its own periodical edition *Russkaia usad'ba* (Russian Estate). Indeed, some of the articles and materials placed in the journal were of scholarly interest, but if one were to judge from multiple editorial columns, comments, and notes, one could not help getting an impression that the principal activity of the society during

Self-fashioning of the elites as "aristocracy," "nobility," or "bourgeoisie." Restaurant and casino club "Crown" (*Korona*) in the center of Moscow. The giant symbol of the royal crown, coated with shiny golden strips, speaks for itself and is perfectly visible from any part of the New Arbat avenue. (Photo by the author, 2000)

the first five years of its existence consisted in organizing evening parties, entertainment events, and banquets in prestigious estates of the former Russian nobility. The biggest of such banquets, as it was mentioned in the journal, was held in 1998 on the occasion of the birthday of the society's director L. Ivanova.

Meanwhile, the rhetoric of "nobility estate as an object of fashion and prestige" successfully permeated and continues to permeate various business enterprises, especially those related to construction and advertising. In the business sphere, however, the real target of this rhetoric is not intellectuals but wealthier and more influential strata, *de facto* bourgeoisie, who can actually buy such estates, not just rent them for occasional evening

Publicity stand advertising a new elite housing project in the suburbs of Moscow. The text at the top reads, "Pokrovskoe-Glebovo: The Nobility Estate of the Twenty First Century." At the bottom: "Elite apartments in the green suburban zone of Moscow. Apartment complex in the style of the nineteenth-century Russian aristocratic estate is located in the Pokrovskoe-Streshnevo park, on the shore of the Khimki lake." (Photo by the author, 2000)

parties or banquets. The picture above is an example of a typical advertisement of a construction company that draws attention of potential buyers to the cultural appeal of what looks like, or at any rate is represented as, an old Russian aristocratic estate.

The allure of the cultural merger of history and old Russian architecture is understood even in the world of finance. The Central Bank of Russia currently sponsors the printing of a series of commemorative coins, characteristically entitled "Monuments of Old Russian Architecture." In addition, the release of every new coin is usually announced in popular newspapers, such as *Moskovskii komsomolets*, which never hesitate to carve out a precious spot in the *Culture* column for a note about the image of another old Russian monastery embossed on a ruble.[2] Moscow's subway system, *Metro*, explicitly represents itself as having significance in terms of the same already familiar rhetoric of history, architecture, and culture. The opening article of *Metro*'s official rules and regulations, posted in every subway car, states, "*Metro* is one of the main systems of public transportation; many *Metro* stations are considered monuments of history, culture, and architecture, and are protected by the government."[3] (Thus, instead of putting an emphasis, say, on *Metro*'s efficiency – for it is indeed the fastest and the most reliable means of transportation in Moscow – the company administration chooses to emphasize the fact that *Metro* has a historical and cultural value, since this emphasis has a definite edge within the present system of cultural representation.) Furthermore, *Metro* is advertised – at least, it was until very recently – by a curious series of little posters containing memorable lines from various nineteenth-century Russian poets (mostly of Slavophile orientation, which is again a notorious but hardly surprising detail, considering the direct connection between *Metro* and Moscow municipal authorities, noted for their heavy ideological investment in the Slavophile political strategy during Yuri Luzhkov's term in the office of city mayor).

Yet another example of the sort is the Russian internal revenue service, commonly known as the tax police, which recently started to remind citizens of itself with the help of giant city posters depicting the figure of Yuri Dolgorukii, twelfth-century Russian prince who, as the story has it, had once united a number of Slavic provinces engaged in internecine warfare into a powerful feudal kingdom and had been thus responsible for the rise and strengthening of Muscovite Russia. The allegory implied in these posters is, of course, rather straightforward, and perhaps it may be even

---

[2] MK Novosti, "Vypuskaetsia moneta s izobrazheniem Nikolo-Ugreshskogo monastyria," *Moskovskii komsomolets*, no.102 (13 May 2000), p.4.
[3] Pravila pol'zovaniia moskovskim metropolitenom. Postanovlenie mera Moskvy no.553-RM, statia 1.1.

Publicity stand on the notorious *Lubianka* square in Moscow with the tax police poster. The text reads, "Revival of Russia is our common task!" (Photo by the author, 2000)

slightly ironic or humorous by intent (if "humorous" is the word to be applied to the tax police). The name "Dolgorukii" in Russian means "long-armed," and prince Yuri was given this informal name precisely as a result of his far-reaching campaigns ("no one would be able to hide from the reach of his hand" meant this name in the popular imagination). The message that the tax police authorities are trying to convey – namely, that they will reach anybody who tries to hide from them – is thus unambiguous. But this is perhaps not so interesting as the fact that, by its very semiotic design, the message again appeals to the knowledge of history rather than to some civil sentiment in citizens (and, one might add, it conveys a hint of threat or punishment, no matter how ironic, hidden behind the lesson of history). The Slavophile content of the message, as well as the traditional rhetoric of revival (call to revive the old society, rather then to build a new one), is also unmistakable.

There are occasional remarks in the press, pointing out to the fact that the intelligentsia seem a bit tired of the Russian Orthodox card played by the politicians, but they are indeed so infrequent and so unconvincing that the conclusion one might draw from them would be still unambiguous: a few are tired of it, but the majority are fond of it. One of the articles published in the *Itogi* magazine in October 2000 even argued that the historicist trend in contemporary Russian architecture was coming to an end and giving way to a neo-constructivist trend. "Luzhkov's historicism is over," stated the author, "there is a new fashion in Moscow architecture ... which reminds one of Moscow of the 1920s and of the architecture of Russian avant-garde, that is of the constructivism."[4] First of all, it has to be said that the prognosis seems a bit too early. True, quite a few buildings that are considered landmarks of the Soviet constructivism have been restored (again and again, one has to repeat, *restored*) in the recent years, but that does not mean that the new fashion has taken over, nor does it mean that

---

[4] Ivan Ezerskii, "Konstruktivizm v tapochkakh," *Itogi*, no.44 (31 October 2000).

the old one has died. Secondly, even if there is an actual change in fashions under way (which could be only welcomed), it is indeed only a change in fashions, not in the general attitude. The general attitude remains distinctively enclosed within the same paradigm of "culture as history" in intellectual thinking. What this change in fashions would rather mean (if it is the case) is that the epoch of the Soviet constructivism finally has become "old" enough, remote enough on the time scale to qualify for a proper place in history and, therefore, proper cultural acknowledgement. The difference is not in the trend, but just in the object. The interests are still directed toward the restoration of something old that had been created before, not toward the creation of something new that has not yet existed.

In any case, architecture functions here not as a legislator of cultural trends but only as their indicator. Cultural trends, at the same time, are still predominantly regressive and conservative. It is difficult to imagine how this could be otherwise, if in the acting federal law on culture in Russia the term "preservation" meaningfully precedes the term "creativity," and references to "history" and "heritage" define the essence of culture. "Cultural activity," states the opening section of the law, "is the activity dealing with preservation, creation and dissemination of cultural values." Creation is emphatically put second to preservation. "Cultural heritage of the peoples of the Russian Federation," continues the section, "consists of material and spiritual values created in the past, as well as of monuments and historical–cultural areas and objects, important for the preservation and development of the unique achievements of the peoples of the Russian Federation."[5] Everything I was trying to explain in this book seems to be explained in these two passages in a more eloquent and more concise manner.

Those who pay attention to the rhetoric of Russian politicians in their domestic debates may still observe that the coin of the past never loses its currency in their speeches, regardless of the actual political line they fol-

---

[5] Zakon Rossiiskoi Federatsii: Osnovy zakonodatel'stva Rossiiskoi Federatsii o kul'ture. No.115-F3 (23.06.1999), razdel 1, statia 3.

low. This has become much less pronounced (and one can only applaud this) in the political vocabulary used by President Putin. Former President Yeltsin's administration, on the contrary, never learned, nor perhaps ever wanted, to talk to the public in terms of new incentives and kept addressing the nation in terms of a cheap yet appealing motive of returning or regaining all those *matreshkas* that people lost under communism. Anti-Yeltsin forces did not offer a radically different perspective. Gennady Ziuganov, aging leader of the communist bloc, is still trying to convince the public in his manifestoes that "we need to take everything from the past in order to ensure that Russia will move ahead."[6] An article by the Reuters analyst Alastair Macdonald provided an informative comment on Boris Yeltsin's public address on November 7, 1998 (the anniversary of the October Revolution of 1917, which used to be a very important, ideologically colored state holiday during the era of socialism). Summarizing the theme and mood of the speech, in which Yeltsin proudly emphasized his role in putting an end to the period of communist history in Russia, the analyst remarked, "The sight of the tired-looking 67-year-old president, speaking on Saturday from the Black Sea resort of Sochi where he has spent more than a week convalescing from exhaustion, gave the impression that the Yeltsin era may be all but over too. Claiming credit for putting paid to authoritarian communism and installing democracy in Russia, the ailing president sounded to many like a man more concerned with history, and his place in it, than with the problems of the present."[7]

The apt concluding remark of the journalist summarized, in fact, not just the personal ambitions of Boris Yeltsin, but rather the symbolic universe of late twentieth-century Russian intellectual culture in one of its typical manifestations. The culture that is not concerned with the problems of the present and strangely continues to address the future in the subjunc-

---

[6] Gennady Ziuganov, "Obrashchenie k narodu," *Zavtra*, no.6 (February 2000), p.1.
[7] Alastair Macdonald, "Yeltsin 'Revolution' May Be Over," *Analysis* (Reuters, Moscow, November 8, 1998).

tive future-in-the-past tense, indeed, seems to be destined to count the passage of time in some circular motion. As long as modernity as a self-contained integral moment remains alien to the intellectual spirit of the society and the cultural discourse remains largely immersed in the idea of restoring and improving the past, one can predict no visible way or direction along which an actual change in the discussed social spheres, such as education, science, and civil policy, might come. However, a growing number of intellectuals, no matter how few, who are tired of the old discourses, emerge these days in various institutions and try to search for ways of establishing new organizational practices and ideals, appropriate to the needs and interests of the present moment. The search until now has been more often a failure than a success, due to the plentitude of surviving bureaucratic and, what turns out to be no less problematic, *cultural* obstacles. But, still, there are positive developments here and there, and many people prefer to remain optimistic. As one of the interviewed academics put it, "Everywhere there is a hidden potential that can be realized and developed into something valuable ... It is important that people not stop looking for new perspectives and trying out unexpected points of view. You never know where the exciting results might come from."[8]

---

[8] Alexei Elfimov, "The State of the Discipline in Russia," p.785.

Bibliography

Afanas'ev, Iurii. 1995. "Reviving the Humanities in Modern Russia." Pp.255–270 in *Remaking Russia*. Edited by Heyward Isham. Armonk, N.Y.: M. E. Sharpe.

Apenin, Vadim. 1996. "Eto strashnoe slovo *rekonstruktsia* – imenno pod ego prikrytiiem unichtozhaetsia staraia Moskva." *Nezavisimaia gazeta*, no.151, August 16.

Azadovskii, Konstantin. 1995. "Russia's Silver Age, Yesterday and Today." Pp.79–90 in *Remaking Russia*. Edited by Heyward Isham. Armonk, N.Y.: M. E. Sharpe.

Bann, Stephen, ed. 1974. *The Tradition of Constructivism*. New York: Viking.

Basilov, V. N. 1998. "Traditsii otechestvennoi etnografii." *Etnograficheskoe obozrenie*, no.2, pp.18–45.

Benjamin, Walter. 1969 [1940]. "Theses on the Philosophy of History." Pp.253–264 in *Illuminations*, by Walter Benjamin. Edited by Hannah Arendt. New York: Schocken Books.

———. 1986 [1929]. "Surrealism: The Last Snapshot of the European Intelligentsia." Pp.177–192 in *Reflections*, by Walter Benjamin. New York: Schocken Books.

Berdiaev, Nikolai. 1992 [1947]. *The Russian Idea*. Trans. by R. M. French. Hudson, N.Y.: Lindisfarne Press.

Blackburn, Robin, ed. 1991. *After the Fall: The Failure of Communism and the Future of Socialism*. London, New York: Verso.

Bobrova, Natalia. 1996. "Anatolii Grebnev: 'Svoboda prikhodit liubaia'." *Moskovskii komsomolets*, no.149, August 10, p.2.

Bourdieu, Pierre. 1988. *Homo Academicus*. Trans. by Peter Collier. Stanford: Stanford University Press.

Bourdieu, Pierre, and Jean-Claude Passeron. 1977. *Reproduction in Education, Society and Culture*. London: Sage.

Boym, Svetlana. 1994. "The Archeology of Banality: The Soviet Home." *Public Culture* 6, no.2, pp.263–292.

Brichkalevich, Irina. 2000. "V raionnykh upravakh Moskvy sidiat potentsial'nye terroristy." *Moskovskii komsomolets*, no.137, June 26, p.3.

Buck-Morss, Susan. 1989. *The Dialectics of Seeing: Walter Benjamin and the Arcades Project*. Cambridge, MA: The MIT Press.

Bychkov, Sergei. 1996. "Akademik Likhachev." *Moskovskii komsomolets*, no.164, August 31, p.2.

Cheshko, Sergei. 1996. *Raspad Sovetskogo Soiuza: Etnopoliticheskii Analiz*. Moscow: RAN IEA.

Clifford, James, and George E. Marcus, eds. 1986. *Writing Culture: The Politics and Poetics of Ethnography*. Berkeley: University of California Press.

Colton, Timothy J. 1995. *Moscow: Governing the Socialist Metropolis*. Cambridge, MA: The Belknap Press.

Dallin, Alexander. 1988. "Soviet History." Pp.5–25 in *Soviet Scholarship Under Gorbachev*. Edited by Alexander Dallin and Bertrand M. Patenaude. Stanford: Russian and East European Studies Publications and Reprints, No.3.

Dallin, Alexander, and Bertrand M. Patenaude, eds. 1988. *Soviet Scholarship Under Gorbachev*. Stanford: Russian and East European Studies Publications and Reprints, No.3.

de Certeau, Michel. 1986. "History: Science and Fiction". Pp.199–221 in *Heterologies: Discourse on the Other*. By Michel de Certeau. Minneapolis: University of Minnesota Press.

Derrida, Jacques. 1993. "Back from Moscow, in the USSR." Pp.13–81 in *Zhak Derrida v Moskve*. Sost. M. Ryklin. Moscow: RIK "Kul'tura".

Dunaev, Sergei. 1997. "Siurrealisty protiv realistov." *Nezavisimaia Gazeta*, no.182, September 27, p.2.

Elfimov, Alexei. 1996. "Razmyshlenia o sud'bakh nauki." *Etnograficheskoe obozrenie* no.5, pp.3–24.

_____. 1997. "The State of the Discipline in Russia: Interviews with Russian Anthropologists." *American Anthropologist* 99, no.4, pp.775–785.

_____. 2000. "Academics and the Production of an Intellectual Discourse of Modernity in Russia." Pp.225–255 in *Para-Sites: A Casebook against Cynical Reason*. Edited by George E. Marcus. Chicago: University of Chicago Press.

Epstein, Mikhail N. 1995. *After the Future: The Paradoxes of Postmodernism and Contemporary Russian Culture*. Trans. by A. Miller-Pogacar. Amherst: University of Massachusetts Press.

Ezerskii, Ivan. 2000. "Konstruktivizm v tapochkakh." *Itogi*, no.44, October 31.

Fedotkina, Tatiana. 1996. "Radi khrama moskvichi kladut zuby na polku." *Moskovskii komsomolets*, no.71, April 13, p.8.

Foucault, Michel. 1970. *The Order of Things: An Archaeology of the Human Sciences*. New York: Random House.

_____. 1972 [1969]. *The Archaeology of Knowledge*. New York: Pantheon Books.

_____. 1980. *Power/Knowledge: Selected Interviews and Other Writings*. New York: Pantheon Books.

———. 1984a. "What Is Enlightenment?" Pp.33–50 in *The Foucault Reader*. Edited by Paul Rabinow. New York: Pantheon Books.

———. 1984b. "Space, Knowledge, and Power." Pp.239–256 in *The Foucault Reader*. Edited by Paul Rabinow. New York: Pantheon Books.

Geertz, Clifford. 1973. *The Interpretation of Cultures*. New York: Basic Books.

Gordon, Colin. 1980. "Afterword." Pp.229–259 in *Power/Knowledge*, by Michel Foucault. New York: Pantheon Books.

Grant, Bruce. 1993. "Dirges for Soviets Passed." Pp.17–51 in *Perilous States: Conversations on Culture, Politics, and Nation*. Edited by George E. Marcus. Chicago: University of Chicago Press.

Gurevich, P. S. 1996. *Kul'turologiia*. Moscow: Znanie.

Hirsch, Francine. 1997. "The Soviet Union as a Work-in-Progress: Ethnographers and the Category *Nationality* in the 1926, 1937, and 1939 Censuses." *Slavic Review* 56, no.2, pp.251–278.

Holmes, Brian, Gerald H. Read, and Natalya Voskresenskaya. 1995. *Russian Education: Tradition and Transition*. New York, London: Garland Publishing.

Husband, William B. 1994. "History Education and Historiography in Soviet and Post-Soviet Russia." Pp.119–139 in *Education and Society in the New Russia*. Edited by Anthony Jones. Armonk, N.Y.: M. E. Sharpe.

Isham, Heyward, ed. 1995. *Remaking Russia*. Armonk, N.Y.: M. E. Sharpe.

Iskander, Fazil. 1995. "Who Are We?" Pp.37–49 in *Remaking Russia*. Edited by Heyward Isham. Armonk, N.Y.: M. E. Sharpe.

Ivanov, Sergei. 1997. "Pod flagom Liberei." *Itogi*, no.39, October 7, pp.52–53.

Jameson, Fredric. 1988. "Architecture and the Critique of Ideology." Pp.35–60 in *The Ideologies of Theory*. Vol.2, "Syntax of History." Minneapolis: University of Minnesota Press.

Jones, Anthony, ed. 1994. *Education and Society in the New Russia*. Armonk, N.Y.: M. E. Sharpe.

Kagarlitsky, Boris. 1988. *The Thinking Reed: Intellectuals and the Soviet State from 1917 to the Present*. London: Verso.

———. 1995. *Restoration in Russia: Why Capitalism Failed*. London: Verso.

Kitaev, Igor V. 1994. "The Labor Market and Education in the Post-Soviet Era." Pp.311–332 in *Education and Society in the New Russia*. Edited by Anthony Jones. Armonk, N.Y.: M. E. Sharpe.

Kochergin, Yurii, and Sergei Samoilov. 2000. "Ostrov nevezeniia: V tsentre Moskvy nachali ukhodit'pod zemliu doma." *Moskovskii komsomolets*, no.114, May 27, p.1.

Konrad, George, and Ivan Szelenyi. 1991. "Intellectuals and Domination in Post-Communist Societies." Pp.337–361 in *Social Theory for a Changing Society*. Edited by Pierre Bourdieu and James S. Coleman. Boulder: Westview.

Kovaleva, Anna. 1996. "Nash gorodok." *Moskovskii komsomolets*, no.150, August 13, p.3.

Likhachev, Dmitrii. 1995. "I Object: What Constitutes the Tragedy of Russian History." Pp.51–64 in *Remaking Russia*. Edited by Heyward Isham. Armonk, N.Y.: M. E. Sharpe.

Lissitzky, El. 1974 [1930]. "Russia: The Reconstruction of Architecture in the Soviet Union." Pp.137–147 in *The Tradition of Constructivism*. Edited by Stephen Bann. New York: Viking Press.

Lunina, Liudmila. 1996. "Bytovoe obaianie russkoi usad'by." *Segodnia*, Saturday, August 24.

Marcus, George E., ed. 1993. *Perilous States: Conversations on Culture, Politics, and Nation*. Chicago: University of Chicago Press.

Marcus, George E. 1995. "Ethnography in/of the World System: The Emergence of Multi-Sited Ethnography." *Annual Review of Anthropology* 24, pp.95–117.

Mirskii, E. 1995. "Zametki o gumanitarnom obrazovanii." *Chelovek*, no.6, pp.154–166.

MK Novosti. 2000. "Vypuskaetsia moneta s izobrazheniem Nikolo-Ugreshskogo monastyria." *Moskovskii komsomolets*, no.102, May 13, p.4.

Nietzsche, Friedrich. 1983 [1874]. "On the Uses and Disadvantages of History for Life." Pp.57–123 in *Untimely Meditations*, by Friedrich Nietzsche. Trans. by R. J. Hollingdale. Cambridge: Cambridge University Press.

Papernyi, Vladimir. 1996. *Kul'tura Dva*. Moscow: Novoe Literaturnoe obozrenie.

Pipes, Richard, ed. 1961. *The Russian Intelligentsia*. New York: Columbia University Press.

Popper, Karl R. 1966. *The Open Society and Its Enemies*. Vol.2, "The High Tide of Prophecy: Hegel, Marx, and the Aftermath." Princeton: Princeton University Press.

Pravila pol'zovaniia moskovskim metropolitenom (Postanovlenie mera Moskvy no.553-RM).

Pristavkin, Anatolii. 1995. "By Candlelight, Near My Beloved." Pp.13–22 in *Remaking Russia*. Edited by Heyward Isham. Armonk, N.Y.: M.E.Sharpe.

Radlov, V. V. 1989. *Iz Sibiri*. Moscow: Nauka.

Rilke, Rainer Maria. 1986. *Letters to a Young Poet*. Trans. by Stephen Mitchell. New York: Vintage Books.

Rokitianskii, V. R. 1994. "Chego zhdat' ot postmodernistskoi etnografii?" *Etnometodologiia*, vol.1, pp.73–93.

Samokhina, M. M. 1996. "Gumanitarizatsia obrazovania: vzgliad iz biblioteki." *Chelovek*, no.4, pp.75–87.

Schapiro, Leonard. 1961. "The Pre-Revolutionary Intelligentsia and the Legal Order." Pp.19–31 in *The Russian Intelligentsia*. Edited by Richard Pipes. New York: Columbia University Press.

Semenov, Y. I. 1998. "Predmet etnografii (etnologii) i osnovnye sostavliayushchie eio nauchnye distsipliny." *Etnograficheskoe obozrenie*, no.2, pp.3–17.

Shandybin, S. A. 1998. "Postmodernistskaia antropologia i sfera primenimosti eio kul'turnoi modeli." *Etnograficheskoe obozrenie*, no.1, pp.14–30.

Shnirelman, Victor A. 1996. *Who Gets the Past? Competition for Ancestors among Non-Russian Intellectuals in Russia*. Washington, D.C.: Woodrow Wilson Center Press.

Sigida, Adelaida. 2000. "Tresnul dom na Bolotnoi naberezhnoi." *Nezavisimaia gazeta*, no.96, May 27, p.2.

Smith, Hedrick. 1991. *The New Russians*. New York: Avon Books.

Sokolov, A. B. 1991. "Raskreposhchenie istorii." *Voprosy istorii* 9–10, pp.250–252.

Sokolov, Nikita. 1997. "Pravoslavie, samoderzhavie, elektorat: Velichestvennoe proshloe Rossii v budushchem prevzoidet samye smelye ozhidania." *Itogi*, no.37, September 23, pp.66–67.

Sokolovski, S. V. 1993. "Etnograficheskie issledovaniia: ideal i deistvitel'nost'". *Etnograficheskoe obozrenie*, no.3, pp.3–14.

Szelenyi, Ivan. 1991. "The Intellectuals in Power?" Pp.269–273 in *After the Fall: The Failure of Communism and the Future of Socialism*. Edited by Robin Blackburn. London: Verso.

Vaillant, Janet G. 1994. "Reform in History and Social Studies Education in Russian Secondary Schools." Pp.141–68 in *Education and Society in the New Russia*. Edited by Anthony Jones. Armonk, N.Y.: M. E. Sharpe.

Verdery, Katherine. 1991. *National Ideology Under Socialism: Identity and Cultural Politics in Ceausescu's Romania*. Berkeley: University of California Press.

Yonin, L. G. 1996. *Sotsiologia kul'tury*. Moscow: Logos.

Zakon Rossiiskoi Federatsii: Osnovy zakonodatel'stva Rossiiskoi Federatsii o kul'ture. No.115-F3 (23.06.1999).

Zelenin, D. K. 1991. *Vostochnoslavianskaia etnografiia*. Moscow: Nauka.

_____. 1994. *Izbrannye trudy*. Moscow: Indrik.

Ziuganov, G. 2000. "Obrashchenie k narodu." *Zavtra*, no.6, February, p.1.

Index

Adamovich, A., 111
Adorno, T., 36, 38
Afanasiev, Y., 137, 155–157
Aitmatov, C., 111
Akademicheskii Proekt, 180
Alexander I, Tsar, 57
Anikeeva, S., 180
Arkhangel'skoe, 127
Aron, R., 180
Auerbach, E., 180
Averintsev, S., 106–107, 110–111, 173
Azadovskii, K., 59

Bakhtin, M., 69–70, 110, 173
Basilashvili, O., 111
Basilov, V., 152
Bataille, G., 178
Baudelaire, C., 21–23
Baudrillard, J., 87
Bauman, Z., 182
Bazhenov, V., 67–70
Bell, D., 174–175
Benjamin, W., 53, 55, 116, 190
Berdiaev, N., 23, 69, 110, 175
Berger, P., 174
Blok, A., 27–28, 69
Boas, F., 178
Bolsheviks, 23–24, 58, 85, 129
Bourdieu, P., 12, 14, 55, 145, 149, 181–182
Brezhnev, L., 37, 79
Bulgakov, M., 62, 122

Bulgakov, S., 69
Bychkov, S., 99–100

Cassirer, E., 175, 180
Chaadaev, P., 22, 69, 110, 175
Chekhov, A., 62, 69, 120, 135, 191
Chernov, V., 9, 159
Cheshko, S., 16, 50, 154, 158, 164–165, 171
Church of Christ the Savior, 74–76, 85
Comte, O., 159
Constructivism, 65–68, 70, 197–198
Culturology, 17, 168–176

Danilevskii, N., 69
de Certeau, M., 102
Derrida, J., 106, 178–179
Derzhavin, G., 69
Dilthey, W., 180
Dneprov, E., 138–139
Dolgorukii, Y., 195–197
Dostoevsky, F., 69–70, 122

Epstein, M., 172–174
Etnograficheskoe obozrenie, 16, 187
Evans-Pritchard, E., 178, 187

Fedorov, N., 69
Foucault, M., 13, 19, 42, 45–46, 49, 52–53, 73, 87–89, 101, 119, 151, 179
Frank, S., 69
Fromm, E., 175

206

Galitsky, V., 77–78
Geertz, C., 62–63, 173
Glinka, M., 69
Gnosis, 178
Gogol, N., 69
Golovnev, A., 184
Gorbachev, M., 9, 54, 58–59, 77, 117, 124, 136, 152
Gorky, M., 27–29
Goya, F., 24
Granin, D., 111, 116–117
Grant, B., 41
Grebnev, A., 117, 136
Greenblatt, S., 178
Grishin, V., 86
Gubenko, N., 111
Gudeman, S., 182
Gurevich, P., 174–176

Hanson, A., 182
Hegel, G., 140

Il'f, I., 26
Iskander, F., 64
Itogi, 7, 98, 197
Ivan Kalita, Tsar, 97
Ivan the Terrible, Tsar, 98
Ivanov, V., 106, 111, 189
Ivanova, L., 193
Ivanovskii, V., 159

Jameson, F., 14

Kagarlitsky, B., 79, 95–96, 101, 112, 118, 122, 189
Karamzin, N., 69

Karlov, V., 171
Kavelin, K., 8
Khrushchev, N., 29, 37, 57
Khvostov, V., 9, 159
Kirsanova, R., 139
Kistiakovskii, B., 9, 159
Kliuchevskii, V., 8
Klykov, V., 93
Knabe, G., 151
Komsomol, 25, 47, 96
Korkunov, N., 159
Kovalev, S., 111–112
Kovaleva, A., 134
Kovalevskii, M., 9
Kremlin, 67–68, 89, 93, 108
Kuhn, T., 19
Kuskovo, 127

Lacan, J., 178–179
Lavrov, K., 111
Lenin, V., 25, 27, 65, 85, 109
Levada, Y., 109
Lévi-Strauss, C., 107, 174, 178
Levit, S., 180
Likhachev, D., 68–70, 99–101
Linton, R., 154
Literaturnaia gazeta, 43
Litfond, 134
Lobachevskii, N., 69
Lodge, D., 12
Lomonosov, M., 69
Losev, A., 173
Lotman, Y., 16, 173
Lunacharsky, A., 27–28
Lunina, L., 127, 130, 133–134
Luzhkov, Y., 74, 98, 195, 197

Macdonald, A., 199
Malinowski, B., 180
Marx, K., 140
Mendeleev, D., 27, 69
Metro, 195
Michelangelo, 19, 21, 24
Mikhaylovsky, N., 118
Mirskii, E., 162–163
Miskova, L., 184
Modérn, 20–21, 70–74
Moiseev, A., 180
Moscow State University, 12, 16, 44, 49, 71–72, 76, 106–108, 112, 140–144, 146–149, 152, 154, 159, 161, 171, 177
Moscow University for Business and Management, 159–160
Moskovskii komsomolets, 74, 117, 194
Muranovo, 99–100
Mussorgsky, M., 69

Nadezhdin, N., 8
Nash Sovremennik, 43
Nashe nasledie, 127
Nauka i zhizn', 48
Nietzsche, F., 52
Nikishenkov, A., 10, 16, 108, 140–142, 151, 152, 154, 157, 158, 165–166, 169–170, 178, 184–185
Nomenklatura, 30, 33, 95, 124, 138, 142, 146, 153
Novalis, 22
Novik, E., 140
Novyi Mir, 43

OIRU, 192

ORT, 161
Ostankino, 127
Ostrovskii, A., 62

Papernyi, V., 44, 87
Parfenov, K., 80
Parsons, T., 169
Peredelkino, 132–134, 192
Peter the Great, Tsar, 93–94, 116
Petrov, E., 26
Polyakov, S., 171
Popov, G., 112
Popper, K., 102, 158
Prokofiev, S., 69
Proust, M., 56
Pushkin, A., 57, 69, 85, 120
Putin, V., 199

Rabelais, F., 70
Rachmaninoff, S., 69
Radlov, V., 8
Rilke, R., 41, 61
Rokitianskii, V., 182
Rorty, R., 182
Rousseau, J., 166
Rozanov, V., 110
Russian State University for the Humanities, 12, 15, 109, 137, 139, 151, 156–157, 167
Russkaia Usad'ba, 192

Sakharov, A., 106, 111
Saltykov, A., 16, 108, 143–144, 149, 183
Scriabin, A., 69
Segodnia, 127, 163

Semenov, Y., 182, 186–187
Shandybin, S., 181
Shcherbakov Palaces, 80–81, 121
Sheremetiev, N., 127
Shostakovich, D., 69
Shtakenshneider, A., 69–70
Shternberg, L., 8
Silver Age, 21–25, 58, 69, 156
Slavophiles, 9, 17, 142, 153–164, 181, 195, 197
Smith, H., 77, 81
Sokolovski, S., 16, 140, 142, 150, 154, 157, 169, 177, 184–186
Solomin, Y., 111
Soloviev, S., 8
Soloviev, V., 69, 110, 175
Soviet constitution, 26
Spencer, H., 159
Spengler, O., 175
Stalin, I., 29, 41, 50, 54, 58, 108
Stankevich, S., 112–114
Starov, I., 69–70
Stasov, V., 69–70
Stepanova, J., 146–147
Swinburne, A., 22
Szelenyi, I., 112

Taganka Theater, 111
Taine, H., 175
Takhtarev, K., 9, 159
Tarkovsky, A., 30–31
Tchaikovsky, P., 69
Terekhova, M., 31
Tolstoy, L., 69, 85, 120, 191
Ton, K., 67
Toynbee, A., 175

Trofimov, A., 81
Tsereteli, Z., 93
Tsvetayeva, M., 191
Turgenev, I., 191
Turner, V., 178

Vainshtein, O., 15, 109, 139–140, 151–152, 163, 177–178, 187
Verdery, K., 14, 46–47
Vernadsky, V., 69
VOOPIK, 79–81, 83, 86, 90
Voprosy Filosofii, 43
Voprosy Istorii, 43
Voronikhin, N., 69–70
Vostochnaia Literatura, 180
Voznesensky, A., 24–25, 37

Weber, M., 150
Westernizers, 9, 17, 153–157, 163–164, 172
Whitman, W., 22
Windelband, W., 175
Writing Culture, 165–166, 182

Yagafova, E., 141
Yazkov, E., 146–148
Yeltsin, B., 9, 54, 95, 108, 113, 138, 199
Yevtushenko, E., 37–38
Yonin, L., 175

Zekhirev, L., 146, 148–149
Zelenin, D., 8
Zhirinovsky, V., 108
Ziuganov, G., 199
Znanie, 174

TRANS
anthropologische texte/anthropological texts

herausgegeben von /edited by Ina-Maria Greverus and George Marcus

Ina-Maria Greverus
Anthropologisch reisen
Das Buch bietet eine Perspektive des anthropologischen Reisens oder einer mobilen Feldforschung, die im sozial- und kulturanthropologischen Diskurs der Gegenwart als Alternative zu einer stationären Langzeitforschung gesehen wird. Die Aufmerksamkeit für den Augenblick oder die Offenheit für das Unerwartete (das Serendipity-Prinzip) spielt dafür eine ebenso große Rolle wie die Aufmerksamkeit für die "zufälligen" Verortungen der globalen Ströme und der Vergleich ihrer Wirkungen auf die Orte, die Länder und die Menschen.
Bd. 1, 2002, 404 S., 20,90 €, br., ISBN 3-8258-5720-4

Göttinger Studien zur Ethnologie
hrsg. vom Institut für Ethnologie der Universität Göttingen
Redaktion: Prof. Dr. Ulrich Braukämper und Prof. Dr. Brigitta Hauser-Schäublin

Veronika Fuest
"A job, a shop, and loving business"
Lebensweisen gebildeter Frauen in Liberia
Formale Bildung in kolonial geprägten Bildungsinstitutionen Afrikas – ein seit über 30 Jahren von verschiedenen akademischen Disziplinen, Politikern und Experten vieldiskutiertes und – wie es scheint – unerschöpfliches Thema. Diese Studie behandelt das Thema aus der Perspektive von gebildeten Frauen auf der Grundlage von Feldforschungsdaten aus den achtziger Jahren (vor dem Bürgerkrieg). Vor dem Hintergrund der spezifischen Kolonialgeschichte, der aktuellen Wirtschaftskrise und der – insbesondere westliberianischen – traditionellen Sozialstruktur wird versucht, ein lebendiges Bild vom Leben gebildeter Frauen aus dem Sekundarschulmilieu außerhalb der Hauptstadt zu vermitteln. Aus einem handlungstheoretischen Blickwinkel ermöglicht die Betrachtung von Alltag, sozialen Beziehungen, ökonomischen Aktivitäten, Prioritäten und Perspektiven die Wahrnehmung dieser Frauen nicht als bloße Opfer fehlgeleiteter Entwicklungen, sondern als versierte soziale und ökonomische Strateginnen, die ihre Handlungsspielräume durch den Faktor Bildung verlagert bzw. erweitert haben und sich, kontext- und interessensabhängig, auf traditionelle oder moderne Orientierungssysteme beziehen.
Bd. 1, 1996, 350 S., 30,90 €, br., ISBN 3-8258-2644-9

Klaus Hesse
Staatsdiener, Händler und Landbesitzer
Die Khatri und der Bazar von Mandi (Himachal Pradesh, Indien)
Diese auf 18monatiger Feldforschung beruhende Studie versteht sich als Beitrag zur Urbanethnologie und Soziologie Indiens am Beispiel von Mandi, der ehemaligen Hauptstadt des kleinen Fürstentums Mandi.
Dazu werden die sozialen und wirtschaftlichen Strukturen der Stadt Mandi und ihres Bazars analysiert. Den Mittelpunkt der Untersuchung bilden die hohe Kaste der Khatri, ihre soziale Struktur, ihre wirtschaftlichen Handlungsfelder, ihr Wertesystem, ihre sozialen und symbolischen Klassifikationen und ihr System des Gabentausches in diachronischer Perspektive. Kaste, Kastensystem, hierarchische Relationen und Klassifikationen sind integraler Bestandteil der Untersuchung.
In dieser Hinsicht ist das Werk auch eine positive und kritische Auseinandersetzung mit der Soziologie Louis Dumonts.
Bd. 2, 1996, 358 S., 35,90 €, br., ISBN 3-8258-2645-7

Martin Rössler
Der Lohn der Mühe
Kulturelle Dimensionen von 'Wert' und 'Arbeit' im Kontext ökonomischer Transformation in Süd-Sulawesi, Indonesien
Wie in vielen Regionen Südostasiens vollziehen sich in der indonesischen Provinz Süd-Sulawesi gegenwärtig tiefgreifende Veränderungen ländlicher Wirtschaftssysteme. Diese Studie befaßt sich mit der Integration einer makassarischen Dorfgemeinschaft in eine regional orientierte bäuerliche Ökonomie. Kennzeichnend sind dabei eine zunehmende Abkehr von der traditionellen Subsistenzwirtschaft und stattdessen eine Hinwendung zur Produktion von *cash crops*, zu Handel und Lohnarbeit. Im Mittelpunkt steht die Analyse der kulturellen Bedingtheit ökonomischer Entscheidungen. Kulturspezifische Wert- und Nutzenempfindungen, Bedürfnisstrukturen und ambivalente Konzeptionen unterschiedlicher Arten von Arbeit sind für Veränderungen oder Konstanz in Konsumtionsmustern und Produktionsstrategien verantwortlich. Dementsprechend liegt kein eindimensionaler Übergang von einer Subsistenzökonomie der Anspruchslosigkeit zu einer 'rationalen' Marktorientierung und Monetarisierung vor. Was als 'Lohn der Mühe' aufgefaßt wird, ist von heterogenen und häufig konträren

L**IT** Verlag Münster – Hamburg – Berlin – London
Grevener Str./Fresnostr. 2 48159 Münster
Tel.: 0251 – 23 50 91 – Fax: 0251 – 23 19 72
e-Mail: vertrieb@lit-verlag.de – http://www.lit-verlag.de

individuellen Überzeugungen abhängig.
Bd. 3, 1997, 592 S., 45,90 €, br., ISBN 3-8258-3434-4

Renate Kulick-Aldag
Die Göttinger Völkerkunde und der Nationalsozialismus zwischen 1925 und 1950
Die Reflexion über die Rolle der Wissenschaften in der Zeit des Nationalsozialismus ist ein (spätes) Gebot der Stunde. Renate Kulick-Aldag ist in ihrer Magisterarbeit der Frage nachgegangen, wie eng die Göttinger Völkerkunde personell und ideologisch, in Lehre und Forschung sowie in Ausstellungen, dem Nationalsozialismus verpflichtet war. Die Arbeit stellt einen wichtigen Meilenstein auf dem Weg der Aufarbeitung der Zeit zwischen den späten zwanziger bis in die fünfziger Jahre dar, die dem Ansehen der deutschen Völkerkunde aufgrund ihrer teils zwiespältigen teils eindeutigen Rolle international einen schweren Schlag versetzt hat, von dem sie sich bis auf den heutigen Tag nicht erholt hat.
Bd. 4, 2000, 136 S., 24,90 €, br., ISBN 3-8258-4469-2

Jutta Borchardt
Von Nomaden zu Gemüsebauern
Auf der Suche nach yörük-Identität bei den Saçıkaralı in der Südwest-Türkei
Die auf Feldforschungen beruhende Studie untersucht den sozio-kulturellen Wandel, der bei südwestanatolischen Kleinvieh- und Kamelnomaden, genannt yörük, im 19. Jahrhundert einsetzte und um die Mitte des 20. Jahrhunderts mit ihrer Übernahme des Bodenbaus und ihrer vollständigen Seßhaftwerdung endete. Mit den Veränderungen ihrer Lebensgrundlagen und wirtschaftlichen Strategien glichen sich zwar zunehmend auch ihre Gesellschaftsnormen, Verhaltens- und Wertvorstellungen denen der gemein-türkischen Kultur an, aber dennoch blieben bemerkenswerte Züge des "Yörük-Seins" der nomadischen Vergangenheit als ein die Gruppenidentität mitbestimmender Faktor bei ihnen erhalten.
Bd. 5, 2001, 200 S., 24,90 €, br., ISBN 3-8258-4470-6

Holger Kirscht
Ein Dorf in Nordost-Nigeria
Politische und wirtschaftliche Transformation der bäuerlichen Kanuri-Gesellschaft
Die Arbeit ist das Ergebnis von rund zwei Jahren intensiver Feldforschung in dem Kanuri-Dorf Marte und seiner Umgebung im nigerianischen Tschadbecken. Der Autor hat mit teilnehmender Beobachtung die Lebens- und Arbeitswelt der Bewohner dieses regenzeitlich teilweise überfluteten Gebietes untersucht und eine umfassende Dokumentation ihrer landwirtschaftlichen Kognitionen, Techniken, Erträge sowie ihrer Konsum- und Vermarktungsstrategien erstellt. Ethnographisch von besonderem Interesse ist die detaillierte Beschreibung eines nach den Gestirnen ausgerichteten Agrarkalenders. Die in der Dorfstudie gewonnenen empirischen Daten werden auf einer Makroebene mit der Analyse der sozioökonomischen und politischen Gegebenheiten des Kanuri-Staates Borno verknüpft. Dabei reicht der historische Untersuchungsrahmen von den 1990er Jahren ins frühe 19. Jahrhundert zurück.
Bd. 6, 2001, 360 S., 30,90 €, br., ISBN 3-8258-4494-3

Michael Dickhardt
Das Räumliche des Kulturellen
Entwurf zu einer kulturanthropologischen Raumtheorie am Beispiel Fiji
Diese Studie leistet einen Beitrag zur aktuellen Debatte um "Raum" als fundamentaler Kategorie menschlicher Praxis. Sie verbindet grundlagentheoretische Arbeit an den Begriffen "Kultur" und "Raum" mit der konkreten Ethnographie Fijis. Ausgehend von einem strukturierungstheoretischen Praxisbegriff und der Kulturphilosophie E. Cassirers wird eine neuartige Konzeption kultureller Räumlichkeit entwickelt. Die ethnographische Umsetzung erfolgt anhand der konkreten Räume des Dorfes, des Landes und der Verortung von Personen und Gruppen eines fijianischen Dorf. Im Rahmen unterschiedlicher Kontexte entsteht so eine differenzierte Sicht kultureller Räumlichkeit. Selbst symbolisch konstituiert, wird diese Räumlichkeit somit auch in ihren konstituierenden Funktionen für die kulturelle Praxis verstehbar.
Bd. 7, 2001, 328 S., 25,90 €, br., ISBN 3-8258-5188-5

Dorothea Deterts
Die Gabe im Netz sozialer Beziehungen
Zur sozialen Reproduktion der Kanak in der paicî-Sprachregion um Koné (Neukaledonien)
Das Phänomen des Gabentausches ist eines der klassischen Themen der ethnologischen Forschung im melanesischen Raum. Die Verknüpfung der sozialen, religiösen, politischen und wirtschaftlichen Bereiche im Gabentausch steht dabei im Vordergrund. Die vorliegende Studie untersucht die Bedeutung des Gabentausches für das soziale Gefüge der Kanak und geht dabei der Frage von sozialer Reproduktion und sozialer Transformation nach.
Die Studie beruht auf einer 15-monatigen Feldforschung in der paicî-Sprachregion um Koné, im Nordwesten der Hauptinsel von Neukaledonien, das bis vor kurzem ein Übersee-Territorium Frankreichs war und seit 1999 einen autonomen Status besitzt. Im Mittelpunkt steht die Analyse der zeitgenössischen Tauschsysteme in den Lebenszykluszeremonien der paicî-Kanak und die

LIT Verlag Münster – Hamburg – Berlin – London
Grevener Str./Fresnostr. 2 48159 Münster
Tel.: 0251 – 23 50 91 – Fax: 0251 – 23 19 72
e-Mail: vertrieb@lit-verlag.de – http://www.lit-verlag.de

Bedeutung der im Gabentausch definierten sozialen Beziehungen für die Tradition und für die Konstruktion einer neuen kulturellen Identität.
Bd. 8, 2002, 336 S., 25,90 €, br., ISBN 3-8258-5656-9

Ulrich Braukämper
Islamic History and Culture in Southern Ethiopia
Collected Essays
Studies on Islam in Ethiopia have long been neglected although Islam is the religious confession of almost half of the Ethiopiean population.
The essays focus on the following topics: *Islamic principalities in Southeast Ethiopia between the 13th and the 16th Centuries; Medieval Muslim Survival as a Stimulating Factor in the Re-Islamization of Southeastern Ethiopia; The Sanctuary of Shaykh Husayn and the Oromo-Somali Connections in Bale; Notes on the Islamization and the Muslim Shrines of the Härär Plateau; The Islamization of the Arsi-Oromo.*
The essays are based on the study of written records and on field research in southern parts of the country carrid out during the first half of the 1970s.
Bd. 9, 2002, 208 S., 20,90 €, br., ISBN 3-8258-5671-2

Brigitta Hauser-Schäublin; Michael Dickhardt (Hg.)
Kulturelle Räume – räumliche Kultur
Zur Neubestimmung des Verhältnisses zweier fundamentaler Kategorien menschlicher Praxis
Das Verhältnis von Raum und Kultur wird zunehmend fragwürdig. Erschienen Kulturen lange Zeit fest in Räumen verankert zu sein, so haben Globalisierung und Postmoderne dazu geführt, dass Raum und Kultur selbst in der Alltagserfahrung schon längst nicht mehr eindeutig aufeinander verweisen. Die feste Verbindung einer Kultur mit ihren definierbaren Territorien und Orten löst sich zusehends – ein Phänomen, das oft mit Schlagworten wie Entterritorialisierung oder Entörtlichung benannt wird. Doch wenn Kultur nicht mehr einem Raum zugeordnet werden kann und wenn Räume in ihrer Bedeutung für Kultur vieldeutig werden – wie kann ihr Verhältnis dann sinnvoll bestimmt werden, um die räumliche Dimension des Kulturellen und die kulturelle Dimension des Räumlichen beschreibbar zu machen? Die Autoren und Autorinnen dieses Bandes versuchen vor diesem Hintergrund, aus einer ethnologischen Perspektive das Verhältnis zwischen Raum und Kultur auf der Grundlage empirischer Studien aus Bali, Neuguinea, Indien, Indonesien und Fiji zu bestimmen. Es zeigt sich dabei, dass Entterritorialisierung und Entörtlichung keineswegs zu einer Enträumlichung des Kulturellen führen: Das Räumliche ist und bleibt fundamental für das Kulturelle, als konkreter Ort genauso wie als formendes Moment menschlicher Praxis. Raum und Kultur sind nach wie vor nur in ihrer wechselseitigen Bezogenheit zu verstehen, auch wenn sie in ihrem Verhältnis zueinander neu bestimmt werden müssen.
Bd. 10, Frühj. 2003, ca. 264 S., ca. 25,90 €, br., ISBN 3-8258-6799-4

Mainzer Beiträge zur Afrika-Forschung
herausgegeben von Thomas Bierschenk, Anna-Maria Brandstetter, Raimund Kastenholz und Ivo Strecker

Ernst Wilhelm Müller; Anna-Maria Brandstetter (Hg.)
Forschungen in Zaire
In memoriam Erika Sulzmann
(7. 1. 1911 – 17. 6. 1989)
Obwohl in Deutschland Frauen bereits im 19. und zu Beginn des 20. Jahrhunderts Forschungsreisen durchführten, dauerte es bis zur Zeit nach dem Zweiten Weltkrieg, daß Frauen wieder eigenständig ethnographische Feldforschungen leiteten. Zu diesen Frauen gehörte auch Erika Sulzmann, die 1951 bis 1954 die erste größere Forschungsreise der Nachkriegszeit leitete, die "Mainzer Kongo-Expedition". Dieser ersten Forschungsreise folgten in den Jahren 1956 bis 1980 noch acht weitere Reisen zu den südwestlichen Mongo in Zaire.
Erika Sulzmann kam im Sommer 1948 als Assistentin an das neueingerichtete Institut für Völkerkunde der Johannes-Gutenberg-Universität in Mainz. 1960 wurde sie zunächst Kustodin der ethnographischen Studiensammlung, dann Akademische Oberrätin und schließlich bis zum Eintritt in den Ruhestand 1976 Akademische Direktorin. Aber auch danach war sie bis kurz vor ihrem Tod im Juni 1989 eine aktive Mitarbeiterin des Institutes.
Erika Sulzmann hat durch ihre eigenen und die von ihr angeregten wissenschaftlichen Untersuchungen viel dazu beigetragen, unsere Kenntnisse über die Bevölkerungen des nördlichen Zaire, deren Sprachen und deren Geschichte zu verbessern, dabei waren diese Forschungen von der früheren ethnographischen Feldarbeit sehr verschieden: sie beruhten auf der Anerkennung der Gleichberechtigung der Partner, auf den Interessen der

L IT Verlag Münster – Hamburg – Berlin – London
Grevener Str./Fresnostr. 2 48159 Münster
Tel.: 0251 – 23 50 91 – Fax: 0251 – 23 19 72
e-Mail: vertrieb@lit-verlag.de – http://www.lit-verlag.de

Erforschten und auf der Achtung ihrer persönlichen Integrität.
Herausgeber und Herausgeberin, Autorinnen und Autoren möchten mit der vorliegenden Gedenkschrift nicht nur Erika Sulzmann ehren, sondern auch einen weiteren Beitrag zur Zaire-Forschung leisten.
Bd. 1, 1992, 480 S., 35,90 €, br., ISBN 3-89473-357-8

Anna-Maria Brandstetter
Leben im Regenwald
Politik und Gesellschaft bei den Bolongo (Demokratische Republik Kongo)
Der Lebensraum der Bolongo ist der äquatoriale Regenwald im Süden des inneren Kongo-Beckens. Seit langem wird dieser als undurchdringlicher, bedrohlicher Urwald imaginiert, bar jeglicher gesellschaftlicher Ordnung und jenseits aller Geschichte, in dem die Menschen, isoliert voneinander, nur mit dem täglichen Kampf ums Überleben beschäftigt sind. Dieser Erdichtung des Lebens im Regenwald widerspricht die historisch-ethnographische Studie der Mainzer Ethnologin Anna-Maria Brandstetter über Politik, Religion und Gesellschaft bei den Bolongo. Sie zeigt, daß die politischen und religiösen Institutionen der Bolongo eine Geschichte haben, die vermittels oraler Traditionen konstruiert werden kann. Wie die anderen Mongo-Gesellschaften, zu denen sie gezählt werden, unterhielten die Bolongo vielfältige Beziehungen zu ihren Nachbarn, mit denen sie neben Prestigegütern auch politische 'Güter' und rituelle Praktiken austauschten.
Die Patriarchen, Häuptlinge und Priester galten als Garanten für den Erhalt und Fortbestand des Lebens. Ihre Vermittlerstelle zwischen dem Diesseits und dem Jenseits erlaubte ihnen, die Beziehungen zwischen der Lebenden und der Toten zu interpretieren und zu manipulieren. Dies verlieh ihnen in der Gesellschaft der Bolongo Macht und Autorität. Orale Traditionen lassen vermuten, daß in der vorkolonialen Gesellschaft der Bolongo auch Frauen Zugang zu diesen Ämtern hatten.
Mit der Einbindung der Bolongo-Gesellschaft zunächst in den Kolonialstaat und später in den unabhängigen Staat Zaire/Kongo kamen neue ökonomische und politische Kräfte ins Spiel. Eine neue Elite, die ihren Führungsanspruch mit ihrer schulischen Bildung, ihrer Beschäftigung im modernen Sektor der Gesellschaft und mit ihrem modernen Lebensstil legitimiert, stellte in den letzten Jahren verstärkt die alte Elite der Patriarchen, Häuptlinge und Priester in Frage.
Bd. 2, 1999, 448 S., 40,90 €, br., ISBN 3-89473-358-6

Chrys Kwesi Sackey
Highlife
Entwicklung und Stilformen ghanaischer Gegenwartsmusik
Zu den modernen Musikformen Afrikas, die weltweite Anerkennung gefunden haben, gehört seit den 40er Jahren der ghanaische *Highlife*. Zusammen mit zahlreichen anderen Musikformen, die auf dem Schwarzen Kontinent gegen Ende der europäischen Kolonialzeit und in deren Nachfolge erschienen, wurde er lange für eine Art Abzweigung europäischer Musik gehalten. Diese Interpretation neuer afrikanischer Musik als Resultat von Einflüssen oder Übernahmen europäischer Instrumente, Strukturformen, Rhythmen, Harmonien beruhte auf einer äußerlichen und eurozentrischen Betrachtungsweise und mißachtete das Eigenleben musikalischer Traditionen in Afrika.
Durch Arbeiten wie die vorliegende wird diese Betrachtungsweise revidiert: Jetzt öffnen sich afrikanische Gesellschaften und geben uns Einblicke in die inneren Vorgänge, auch in die Entstehung kontemporärer Musik. Dies ist eine Darstellung der Entstehung und Entwicklung des Highlife-Phänomens aus der Sicht eines afrikanischen Beteiligten. Sie bedient sich der Methoden und Techniken heutiger Ethnologie, Musikologie, Linguistik und Computerwissenschaft.
Bd. 3, 1997, 536 S., 40,90 €, br., ISBN 3-89473-779-4

Matthias Krings
Geister des Feuers
Zur Imagination des Fremden im Bori-Kult der Hausa
Die Geister des Feuers, oder auch Europäergeister, bilden die kulturhistorisch jüngste Geisterkategorie im Pantheon des Bori-Kultes der Hausa. Sie erschienen zu Beginn der Kolonialzeit in den Besessenheitsritualen des Kultes, wo sie von ihren Adepten nach den Vorbildern der kolonialen Militärs und europäischen Verwaltungsbeamten verkörpert wurden.
Die vorliegende Arbeit basiert auf einer insgesamt vierzehnmonatigen Feldforschung in der nordnigerianischen Großstadt Kano. Im Zentrum der Arbeit steht die rezente Praxis des Kultes, vor allem aber das Bild der Geister, wie es von den Geistmedien und Musikern des Kultes in Erzählungen, Preisgesängen und nicht zuletzt auf dem Tanzplatz entworfen wird. In einem historischen Exkurs wird das Auftreten der Europäergeister in verschiedenen Regionen des Hausalandes, im Niger und in Nigeria, über sieben Jahrzehnte verfolgt. Dabei wird deutlich, daß sich die Mitglieder des Kultes heute bei der Repräsentation der Geister nicht mehr allein auf die eigentümliche Kultur der europäischen Kolonialisten

LIT Verlag Münster – Hamburg – Berlin – London
Grevener Str./Fresnostr. 2 48159 Münster
Tel.: 0251 – 23 50 91 – Fax: 0251 – 23 19 72
e-Mail: vertrieb@lit-verlag.de – http://www.lit-verlag.de

beziehen, sondern ebenso auf die gleichermaßen anziehend und abschreckend wirkende Kultur des nigerianischen Militärs. Das rituell entworfene Bild der Geister gestattet dem Leser einen Blick über die Schultern der Akteure, einen Blick auf die Wahrnehmung und Bewertung des europäischen Fremden und des nigerianischen Soldaten durch die Mitglieder des Kultes.
Bd. 4, 1998, 200 S., 19,90 €, br., ISBN 3-8258-3399-2

Ernst Wilhelm Müller
Kultur, Gesellschaft und Ethnologie
Aufsätze 1956 – 2000
I. THEORIE UND GESCHICHTE DER ETHNOLOGIE
1. Die Koreri-Bewegung auf den Schouten-Inseln (West-Neuguinea), 1961; 2. Die Ethnologie und das Studium komplexer Gesellschaften, 1973; 3. Die Verwendung der Begriffe emisch/etisch in der Ethnologie, 1983; 4. Ethnologie als Sozialwissenschaft, 1984; 5. Sozialwissenschaft als Ethnologie, 1986; 6. Mühlmann † (1.10.1904 Düsseldorf – 11.5.1988 Wiesbaden), 1989; 7. Der Begriff 'Volk' in der Ethnologie, 1989; 8. Naturvölker? – Nein! 1990; 9. Die Bılimá der Móngo, 1992; 10. Plädoyer für die komparativen Geisteswissenschaften, 1993; 11. Ethnologie, Rassismus und Negritude, 1996/2000
II. RECHT UND HERRSCHAFT
1. Eine zentralafrikanische Herrschaftsinstitution in idealtypologischer Betrachtung, 1957; 2. Moderne Wandlungen im afrikanischen Bodenrecht, 1961; 3. Problematik des Gebrauchs juristischer Kategorien bei der Aufnahme und bei der Kodifizierung von Eingeborenenrecht, 1962; 4. Ethnologische Bemerkungen zu einem belgischen Entwicklungsprojekt bei den Ekonda, 1963; 5. Eigentums- und Nutzungsrechte am Boden bei den Móngo: Ein Problem der Allgemeinen und angewandten Rechtsethnologie, 1980; 6. "Kritik und Vertrauen": Das Entschädigungsurteil des Bundesgerichtshofes von 1956, 1990.
III. VERWANDTSCHAFT
1. Soziologische Terminologie und soziale Organisation der Ekonda 1956; 2. Die Anwendung der Murdockschen Terminologie auf Felderbgebnisse (Ekonda, Belgisch Kongo) 1959; 3. Über Grundformen der Verwandtschaft 1966; 4. Der Vater in Afrika 1979.
Bd. 5, 2001, 384 S., 40,90 €, br., ISBN 3-8258-4325-4; 65,90 €, gb., ISBN 3-8258-4326-2

Anna-Maria Brandstetter;
Dieter Neubert (Hg.)
Postkoloniale Transformation in Afrika
Zur Neubestimmung der Soziologie der Dekolonisation
Dieser Band geht die Analyse des Übergangs vom Kolonialismus zu souveränen Nationalstaaten und den damit verbundenen politischen, gesellschaftlichen und ökonomischen Entwicklungen in Afrika in einer ungewöhnlichen Weise an. Ausgangspunkt ist der von Grohs/Tibi 1973 herausgegebene Band „Zur Soziologie der Dekolonisation in Afrika". Im erweiterten Rahmen der postkolonialen Transformation und auf der Basis aktueller Kenntnisse bieten Mitwirkende am Grohs/Tibi-Band sowie neue Autorinnen und Autoren die Aufarbeitung der alten Dekolonisierungsdebatte sowie ein Stück selbstreflexiver Wissenschaftsgeschichte: D. Berg-Schlosser, A.-M. Brandstetter, G. Grohs, C. Lentz, U. Luig, P. Meyns, D. Neubert, A. v. Oppen, R. Tetzlaff, I. Varga, H. Weiland.
Bd. 6, 2002, 208 S., 20,90 €, br., ISBN 3-8258-4479-x

Jean Adanguidi
Réseaux, marchés et courtage
La filière igname au Bénin (1990 – 1997)
Au Bénin, l'igname est à la fois une culture vivrière et une culture commerciale. Elle joue également un rôle important à l'échelon socioculturel. Contrairement aux statistiques officielles et à certains travaux, sa production a baissé ces dernières années. Paradoxalement, sa consommation a augmenté dans les villes du Sud-Bénin. Le présent travail, à travers une analyse tridimensionnelle de la production, de la commercialisation et de la consommation de l'igname, a analysé en profondeur ce paradoxe. L'importance des réseaux marchands dans l'approvisionnement des villes a été mise en exergue. La principale thèse de l'auteur est que le marché de l'igname est régulé non seulement par lex prix mais aussi par les facteurs sociaux.
Bd. 7, 2001, 328 S., 25,90 €, br., ISBN 3-8258-5421-3

Katrin Langewiesche
Mobilité religieuse
Changements religieux au Burkina Faso
Die vorliegende Arbeit beschäftigt sich mit religiösem Wandel in Burkina Faso. Sie behandelt im Besonderen die Provinz Yatenga seit den sechziger Jahren. Der Schwerpunkt der Analyse liegt auf der historischen Konstruktion einer Situation religiöser Pluralität und der Interpretation von individuellen Konversionsgeschichten, die in diesen Kontexte eingebettet sind. Der erste Teil der Arbeit privilegiert eine historische Darstellung, der zweiten Teil stützt sich auf empirische Feldforschung und beschreibt die zeitgenössische Situation an Hand einer Fallstudie (der Trauerfeier eines Dorfchefs) und Konversionsgeschichten. Beide Teile analysieren vergleichend die Entwicklungen des Islam, des Katholizismus und des Protestantismus in ländlichem Gebiet.

LIT Verlag Münster – Hamburg – Berlin – London
Grevener Str./Fresnostr. 2 48159 Münster
Tel.: 0251 – 23 50 91 – Fax: 0251 – 23 19 72
e-Mail: vertrieb@lit-verlag.de – http://www.lit-verlag.de

Bd. 8, Frühj. 2003, ca. 376 S., ca. 35,90 €, br.,
ISBN 3-8258-5679-8

Nikolaus Schareika
Westlich der Kälberleine
Nomadische Tierhaltung und naturkundliches
Wissen bei den Wodaabe Südostnigers
Bd. 9, Frühj. 2003, ca. 352 S., ca. 25,90 €, br.,
ISBN 3-8258-5687-9

Ivo Strecker; Baye Yimam (Eds.)
Cultural Contact, Respect and Self-Esteem in Ethiopia
Ethiopia with its great variety of languages, nationalities, cultural heritage and social memories, constitutes an area where people carry many diverse mental and emotional maps in their heads and hearts. Here, the future of all parties involved lies, just as in the international arena with which the Unesco resolution is concerned, in a fruitful transformation of existing cultural and social differences.
Both psychological and anthropological studies of alterity have shown that the contact with the cultural other always involves a tension between the opposites of attraction and rejection. That's to say, the desire to value, accept and incorporate the other, as against the desire to downgrade, reject or even annihilate the other. Only if neither of the two tendencies is allowed to dominate, can a harmonic relationship develop where all parties involved can maintain their respective identities while engaging in common projects with each other.
Bd. 10, Frühj. 2003, ca. 304 S., ca. 30,90 €, br.,
ISBN 3-8258-6122-8

Kölner ethnologische Studien
herausgegeben von Prof. Dr. Ulla Johansen
und Prof. Dr. Thomas Schweizer †

Michael Bollig
Die Krieger der gelben Gewehre
Intra- und interethnische Konfliktaustragung bei den Pokot Nordwestkenias
Der Osten Afrikas ist in den letzten Jahrzehnten zu einem Krisenherd par excellence geworden. Zwischenstaatliche Kriege, ethnische Konflikte und Banditentum prägen Wirtschaftsweisen und politische Organisationen auf lokaler Ebene. Die Studie beschreibt das Management intra- und interethnischer Konflikte bei den Pokot, einer Gruppe mobiler Viehhalter im Nordwesten Kenias und sucht nach Erklärungen für friedliche und gewaltsame Konfliktaustragungsmuster. In einer Phase rapider Militarisierung und wachsender Spannungen zwischen nationalstaatlichem Zentrum und peripheren Wirtschaftsräumen gelingt es den Pokot weiterhin, interne Konflikte weitgehend friedlich beizulegen. Eine engmaschige wirtschaftliche und soziale Vernetzung der nomadischen Haushalte, Nachbarschaftsräte und auf Schlichtung spezialisierte rituelle Experten helfen, den inneren Frieden zu bewahren. Dagegen werden Konflikte mit anderen ethnischen Gruppen häufig gewaltsam ausgetragen. Die Konkurrenz um Weiden und Viehbesitz, Kriegerideale und fehlende Vermittlungsinstitutionen lassen kleinere Interessensgegensätze eskalieren und in lange andauernde, verlustreiche Kriege ausarten.
Bd. 20, 1992, 400 S., 35,90 €, br., ISBN 3-89473-364-0

Barbara Jacobs
Kleidung als Symbol
Das Beispiel der Altgläubigen Südsibiriens im 19. und beginnenden 20. Jahrhundert
Sprache dient der verbalen Kommunikation, Kleidung hingegen vermittelt nichtverbale Informationen ihres Trägers. Kleidung ist für denjenigen eine Sprache, der ihre einzelnen Zeichen versteht, ihre einzelnen Elemente und ihre Kombinationen untereinander zu entziffern weiß. Sie ist ein Abzeichen der Kultur, der der Einzelne angehört. Kleidung gibt Aufschluß über individuellen Status und soziale Rollen; durch sie werden also Beziehungen der Menschen untereinander deutlich. Hinter den äußeren Erscheinungsbild stehen Vorschriften, welche die Bekleidungsetikette für alle Angehörigen einer Gesellschaft verbindlich regeln, die für einen bloßen Betrachter allerdings unsichtbar bleiben. Erst durch eine intensive Beschäftigung mit der Kultur vermag der Betrachter diesen Kleidungscode zu entschlüsseln und Aussagen darüber zu geben, von welchen religiösen und sozialen Vorstellungen dieses Kleidungsverhalten geprägt ist. Die Beharrlichkeit, mit der sich Trachten in vielen Gesellschaften über längere Zeiträume hinweg halten, ist Ausdruck von Tradition. In dieser Arbeit wird durch eine Analyse der Trachten der Altgläubigen Südsibiriens versucht, Einsicht über die ihnen eigenen Normen und Werte, insbesondere aber über ihr religiöses Weltbild zu erlangen. Bis heute ist eine solche Analyse ihrer Kleidung noch nicht erfolgt.
Bd. 21, 1993, 220 S., 24,90 €, br., ISBN 3-89473-571-6

Susanne Knödel
Die matrilinearen Mosuo von Yongning
Eine quellenkritische Auswertung moderner chinesischer Ethnographien
Die matrilinearen Mosuo, eine tibetobirmanische Ethnie Südwestchinas, haben eine außergewöhnliche Form der sozialen Organisation. Formelle Ehen sind bei ihnen zwar bekannt, aber selten.

LIT Verlag Münster–Hamburg–Berlin–London
Grevener Str./Fresnostr. 2 48159 Münster
Tel.: 0251 – 23 50 91 – Fax: 0251 – 23 19 72
e-Mail: vertrieb@lit-verlag.de – http://www.lit-verlag.de

Die sozial erwünschte Form der Mann-Frau-Bindung ist die "Azhu-Beziehung", die ohne Mitwirken Dritter aufgenommen und beendet wird. Der Mann besucht die Frau nur über Nacht, beide bleiben Vollmitglieder ihres mütterlichen Haushalts. Kinder aus einer solchen Beziehung gehören ausschließlich der Mutterseite an. Trotz großen Drucks von Seiten der kommunistischen Partei haben die Mosuo ihre Lebensform auch nach Gründung der Volksrepublik bewahrt. Die vorliegende Arbeit beschreibt die sozialen Institutionen der Mosuo sowie das wirtschaftliche und ethnische Umfeld, in dem ihre Gesellschaft sich befindet.
Bd. 22, 1995, 370 S., 30,90 €, br., ISBN 3-89473-805-7

Castulus Kolo
Computersimulationen als Instrument der Prozeßanalyse in der Ethnologie
In fast allen wirtschaftlichen Disziplinen werden heute zunehmend Computersimulationen zur Untersuchung komplexer Prozesse eingesetzt; insbesondere dann, wenn deren Ablauf nicht auf experimentelle Weise erfaßt werden kann. Auch für den Forschungsgegenstand der Ethnologie legen verschiedene Aspekte der Komplexität, wie etwa die starke Vernetzung kultureller, demographischer und ökologischer Zusammenhänge sowie die Vielzahl möglicher Entwicklungspfade, ein Nachdenken über neue Hilfsmittel des Prozeßverstehens nahe. Neben einer allgemeinen Einführung in die Methodik und Terminologie von Computersimulationen werden anhand konkreter Anwendungsbeispiele die fachspezifischen Möglichkeiten bzw. Grenzen diskutiert. Auch dem mathematischen Laien werden dabei Kriterien vermittelt, um den eigenen Einsatz von Simulationsmodellen planen bzw. die Ergebnisse fremder Simulationsstudien besser beurteilen zu können.
Bd. 23, 1997, 232 S., 24,90 €, br., ISBN 3-8258-3321-6

Susanne Spülbeck
Biographie-Forschung in der Ethnologie
Im Mittelpunkt der ethnologischen Methode steht die Begegnung zwischen einem Ethnologen und seinem Gegenüber, dessen Lebenswelt es zu verstehen gilt. Nicht zuletzt deshalb hört der Ethnologe immer wieder biographische Erzählungen, zeichnet sie auf und kann im Forschungsprozeß häufig noch nicht genau absehen, welche Rolle sie in der Auswertung spielen werden. Genau hier setzt der vorliegende Überblick an: wie kann biographisches Material interpretiert werden, um etwas über soziale Prozesse zu sagen? Welche Rolle spielen die Entstehungsbedingungen der biographischen Erzählung dabei? Wie kann ein biographischer Text sinnvoll in einer ethnologischen Studie dargestellt werden? Dabei geht es vor allem um das Verhältnis von biographischer Erzählung, ethnologischer Begegnung und Wirklichkeit.
Bd. 25, 1998, 176 S., 12,90 €, br., ISBN 3-8258-3401-8

Christoph Brumann
Die Kunst des Teilens
Eine vergleichende Untersuchung zu den Überlebensbedingungen kommunitärer Gruppen
Kommunitäre Gruppen – Gemeinschaften, die freiwillig alles gemeinsam haben – treiben das Teilen ins Extrem. Wie alle Formen der Kooperation, in denen Zwang (Staat) und individuelle materielle Anreize (Markt) ausgeschlossen sind, macht sie dies anfällig für den Egoismus ihrer Mitglieder. Die meisten dieser Experimente scheitern denn auch schnell, doch einige blühen über Jahrzehnte oder gar Jahrhunderte und unternehmen mutige, oft utopische kulturelle Experimente. Anhand eines Vergleichs von 43 Gruppen aus den letzten drei Jahrhunderten – darunter so bekannte wie die Hutterer, die Kibbutzim, Oneida, die Shakers und die Bruderhof-Gemeinschaften – klärt Christoph Brumann die Gründe für die seltenen Erfolge. In Bereichen wie Größe, Zweigstrukturen, Ehe und Familie, charismatischer Führung und Überzeugung entdeckt er überlebensförderliche und -hemmende Bedingungen, die er in integrierten Modellen zusammenfaßt. Statt der in Kulturvergleichen sonst üblichen statistischen Verfahren nutzt er dazu intensive Fallanalysen und die Möglichkeiten der Implikationslogik. Es zeigt sich, daß es eine Reihe von Gesetzmäßigkeiten gibt, die sich unabhängig von den offiziellen Überzeugungen der Gruppen auswirken, mitunter ohne diesen überhaupt bewußt zu sein.
Diese Studie ist ein Plädoyer für die empirisch orientierte, vergleichende Erforschung von Kooperation. Oft scheitert Kooperation nicht am mangelnden Idealismus, sondern am falschen Design. Wer Menschen dazu bringen möchte, zu teilen – ob nun Güter, Arbeitsplätze oder Aufmerksamkeit –, sollte daher die bereits gemachten Erfahrungen nicht ignorieren. Kultur- und Sozialwissenschaftler aller Disziplinen sind mit diesem Thema angesprochen.
Bd. 26, 1998, 368 S., 30,90 €, br., ISBN 3-8258-3732-7

Julia Pauli
Das geplante Kind
Demographischer, wirtschaftlicher und sozialer Wandel in einer mexikanischen Gemeinde
Bd. 27, 2001, 392 S., 35,90 €, br., ISBN 3-8258-5120-6

LIT Verlag Münster – Hamburg – Berlin – London
Grevener Str./Fresnostr. 2 48159 Münster
Tel.: 0251 – 23 50 91 – Fax: 0251 – 23 19 72
e-Mail: vertrieb@lit-verlag.de – http://www.lit-verlag.de